CW01375892

ISBN: 9781314368567

Published by:
HardPress Publishing
8345 NW 66TH ST #2561
MIAMI FL 33166-2626

Email: info@hardpress.net
Web: http://www.hardpress.net

Aberdeen University
Studies : No. 37

The Science and Philosophy of the
Organism

With Mr. P. J. Anderson's Compliments

The University Library
  Aberdeen

University of Aberdeen.

COMMITTEE ON PUBLICATIONS.

Convener: Professor JAMES W. H. TRAIL, F.R.S., Curator of the Library.

UNIVERSITY STUDIES.

General Editor: P. J. ANDERSON, LL.B., Librarian to the University.

1900. No. 1.—*Roll of Alumni in Arts of King's College*, 1596-1860. P. J. Anderson.
 " No. 2.—*Records of Old Aberdeen*, 1157-1891. A. M. Munro, F.S.A. Scot. Vol. I.
 " No. 3.—*Place Names of West Aberdeenshire*. James Macdonald, F.S.A. Scot.
1901. No. 4.—*The Family of Burnett of Leys*. George Burnett, LL.D., Lyon King of Arms.
 " No. 5.—*Records of Invercauld*, 1547-1828. Rev. J. G. Michie, M.A.
1902. No. 6.—*Rectorial Addresses in the Universities of Aberdeen*, 1835-1900. P. J. Anderson.
 " No. 7.—*The Albemarle Papers*, 1746-48. Professor C. S. Terry, M.A.
1903. No. 8.—*The House of Gordon*. J. M. Bulloch, M.A. Vol. I.
 " No. 9.—*Records of Elgin*. William Cramond, LL.D. Vol. I.
1904. No. 10.—*Avogadro and Dalton*. A. N. Meldrum, D.Sc.
 " No. 11.—*Records of the Sheriff Court of Aberdeenshire*. David Littlejohn, LL.D. Vol. I.
 " No. 12.—*Proceedings of the Anatomical and Anthropological Society*, 1902-04.
1905. No. 13.—*Report on Alcyonaria*. Professor J. Arthur Thomson, M.A., and others.
 " No. 14.—*Researches in Organic Chemistry*. Prof. F. R. Japp, F.R.S., and others.
 " No. 15.—*Meminisse Juvat: with Appendix of Alakeia*. Alexander Shewan, M.A.
 " No. 16.—*The Blackhalls of that Ilk and Barra*. Alexander Morison, M.D.
1906. No. 17.—*Records of the Scots Colleges*. Vol. I. P. J. Anderson.
 " No. 18.—*Roll of the Graduates*, 1860-1900. Colonel William Johnston, C.B., LL.D.
 " No. 19.—*Studies in the History of the University*. P. J. Anderson and others.
 " No. 20.—*Studies in the History and Art of the Eastern Provinces of the Roman Empire*. Professor Sir W. M. Ramsay, D.C.L., and pupils.
 " No. 21.—*Studies in Pathology*. William Bulloch, M.D., and others.
 " No. 22.—*Proceedings of the Anatomical and Anthropological Society*, 1904-06.
 " No. 23.—*Subject Catalogues of the Science Library and the Law Library*. P. J. Anderson.
 " No. 24.—*Records of the Sheriff Court of Aberdeenshire*. David Littlejohn, LL.D. Vol. II.
1907. No. 25.—*Studies on Alcyonarians and Antipatharians*. Prof. Thomson, M.A., and others.
 " No. 26.—*Surgical Instruments in Greek and Roman Times*. J. S. Milne, M.A., M.D.
 " No. 27.—*Records of the Sheriff Court of Aberdeenshire*. David Littlejohn, LL.D. Vol. III.
 " No. 28.—*Flosculi Graeci Boreales*. Ser. II. Professor John Harrower, M.A.
 " No. 29.—*Record of the Quatercentenary*, 1906. P. J. Anderson.
 " No. 30.—*The House of Gordon*. J. M. Bulloch, M.A. Vol. II.
1908. No. 31.—*The Miscellany of the New Spalding Club*. Vol. II.
 " No. 32.—*The Religious Teachers of Greece*. James Adam, Litt.D. (Gifford Lectures, 1904-06.)
 " No. 33.—*The Science and Philosophy of the Organism*. Hans Driesch, Ph.D. (Gifford Lect.)
 " No. 34.—*Proceedings of the Anatomical and Anthropological Society*, 1906-08.
 " No. 35.—*Records of Elgin*. Vol. II. Rev. S. Ree, B.D.
 " No. 36.—*Pigmentation Survey of School Children*. J. F. Tocher, B.Sc.
1909. No. 37.—*The Science and Philosophy of the Organism*. Hans Driesch, Ph.D. Vol. II (Gifford Lectures, 1908.)

The Science and Philosophy of the Organism

GIFFORD LECTURES DELIVERED AT ABERDEEN
UNIVERSITY, 1908

By

Hans Driesch, Ph.D.

Heidelberg

VOLUME II.

Aberdeen
Printed for the University
1909

B
3218
S5
1908
v.2

PREFACE

THE second—and final—volume of this work consists of two portions. I first bring to a conclusion the discussion on which I embarked in Volume I., regarding the subject from the point of view of "Science," and then in the longer and more important portion I proceed to the "Philosophy" of the Organism.

The third part of the scientific section, with which this volume opens, is, so to say, an enlarged and improved second edition of my work, *Die " Seele " als elementarer Naturfaktor* (1903). In the course of the argument it will become apparent why the word *Seele* was put in inverted commas in the German title.

Of the philosophical section only Part I. *B* 1 and 2 (pp. 162-188) contains matter that I have already published elsewhere—in Part I. of my *Naturbegriffe und Natururteile* (1904)—and even this part is here presented to the reader in a form very different from what it was. All the rest is new and hitherto unpublished.

I may say here that I myself regard Part I. *B* 3 to 5

SECTION B.—THE PHILOSOPHY OF THE ORGANISM

INTRODUCTORY DISCUSSIONS—

	PAGE
1. PHILOSOPHY OF NATURE IN GENERAL	125
2. THE CONCEPT OF TELEOLOGY	129
Teleology in General	129
The Two Classes of Teleology	135
3. THE CHARACTERISTICS OF ENTELECHY	137
Extensive and Intensive Manifoldness	137
Secondary and Primary Knowing and Willing	139
Entelechy and the "Individuum"	145
The Classes of Bodies	146
The Order of Entelechies. Entelechy and Machine-Work	150
Conclusions and New Problems	151

PART I.—THE INDIRECT JUSTIFICATION OF ENTELECHY

A. ENTELECHY AND UNIVOCAL DETERMINATION	153
B. ENTELECHY AND CAUSALITY—	
GENERAL INTRODUCTION	156
Difficulties	156
Different Forms of the Principle of Causality	158
Our Theme	160
1. ENTELECHY AND THE PRINCIPLE OF THE CONSERVATION OF ENERGY	162
α. THE PRINCIPLE	162
β. THE PRINCIPLE IN ITS RELATION TO ENTELECHY	164
Certain Facts	166
On a Supposed Vital Energy	167
Entelechy not Energy	168
2. ENTELECHY AND THE "PRINCIPLE OF BECOMING"	171
α. THE "SECOND" PRINCIPLE OF ENERGETICS	171
The True Principle of Becoming	172
"Dissipation" as a "Third" Principle	174
On Catenation of Energy	175
β. THE PRINCIPLE OF BECOMING IN ITS RELATION TO ENTELECHY	176
Again: Entelechy not Energy	177
The Relation of Entelechy to the Intensities of Energies	178
The Action of Entelechy in "Suspending" Possible Becoming	179

3. ACTION . . . .
    α. PRELIMINARIES . . . . . .
        No Pseudo-psychology . . . .
        General Definition of Action. Classes of Movements which are not Actions . . .
        The Distribution of Acting . . .
    β. THE FIRST CRITERION OF ACTING. THE HISTORICAL BASIS OF REACTING . . . .
        The Origin of the Acts of Volition .
        The Different Types of Historical Bases
        "Association" . . . . . .
    γ. THE SECOND CRITERION OF ACTING. "INDIVIDUALITY OF CORRESPONDENCE" . . .
    δ. A NEW PROOF OF THE AUTONOMY OF LIFE .
        Preliminary Remarks . . . .
        The Union of the two Chief Criteria of Acting
        So-called "Analogies" to Acting . .
        Conclusions . . . . . .
    ε. THE "PSYCHOID" . . . . .
    ζ. THE "SPECIFIC ENERGY" OF THE SENSORY NERVES .
    η. SOME DATA FROM CEREBRAL PHYSIOLOGY .
        The Connecting Function . . .
        Specific Functions in the Adult . .
        Are there Specific Functions in the Newly Born?
        The "Centre" in General . . .
        The Brain and the Psychoid in General .
        The Brain's Part in Association . .
    θ. REGULABILITY OF MOVEMENT WITH REGARD TO THE MOTOR ORGANS . . . .
    ι. THE LOWER BRAIN CENTRES IN VERTEBRATES .
    κ. DIFFERENT DEGREES OF ACTING IN DIFFERENT ANIMALS
        Man and the Highest Animals Contrasted .
        Higher Invertebrates . . . .
        The Lowest Forms of Acting . .
    λ. "PSYCHO-PHYSICAL PARALLELISM" REFUTED .
    μ. THE SUPRA-PERSONAL FACTOR OF ACTING IN HISTORY .
        No Supra-personal Factor known in History Proper .
        Morality as a Supra-personal Factor .

CONCLUSIONS OF SECTION A . . . . .

CONTENTS OF THE SECOND VOLUME

SECTION A.—THE CHIEF RESULTS OF ANALYTICAL BIOLOGY (*Continued*)

PART III.—ORGANIC MOVEMENTS

	PAGE
INTRODUCTORY REMARKS	3
1. THE MOST SIMPLE TYPES OF ORGANIC MOVEMENTS	8
α. THE SIMPLE REFLEX	8
β. THE DIRECTIVE MOVEMENTS	9
Tropism	9
"Taxis"	13
γ. THE WORK OF H. S. JENNINGS. "TRIAL AND ERROR"	16
The Resolution of "Taxis"	17
The Single Motor Acts. The "Movement at Random"	20
The Modifiability of Single Motor Acts	21
δ. CO-ORDINATED MOTIONS	26
The Concepts of von Uexkuell	27
The Classes of Co-ordination	29
2. INSTINCT	35
α. INSOLUBLE PROBLEMS	36
β. THE ACTUAL PROBLEM. DEFINITIONS	38
γ. THE WORK OF J. LOEB	40
δ. THE PROBLEM OF THE STIMULI OF INSTINCTS	41
ε. THE PROBLEM OF THE REGULABILITY OF INSTINCTS	45
ζ. CONCLUSION	50

philosophy of the Organism and not a general philosophy. For that reason problems of general philosophy—and even of the general philosophy of Nature—are only shortly alluded to.

The general standpoint of this work is subjective-idealistic; but idealism is here nothing more than a method, and I no longer regard subjective idealism as final; there does exist the possibility of metaphysics, *i.e.* of at least a certain knowledge about absolute reality.

Once more I thank my friends in Aberdeen for their great kindness. Once more I am indebted to my anonymous English friend at Heidelberg for his very reliable linguistic assistance, and to my publishers for their well-known courtesy.

HANS DRIESCH.

HEIDELBERG, 27*th August* 1908.

(pp. 189-226), and the whole of Part II. (pp. 266-339) of the philosophical section as the most important final results of my analysis, and therefore especially invite criticism of them. The last named part is, so to speak, the keystone of the whole building, and is written from an unusual point of view. I possess German manuscripts of the theoretical contents of this part dated as early as 1895 and 1897; but I always delayed publishing as the subject is extremely subtle.

The philosophical terminology employed in this work is that in general use. Nobody can feel more strongly than myself how greatly we need a new and immediate denomination of philosophical concepts—a "characteristica universalis" in the sense of Leibniz. But this work was not the right place to introduce it, and there was nothing to adopt from others, for modern "symbolic logic" so far relates only to formalities. I must therefore ask the reader to understand by the terms "substance," "causality," "objective," etc. etc., nothing but what he is instructed by my definitions, and not to confuse what I *have* said with what I *might* have said but did not. I ask the reader to understand my words as they are written, and to conceive the problems only as they are stated, and not as the terminology—steeped as it is in historical reminiscences—might possibly suggest.

It should never be forgotten that this work is a

xii   SCIENCE AND PHILOSOPHY OF THE ORGANISM

	PAGE
The Rôle of Entelechy in the Continuity of Life	181
Entelechy and Chemism	181
An Explanation of the Limits of Regulability and of Life in General	182
Entelechy Burdened with as Little as Possible	184
Entelechy and "Catalysis"	186
Conclusions	187

3. ENTELECHY IN ITS RELATION TO THE DISTRIBUTION OF GIVEN ELEMENTS 189

   α. SOME APPARENT CONTRADICTIONS BETWEEN ENTELECHY AND THE TRUE SECOND AND THE THIRD EMPIRICAL PRINCIPLE OF ENERGETICS 189

The Problem	189
A Partial Solution	190

   β. THE ELEMENTAL RÔLE OF ENTELECHY IN CREATING "DIVERSITIES OF DISTRIBUTION" . . . 191

The Rôle of Entelechy in Morphogenesis	191
The Rôle of Entelechy in Acting	193

   γ. THE RÔLE OF ENTELECHY DOES NOT CONTRADICT THE PRINCIPLES OF THE INORGANIC AS THEY ARE, BUT AS THEY MIGHT BE FORMULATED . . . 195

   δ. BUT THE RÔLE OF ENTELECHY AGREES WITH A CERTAIN GENERAL ONTOLOGICAL PRINCIPLE . . . 197

   ε. THE "DEMONS" OF MAXWELL 198

4. PROVISIONAL REMARKS ON ENTELECHY AND THE CLASSES OF NATURAL AGENTS 201

On "Phenomenalism"	201
The "Constants"	202
Negative Characteristics of Entelechy	204
A Gap in the Scale of Natural Factors	205
A Few Words on "Explaining"	206

5. ENTELECHY AND MECHANICS 208

   α. THE FOUNDATIONS OF MECHANICAL PHYSICS . 208

On a Possible Qualitative Science that is Complete	208
The Epistemological Character of Universal Mechanics	209
The Psychological Basis of Universal Mechanics	212

   β. THE DIFFERENT FORMS OF UNIVERSAL MECHANICS . 214

Mere Movement and the Causation of Movement	215
The Forms of Mechanical Causation	216
Pure Kinetics Negligible	217

CONTENTS

xiii

	PAGE
γ. ENTELECHY AND DYNAMICAL MECHANICS	218
Entelechy in its Relation to the two Forms of Mechanical Energy	219
Entelechy as Transporting Mechanical Energy	222
The Suspending and the Transporting Action of Entelechy Discussed Together	223
Entelechy in Contrast to General Mechanics	224
δ. CERTAIN BRITISH AUTHORS ON LIFE AND MECHANICS	225
6. HOW ENTELECHY IS AFFECTED	227
α. THE PRINCIPLE OF ACTION AND REACTION AS RELATED TO ENTELECHY	227
β. THE TYPES OF AFFECTION OF ENTELECHY	228
Morphogenetic Entelechy	229
The Affection of the Psychoid	231
γ. THE CONTRAST BETWEEN AFFECTION IN THE ORGANIC AND THE INORGANIC	232
GENERAL CONCLUSIONS	234
Entelechy Related to Space and therefore Belonging to Nature, but Entelechy not in Space	234
The Problem of "Entelechy and Causality" only partly Solved	235
Justification of our Cautiousness	236
The "Moment of Regulation"	237

C. ENTELECHY AND SUBSTANCE—

α. THE CATEGORY OF SUBSTANCE AND ITS APPLICATION IN GENERAL	238
Inorganic Substance	239
Inorganic Substance of any Type Relates to Extensity	241
β. ORGANIC "ASSIMILATION"	242
Respiration	242
"Assimilation" and "Dissimilation"	245
The "Living Substance" in the Chemical Sense	246
Negative Results only	248
γ. ENTELECHY INCOMPATIBLE WITH A "LIVING" CHEMICAL SUBSTANCE	249
No Chemical Substance Possible as the Basis of Entelechy	250
No Constellation of Chemical Substances Possible as the Basis of Entelechy	251
Entelechy and Physiological Chemistry	254
Ancient Problems	255
δ. SUBSTANCE AS A CATEGORY IN ITS RELATION TO ENTELECHY	256
The Concept of Divisibility not Applicable to Entelechy	257

xiv SCIENCE AND PHILOSOPHY OF THE ORGANISM

	PAGE
The Concept of Localisation or Seat not Applicable to Entelechy	258
"Entelechy" so far a Mere System of Negations	259
ε. INSOLUBLE PROBLEMS	260
The Origin and the End of Individual Life	260
The Origin of Life in General	262
CONCLUSIONS OF PART I.	264

PART II.—THE DIRECT JUSTIFICATION OF ENTELECHY

A. THE DIRECT PROOF OF THE AUTONOMY OF LIFE BASED UPON INTROSPECTIVE ANALYSIS OF COMPLETE GIVENNESS—

1. ANALYTICAL PART 266
   - α. A CASE FROM COMMON LIFE 267
     - The Case 267
     - What Common Life Learns from the Case . 269
   - β. THE SAME CASE IN A SCIENTIFIC FORM . . 270
     - An Hypothesis 271
     - The Case Once More 271
   - γ. THE DIFFERENT TYPES OF ELEMENTS IN GIVENNESS . 273
     - Spatial and Non-Spatial Elements . . . 273
     - The Elements of Givenness in their Relation to the Brain 275
     - Spatial and Non-Spatial Elements among those which do not Relate to the Brain 276
   - δ. THE CONNEXION BETWEEN THE CEREBRAL PORTIONS OF ELEMENTS 277
     - The Last Cerebral Element of the First Portion. Relations to the Scientific Analysis of Acting . 277
     - On "Identification" 279
     - The "Intra-psychical Series" 280
   - ε. THE DIRECT PROOF OF VITALISM . . . 281
     - My Body as my "Object" 282
     - Other Living Bodies 283
     - "Understanding" Vitalism 284

2. POLEMICAL PART 287
   - α. THE IMPOSSIBILITY OF THE VARIOUS CURRENT FORMS OF PSYCHO-PHYSICAL PARALLELISM . . . 287
     - Metaphysical Parallelism already Refuted . . 287
     - Pseudo-idealistic Parallelism Refuted . . 289
     - Parallelism Impossible on a Truly Idealistic Basis . 291

CONTENTS

	PAGE
β. A NEW FORM OF PARALLELISM	293
CONCLUSIONS	294

B. THE CATEGORY "INDIVIDUALITY"—

α. CATEGORIES IN GENERAL	296
Definitions	296
Fundamental Difficulties	298
An Irreducible Kind of "Experience" the Foundation of Categories	300
A Few Remarks on Categories and Ordinary Experience	301
The Problem of the System of Categories	302
β. THE CATEGORY OF NECESSITY	303
The Fundamental Paradox	303
"Freedom" a Mere Negation	304
γ. THE CATEGORIES OF RELATION	305
Introspective Psychology and the Categories of Substance and Causality	306
The Problem of a New Category of Relation	308
δ. THE CATEGORY "INDIVIDUALITY"	310
Previous Preparatory Work	310
"Individuality"	312
"Finality" a Subclass of Individuality	313
ε. CERTAIN DIFFICULTIES IN THE CATEGORICAL CONCEPT OF INDIVIDUALITY	314
An Analogy to a Mere Functional Conception of Causality	314
No "Causa Finalis"	315
Entelechy and Causality	316
Entelechy Supra-personal	317
ζ. CATEGORIES AND FACTORS IN "NATURE"	318
"Ideal Nature." The "Ontological Prototype"	318
Organic Nature	319
Conclusions	323
η. RATIONAL SCIENCE	324
Rational Science and "Ideal Nature"	324
Rational Science and "Causal" Science	324
Ideal Nature and Natural Factors	325
The Problem of Entelechian Systematics	327
θ. A FEW REMARKS ON THE PROBLEM OF TIME	329

CONCLUSIONS OF PART II. 335

Summary	335
The Method Applied	337
Definition of the Organism	338

PART III.—THE PROBLEM OF UNIVERSAL TELEOLOGY

	PAGE
α. RETROSPECT	340
Consequences of the "Machine-Theory"	341
Different Types of Entelechian Effects	342
General Plan of what Follows	343
β. THE PROBLEM OF SUPRA-PERSONAL TELEOLOGY IN THE REALM OF LIFE	344
History in General	344
The History of the Individual	346
Phylogeny	346
The Significance of Propagation	347
γ. HARMONY IN NATURE	348
δ. THE PROBLEM OF A REAL INORGANIC INDIVIDUALITY	350
ε. CONTINGENCY AND TELEOLOGY	352
The Concept of Contingency	352
The Concept of a Limited Teleology	353
ζ. MORALITY	355
Morality as a Standard of Measurement of Universal Teleology	355
Morality as a Category	356
Morality and Vitalism	357

PART IV.—METAPHYSICAL CONCLUSIONS

INTRODUCTORY REMARKS	359
α. THE THREE WINDOWS INTO THE ABSOLUTE	361
Morality : the Thou	361
The Nature of Memory : the Ego	361
The Character of Givenness : the It	362
β. THE "POSTULATE"	363
γ. TELEOLOGY AND THE ABSOLUTE	365
The Concept of a Limited Teleology once more	365
The Domain of Teleology	368
δ. THE PRIMARY ENTELECHY IN THE UNIVERSE—AN ETERNAL TASK OF SCIENCE	370
ε. METALOGICAL CONSIDERATIONS	372
CONCLUSIONS: *THE ROUTE TRAVERSED*	374
INDEX	377

SECTION A—*Continued*

PART III

ORGANIC MOVEMENTS

PART III

ORGANIC MOVEMENTS

Introductory Remarks

Our study of morphogenesis has led us to a very important result. We have become convinced of the autonomy of life, as far as the origin of the individual living form is concerned. The short surveys that we devoted to the physiology of metabolism and to biological problems of the systematic and historical kind have not proved so successful. Physiology afforded us but few indicia of a future vitalism, and in the large fields of systematics and history we found that there was very little to be learnt at all.

We now begin the second half of our lectures, and shall first conclude the factual or analytical or purely scientific section: the analysis of the physiology of organic movement has still to be attempted. The study of animal movement will be as instructive as the study of morphogenesis has been; it will bring us into close contact with philosophical questions again. And when we have finished it we shall have completed our purely scientific work, and may then enter the sacred halls of pure philosophy.

The physiology of organic movement may raise the following questions, and, indeed, every text-book of physiology shows us that it actually has raised all of them. All movements, in some way, are reactions to external stimuli, *i.e.* are changes of the organic body in question with regard to its external surroundings. In other words, there is a line of processes, the first of which leads from without to within, whilst the last one leads from within to without; and besides these there are intermediate processes. We now may ask: What happens in the organism when it receives the external stimuli, what is the final effect of these stimuli, and what is there between the stimulus and the final effect?

The physiology of the so-called sense organs would give us the answer to our first question; it would teach us to what sorts of stimuli the organisms are responsive and by what means of their organisation and function they are so. The physiology of locomotory organs takes account of the question about the final acts in the process of movement: the contraction of the muscle is studied, but so is also the ciliary movement in infusoria, or the strange process of secretion and absorption of gases by which the movements of Siphonophora or of Radiolaria are carried out.[1] And all intermediate processes concerned in organic movements would come under the physiology of the nerves and nerve-centres. Not very much is actually known about this subject. Scarcely anything has been ascertained with regard to the so-called "centres"; and as to the nerves themselves we know little except that nervous conduction

[1] Rhumbler shares the merit of having studied very extensively the means of movement in the lowest Protista. Even if he is wrong in many points of his interpretation (Jennings, Heidenhain) he has done good work in clearing the problems. But I beg to lay stress upon the fact that he *only* has studied *means* of movement—nothing more.

takes time, that it is accompanied by electric changes, and that it is probably of a chemical nature.

Now we should hardly gain very much for our philosophical purposes, if in our analysis of movement we were to follow the lines of ordinary physiology, which we have shortly sketched here. Moreover, there is wanting something very important in our sketch, and when looking back to it we may be reminded of the words of Goethe: " Dann hat er die Teile in seiner Hand, fehlt leider nur das geistige Band." Ordinary physiology indeed does not offer us much more than " die Teile." But *is* there anything besides them; is a specific motor act of an organism as such anything in itself, is it not merely a sum or aggregate? It seems to me that this is the central *problem* of motor physiology; in other words, it seems to me that the question about the " wholeness " of the act of moving must come up at the beginning of the analysis. It certainly is impossible to neglect this question from the very beginning.

We therefore shall not follow the lines of ordinary physiology in our analytical studies, but shall turn the questions into a somewhat different shape. And, indeed, we know already from our previous researches *how* we may turn them in order to be successful: let the concept of " regulation " again be made the centre of our discussion, though in a slightly different and more complicated sense than when we were speaking of the physiology of morphogenesis and metabolism. There is indeed no properly " normal " state of organisation or function that could be said to be restored or regulated by organic movements. But in spite of that, there is something in these movements that bears the character of a *correspondence* to a change or variation of the medium or the organism, just as in the case of regulation proper.

An actual instance will give you perhaps a better idea of what I am thinking of, than mere abstraction can do. Take a dog and ask what characters resembling regulations, if not regulations themselves, may occur in his movements. The dog is running towards a certain place along the direct line that leads to it, a carriage is crossing this line just when the dog has to pass: the dog will run a little more quickly and will make a curve in order to avoid the carriage. Another dog has undergone an operation involving the loss of a part of one hemisphere of the brain: at first his movements are very defective, but after a certain time, as the experiments of Goltz and others have shown, they become much less so than they were immediately after the operation. And a third dog is injured in one of his legs so that he is forced to run on three legs only: yet he manages to reach the place he wants to get to, by using his three legs in a manner somewhat different from the normal.

Here we have instances of all possible kinds of regulation, or, if you prefer to say so, of the correspondence between the sum of conditions and the sum of single effects concerned in movement, which may occur in the field of motor physiology, no matter by what means or organs movement is carried out, be it by cilia, muscles, or threads of protoplasm. In the first instance the dog's goal was reached, in spite of a change in the outer conditions, by means of a change in certain single acts of movement: the dog ran round the carriage instead of following the straight line. In the second instance we do not know very much about the change of function that follows the change effected in the dog's brain, but we may assume hypothetically, that other lines of nerves have been used for carrying out what there was to be done. In the third instance the change from without affected the organs which perform the movement itself, and this change was followed by a change in the use of these organs: for it is clear that the work done in walking by every single leg when there are four legs at the disposal of the organism does not remain the same when there are only three.

Reviewing our three instances, we may say that in the first case there was a variation in the totality of the external stimuli, followed by a corresponding variation in the effect, whilst such a corresponding variation followed a change of the intermediate organs in the second case, and a change in the general condition of the proper effectuating organs in the third. We observe, then, a co-ordination of our three instances to the three fundamental branches of ordinary motor physiology already mentioned. It is not this co-ordination, however, but the existence of something like *regulation* in organic movement that interests us chiefly, and here we have the starting-point of our future researches.

All changes, whether in the external conditions, or in the intermediate organs, or in the effectuating organs, may be described as changes of motor stimulation in general, and we may therefore say that *the relation between motor stimuli and movement as such* is in fact our general problem. Are there sums or aggregates on both sides or not? If not, what *is* there? These are the questions we have to answer.

Let us now review the great variety of actual organic movements, with the object of discovering the kinds of relation between cause and effect in every class.

1. The Most Simple Types of Organic Movements

When I first tried, six years ago,[1] to classify organic movements according to their degree of complication, it seemed inevitable that the classification must start from two types, which in different respects are the most simple ones: the so-called *simple reflex*, and the simple free directive motion called "*taxis*."

Modern investigations have proved that these two groups of movements, though the most simple in concept, are far from being the most fundamental in fact, and therefore a classification of organic movements at the present day will have to follow other lines of analysis. But in spite of that, for historical interest, a short survey of the theory of the simple reflex and of the simple directive movement may introduce the present chapter.

a. THE SIMPLE REFLEX

The simple reflex occurs in plants, in the Mimosa for instance, as well as in animals, and in the latter both when they possess a well localised brain and nervous system and when they do not. Coughing and sneezing are among the most universally known phenomena of this class. A stimulus applied to a specified point of the body is followed

[1] *Die "Seele" als elementarer Naturfaktor*, Leipzig, 1903.

here by a specified movement of another specified part. And the same holds for some, though not very many, movements of Invertebrates.

It is the *invariability*, the absolute fixation of the relation between a simple cause and a simple motor effect or reaction, with regard to quality as well as to localisation, that characterises this type of the simple reflex;[1] indeed, a simple reflex occurs with the precision of machinery. Nothing in fact speaks against the real existence of such machinery: we therefore may assume hypothetically that true simple reflexes are machine-like in every respect, and with this assumption we may now leave this type of organic movement, which affords us no theoretical problems of a complicated kind.

β. THE DIRECTIVE MOVEMENTS

In the simple free directive movement or "taxis" it is the typical relation between the direction of the stimulus and the direction of the effect, with regard to the main axis or the plane of symmetry of the organism, which separates this type of motion from others. The significance of this will best be illustrated by certain phenomena which do not properly belong to the class of free movements we are dealing with here, but which more correctly belong to the physiology of growth: the so-called "*tropisms.*"

Tropism

Let us first devote a few words to the chief characteristics of these "tropisms." We did not discuss them whilst

[1] Of course the general type of a simple reflex is not changed, if the locality of the cause and of the effect is the same.

analysing morphogenesis and growth in particular, since their most prominent feature is not growth but typical motion.

All of you know that the stem of a tree turns away from the ground, whilst the root enters it. We speak of negative and of positive *geotropism* in this case, for it has been proved that it is gravity which determines the direction of stem and of root here, in a manner that has been very much elucidated by modern authors.[1] And in the same style we call it positive and negative *heliotropism*, if a stem of a plant turns toward the sun or any other source of light, and if a root turns away from such sources. Thermotropism, rheotropism, and chemotropism are similar phenomena; their names show most decidedly in what they consist. There are a few similar phenomena in the so-called stolons of hydroids. As we have said, it is only on *growing* parts of *fixed* organisms that tropisms of all sorts are to be observed. A marked correspondence of the directions of the cause and of its immediate effect is exhibited in all of them.

Let us first state in a few words in what cases we may speak of a real "direction" peculiar to an agent of the medium. That a specific direction is given in the effect of gravity and the rays of light going out from a radiant body is clear without much explanation; but there may be direction in natural agents even when they cannot properly

[1] I refer to the work done by Noll, Nemeč, Haberlandt, and many others during the last ten years. Of more than usual importance seems to be the discovery of Fitting (*Jahrb. wiss. Bot.* 44, 1907) that phototropic stimulation may be transferred along broken (zigzag) lines, and that this stimulation itself probably consists in a real induction of polarity in each cell established from without. There is no machine-like apparatus simply set going.

be spoken of as rays. Take the distribution of heat, not by radiation but by conduction, take the diffusion of chemical substances in solutions, and, last not least, take the electric current; in all these cases we may speak of the existence of "potentials," in the broadest meaning of the word, and similarly we may speak of the existence of "lines of force." These lines of force, existing in all those processes, not only in galvanism but in diffusion and also in thermic conduction, allow us to speak of *directed* agents in every case where these lines exist, and in this way the realm of directed agents of the medium becomes very large. In fact, the directed movements we shall speak about, have been found to exist in correspondence with almost all of the directed agents of the medium in this broadest sense.

A "tropism," then, is a directed movement of a growing part of a plant or hydroid determined by the direction of a directed agent.

The theory of tropisms [1] would be a very simple thing if there were nothing but typical cases say of geotropism or of heliotropism, *e.g.* such cases as the bending of a branch to any source of light, and the invariable bending of roots towards the ground.

But there are two classes of complications, each of them consisting of two parts.

There are many cases where the "sense" of a tropism, that is to say, its being positive or negative, is changed by the intensity say of the light or of the chemical stimulus. An organ that is positive under ordinary conditions begins to bend away from the source of stimu-

---

[1] In Pfeffer's *Pflanzenphysiologie* (vol. vii. p. 546) an excellent account of the theory of tropisms will be found.

lation if the stimulus reaches a certain intensity, and conversely. This is a rather simple complication, but an additional phenomenon appears if the increased intensity of the stimulus has lasted for some time. Then the organism becomes adapted, or rather *acclimatised*, to this intensity, and resumes the positive irritability it had before.

Let us remember on this occasion what was said on irritability and its restoration after irritation in the first part of this work: all tropistic irritability follows the so-called law of Weber, that is to say, an increase of the intensity of the stimulus always acts only in proportion to the intensity already present. This law resembles the so-called " action of masses " in chemistry, and tends to prove that something chemical is connected with tropisms. Also the reversion of tropisms might be explained in the same simple manner. But the change of the *point* of reversion is another thing—a real " acclimatisation," unknown to us in its details, a real " secondary regulation," which, though not proving vitalism in itself, is in any case very remarkable.

The second complication in the theory of tropisms appears whenever the general conditions of life are altered. In this case a change say of the general temperature of the medium changes the " sense " of say heliotropism; a fact that has been named "heterogeneous induction " by Noll. This change of the sense of a tropism very often plays a true morphogenetic, or, rather, restitutive rôle: if a pine is decapitated, one of the side branches assumes the negative geotropism of the lost main axis, and a similar phenomenon holds for roots. The general organisatory state of the organism is the "general condition" that was altered in this case. Whenever parts of a plant change the sense of a tropism, according to their age or state of fertility, we find something very similar. Here already the concept of the "whole" with regard to functioning in its relation to outside factors presents itself, though perhaps not in a manner sufficient to refute the "machine theory" of life.[1]

The last step of complication is reached if two or more stimuli are in competition with one another. This case is best shown by the behaviour of roots in the ground; gravity, moisture, heat, chemicals are the principal stimuli concerned here. The effect is not a simple sum or resultant, but a sort of unity of a very peculiar kind: each single component may change the organism's sense of irritability, or "Stimmung," towards any other component. A certain sort of innate direction relative to the axis may be among the components that influence the behaviour of a certain organ ("autotropism"). It would at least be difficult to apply the machine theory of life in these cases.

So much on tropisms.

Are the directive movements in freely moving Protista or animals, called "taxis," explainable in the same way as tropisms?

"*Taxis*"

It is clear that the direction and the movement are two different things. It is the direction only that is considered here, and so we may better say: "taxis" signifies the specific orientation of a specific axis of the organism with regard to the direction of any directed agent of the medium.

[1] A very strange case belonging here is discussed by Francé (*Zeitschr. f. d. Ausbau d. Entwickelungslehre*, i. 4, 1907).

If the taxis is combined with or followed by movement, there will, of course, be a specific direction in this movement also.

The word "taxis" thus applies only to the correspondence of directions. It does not say the least thing about the means of movement, by which the orientation of the organism goes on; it does not even seek to point out that the process of orientation is quite a simple process. In fact, a very easy consideration shows that the process of "taxis" is by no means simple in many cases.

Imagine an organism,—say a protozoon or a crayfish, in order to show from the beginning that the particular motor organs in question are of no consequence—and imagine it placed with its long axis at a certain angle towards the direction say of the rays of light proceeding from a radiant point. Then "taxis," in this case "phototaxis" or "heliotaxis," would be said to occur, if the organism carries out some sort of turning movement so long as there is any deviation between the direction of its axis and the rays of light; the movement being performed equally well by the cilia of the protozoon or by the legs of the crayfish. Certainly the "taxis" here is neither immediate nor simple; it is a *combination* of very many single motor acts, leading to taxis as a *result*, though this result must be said to have been reached in an unbroken line. We have to assume that the motor organs of one side of our organism are stimulated by the rays of the light as long as there is no symmetrical arrangement of both of its sides with regard to the direction of the light; of course, the result of stimulation of this kind would be finally a symmetry of orientation.

Nothing of course would be *explained* by calling any process of movement of this sort "taxis": but "taxis" certainly would be a good name for *embracing* a rather simple class of co-ordinated movements, which have a very apparent common feature in the fixed relation of the directions between the stimulus or cause and the final effect, reached without any interruption in an unbroken line.

It is true, the phenomena of this so-called taxis were known not to be so simple as described here; there were all the kinds of complications known from the phenomena of tropisms. Taxis was called "positive" in the case when the anterior end of the organism was finally placed towards the stimulating source, and it was called "negative" in the opposite case. Now it was found that the same organism, which had proved to be positively phototactic or chemotactic, could react negatively when the intensity of the stimulus increased, and conversely. But the point of this change was by no means fixed for a given individual; the organism could become adapted or acclimatised to a stimulus which at first had caused the avoiding or negative reaction, and could thus become positive without any change of the medium. But other conditions of the medium, such as its salinity or temperature, were also found to have an influence upon the "sense" of taxis, say with regard to the rays of the sun (J. Loeb).

That was the general state of the apparently well established theory of taxis about six years ago. Was it possible to explain all these facts as being simple and machine-like in the same way as simple reflexes? The difficulties, as with tropisms, lay in the variability of the point of changing the tactical sense and in the phenomena of simultaneous irritation by different stimuli.[1] But these difficulties might perhaps not be regarded as sufficient to *force* us to accept vitalism, *though, of course, to deny the logical necessity of a vitalistic conception of biological facts does not imply the impossibility of vitalistic agents being actually at work in them.*

So much about the aspect of the theory of "taxis" a few years ago.

γ. THE WORK OF H. S. JENNINGS. "TRIAL AND ERROR"

Now it is very important for our present purposes to observe that "taxis," in the sense we have analysed, seems to occur to a rather limited extent only. There is a true and real "galvanotaxis" amongst Infusoria, and there are a few "tactical" phenomena in animals, as for instance when *Hydra* or a flatworm turns its head towards a strong light or towards a mechanical stimulus. But very much of what had been called phototaxis or chemotaxis or thermotaxis, among Protozoa as well as among higher animals, has actually been shown to be not taxis at all, that is, not a final correspondence of direction reached in an unbroken line comparable to the tropisms in plants, but something very different. It therefore must be regarded as possible at least, that in the future still more cases of "taxis" will prove to be illusory, though, as must be mentioned, J. Loeb and certain other writers only

[1] Compare the suggestive article, "Die Lichtsinnesorgane der Algen," by R. H. Francé, Stuttgart, 1908. Francé's conception of "Reizverwertung" —originally created by Kohnstamm in a purely psychological sense—is very well descriptive of what happens.

concede a very limited validity to the views recently brought into the field, and maintain the old "taxis"-theory.

The *new* doctrine of "taxis," and at the same time quite a new theory of the elements of animal movements in general, is due to Herbert Jennings.[1] Jennings made his important discoveries by studying not only the final result of any directed agent acting upon the organism, *but also the moving individual itself in the very act of moving.* This very act of moving, especially in the case of Protozoa, was proved to be anything but a single and unbroken act of turning. "Taxis" thus became a mere resultant of the most various single motor acts, and, with the sole exception of galvanotaxis, ceased to be a proper name for the process.

I shall be only following the historical line of events, if I now try first to give a short sketch of Jennings' solution of the problem of taxis, and then begin the real systematics of animal motions.

The Resolution of "Taxis"

The infusorium *Paramecium* is "positively chemotactic" to a weak solution of acetic acid, that is to say, a number of these Protista living in a dish that contains a drop of such a solution in any part of the water after a certain time will be found to be all in a certain region around this drop, which, of course, is slowly diffusing into the surrounding water. The old theory would say in this case, that the

---

[1] Compare his work, *Behaviour of Lower Organisms* (New York, 1906), where the full literature is to be found.

lines of diffusion of the acetic acid orient the *Paramecia* positively according to their direction, and that thus the *Paramecia* reach the solution by simply swimming forward after the orientation is completed. But that would be far from the truth. Jennings found, on the contrary, by observing the single individuals, that all the Infusoria swim *at random* and enter the solution at random also, but that then they are kept within the limits of a certain concentration of the diffusing acid by a very strange feature: as soon as they reach those limits the passing of which would bring them out of the region of the acid, they give a certain very typical motor reaction, which makes them remain in the region where they were. The reaction consists in a swimming backward, combined with a revolution round the long axis and a turning to the aboral side.

And quite the same holds for "negative chemotaxis," as happening, for instance, in the presence of a solution of ordinary salt. All of the animals which by their ordinary forward motion would reach the region of a certain concentration of the diffusing chloride of sodium, perform the reaction just named in the very moment of entering this region. Thus they never really penetrate to this region, for the reaction may be repeated as often as necessary; but the few organisms which were in the region of the salt at the beginning of the experiment may freely leave it. In the end, of course, all the animals are out of range of the solution, just as in "positive chemotaxis" all the animals were in range.

It must be granted that Loeb, in establishing what he called "Unterschiedsempfindlichkeit," *i.e.* the reactions of animals to differences of intensity say of light, came very near to the views sketched here, though he was (and is) far from admitting the resolution of *all* kinds of "taxis" in this way.[1]

Chemotaxis thus is proved by Jennings to be a mere resulting effect of many different single performances, and is not a simple and immediate process of orientation at all.[2]

And what holds with regard to chemicals is also true with regard to heat, light, contact, and any other stimulus except the galvanic current, and applies not only to Infusoria, but also to Flagellata, and Bacteria, and Rotatoria, and all other sorts of invertebrate animals; as far at least as experiments in the style of Jennings have been carried out. Therefore, though we cannot say at present that *no* case whatever of "taxis" exists (except galvanotaxis), we shall not, I believe, be very far wrong in saying that probably the range of "taxis" will prove finally to be at least very restricted.

It now might seem that the typical motor reaction shown by *Paramecium*, either in leaving or in entering the solution applied in the experiment, is of the type of a true reflex of the most simple kind, and that, therefore, in spite of the resolution of the concept of "taxis," as maintained by Jennings, the simple reflex would be the actual basis of

[1] I cannot agree with Walter (*Journ. exp. Zool.* 5, 1907.—Here full literature on the subject), when, in his studies on the reactions of *Planaria* to light, he applies the term "Phototaxis" to reactions of this worm towards differences of the intensity of illumination. The word "taxis" strictly depends on the theory that refers to the *direction* of a stimulus exclusively.

[2] I should not believe that the resolution of "taxis," according to the analysis of Jennings, would apply to the phenomena of the wandering of embryonic cells to specific localities in the case of "directive stimuli" (see vol. i. p. 104). The old theory might also hold perhaps in cases of "inflammation" and the protective migrations of cells in general (Metschnikoff; see also vol. i. p. 206).

all movement whatever. So indeed Jennings thought in the first period of his work, but a more thorough study taught him very differently.

The Single Motor Acts. The " Movement at Random "

This now is the right point to begin the systematic study of the types of animal movements; let us consider, in the first place, what may be called *single motor acts*.

The " simple reflex " is one of these acts, but it is far from being the most original or the most widely distributed of them; it seems to be restricted to certain specific types of motion among the higher classes of animals; even what is performed by our *Paramecium* is not a simple reflex.

The most original motor act, that is to say, the most elemental one both ontogenetically and systematically (" phylogenetically "), is *" motion at random," i.e.* an indefinitely variable motor effect following some sort of a stimulus and having no specific relation to the locality of the latter, whether the locality of possible stimulation be a limited and fixed one, as for instance in many Infusoria, or not, as in many higher animals and in all Amoebae.

There are two classes of original movements at random requiring to be distinguished. The first consists of such single motor acts as show an absolute contingency, the second of those which show a relative one. All Amoebae are a good instance of the first type: any stimulation may be followed by every possible movement in every geometrically possible direction out of a strictly indefinite number of possibilities; the same holds for many worms. But in Infusoria, as in all animals that are more specifically organised with regard to their locomotory organs, the number of motor possibilities is more restricted: *Paramecium* for instance always swims backward, revolves round the axis, and turns to the aboral side. That might seem to be a typical reflex, but in fact is far from being so. *One* of the components of the motor reaction allows an indefinite variety of motions at random even here—the revolving round the long axis. This act may be performed to any possible amount, and, of course, the slightest variety in performing it would bring the animal to quite a different part of the dish in the course of its subsequent movements. Jennings has introduced the appropriate name of "action system" to signify the typical restriction of possible movements, indefinite [1] in spite of it, which are founded upon the typical locomotory organisation: it is clear that all higher animals possess such a system, and that man for instance is restricted by it from flying.

Thus then all single motor acts that could be actually observed were found to be of the type of "movement at random," occurring either on a definite action system or on an absolutely indefinite one. There was scarcely any reflex of the *true* kind, in the sense of an *absolutely* fixed correspondence of locomotory cause and effect.

The Modifiability of Single Motor Acts

The concept of the contingency of single motor acts embraces the fact of their modifiability. But as our mind is forced to conceive all that happens as being univocally

[1] We might speak here of an indefiniteness of different orders, as mathematics does.

determined, the problem at once arises, by what factors or conditions the actual performance of a particular movement in a particular case is actually determined as such.

Let us first remark that motion in itself by no means requires a separate external cause for each of its single phases. On the contrary, not only can periodic movements like those in medusae or in the heart of animals be said to be due to innate causes or stimuli, and to be, so to say, the normal permanent state of the animal or the organ, but *changes* of the specific type of random-movements may also occur from within. In *Hydra* such an innate change of different contingent motions may be studied with the greatest advantage.

This possibility of a change of single random-motions from within now gives us the key to an understanding of their change as occurring in response to an external stimulus. It is always the interior general state of the organism that determines which particular motor performance is to go on, whether the state of rest is to be changed into a state of some possible movement, or whether permanent motion is to change its type.

Yet we may speak of motions occurring "at random" although we know that they are determined, provided that we know *nothing specific* about the general state of the organism in question. In fact, the movements of an animal which otherwise would not move at all, or the changes of motion in a permanently moving organism, may properly be called "random," if they do not follow any specific law with regard to their *sequence*, if they go on until the stimulus from without, that has caused them, is escaped quite accidentally during and by the moving.

Jennings has spoken of the method of "trial and error" in these cases as well as in others to be studied hereafter. I should like to avoid this term, for, besides its psychological aspect, which seems to be out of place here, the word "trial" seems to me to imply some sort of so-called "experience." But *here* in the simple fact of movement at random there is nothing of that sort as far as we know; it only *might* be, that the true random-motions might offer the material *for* "experience," as will be seen on a later occasion.

Contingency thus is the leading characteristic of the performance of all these most elemental single motor acts, as well as of their being stopped.

But there are cases where something more definite may be said about the factors that determine the type of each single motion. Typical interior states — not only quite generally conceived ones—may change the type of reaction as well as stop motion altogether in spite of the external stimulus being still present. Thus it is well known, especially from the studies of Coelenterata, that a hungry animal reacts otherwise or not at all, if compared with a fed one, with regard to the same stimulus, and there are also differences of reaction corresponding to the different embryonic stage or the age of an organism.

And moreover we find that a competition among various external stimuli may determine the type of reaction. The effect of a second external stimulus may be either that there is no longer any reaction to the original stimulus, or that a sort of resultant reaction goes on, or that the type of the original reaction is otherwise changed. Here we must recall attention to the so-called reversal of the "sense" of the reaction, as asserted by the theory of "taxis" to occur if the intensity of the original stimulus was increased, or if other stimuli came into play. The facts were quite true, but their real explanation now proves to be of a much more general kind. In fact, there may also be "acclimatisation," say to chemical stimuli; then the avoiding reaction shown at first will not be shown any longer after a certain time: "negative chemotaxis" will cease to exist. And other kinds of stimuli, coming into competition with the original one, may result in the same effect.[1]

But now we come to two classes of modifications of single motor acts, which possess a great importance for all that is to follow.

There may be a typical series of consecutive *different* single motor reactions, whenever the first or any following one of these reactions has not avoided the external stimulus or has not reached the condition "desired," and this typical series may go on until the "desired" state is actually reached. Such typical lines of different single reactions have been well studied by Jennings and his followers in many cases, the most typical ones occurring in the infusorium *Stentor* and in Actinians. If a *Stentor* is disturbed, say by some sort of light powder falling upon it, it *first* bends to one side

[1] A very remarkable fact of this class has recently been discovered by Minkiewicz (*Arch. Zool. exp. et gén.* 4 sér. 7, notes, 1907): the crab *Maia* may change the *quality*—not the "sense"—of its "chromotropism," which is independent of its reaction to light in general, according to the colour of the ground it lives upon, and another crab, *Hippolyte*, changes its colour and its chromotropism correspondingly. In this case the whole phenomenon falls most markedly under the concept of what we have called "physiological adaptation" in the first volume of this book. Indeed, the question may arise, whether all modifications of primitive motor irritability may not be considered under this heading in further analytical studies. Of course, what Minkiewicz calls chromo-"tropism" ought rather to be styled chromo-"taxis," and, most probably, is no *real* "taxis."

several times, but, if it is not freed from the stimulus, a *second* type of reaction sets in: the direction of the ciliary movement is reversed. Again without success; even the *third* type of reaction, contraction into the tube, is unsuccessful, and it is only the *last* kind of motion, swimming away, that definitively frees our animal from the "disliked" condition. Here quite decidedly the fact that one type of movement has occurred determines the type of the next reaction: the word "trial," though not quite correct even here, seems at least to have a better meaning than if applied to mere movement at random.

It also might seem to be a typical sequence of reaction types, if to a very weak stimulus our *Stentor* first answers in its usual original manner, and after that does not react any more: but it seems to me that here we have nothing but the well-known fact of acclimatisation.

To the last typical class of modifiability of simple motor acts only a few words may be devoted in *this* connexion. If *Stentor*, after going through the whole series of possible reactions, is stimulated in exactly the same way once more, it answers with the *ultimate* reaction at once, supposing the intermediate time has not been very long. And similar features in simple motor actions have been observed in other Protozoa, in Actinians, and some worms. Did these animals acquire any "experience," even of the most simple kind? And what does "experience" mean in natural science? A later chapter will have to deal with this most fundamental question.

Looking back upon the whole of the work done, especially by Jennings, we see that there is nothing very fixed about the most primitive types of animal movement, but something very variable. In some cases we understand the laws and principles of such variability, in others they either do not exist or they escape us by reason of the minuteness of the objects in question.

Shall we by adopting the "machine-theory" of life be able to understand all that has been observed regarding the most simple movements? Most of it, certainly, *might* be understood in such a manner, at least in principle, and as long as no greater complexity is discovered. But to prove that the fact of so-called "experience" is beyond the limits of such an explanation, will be the object of a special discussion in the future. Of course, as mentioned before, to affirm the *possibility* of *mechanical* explanation is not to affirm the *impossibility* of *vitalistic* actuality: for methodological reasons we always hold the "machine-theory" of life as long as possible—this theory *may* be actually wrong even in the apparently most simple phenomena in organisms.

δ. CO-ORDINATED MOTIONS

We now leave the work of Herbert Jennings and turn to a short survey of the possible classes of so-called *co-ordinated motions*.

Much has long been known about the elemental processes that go on in the nervous system of a moving animal, or, rather, much has been *attributed* to this system in the form of a so-called "property" or "functional state." For it must be well understood that the *immediate* subject of experimental study always and in every case has been the state of the motor organs as such; so-called nervous states or conditions have been *inferred* from this study, and, so to say, have been projected upon the nervous system. It was seen that simple nervous conduction would not suffice to explain what happens here, and the word "centre" therefore played a great though rather mysterious rôle. "Centres" were identified with the anatomical ganglia until Bethe showed that in crabs some typical reflexes may go on even after the ganglia have been extirpated. A certain school of modern physiologists then thought they might drop the concept of a "centre" altogether, but more recently a sort of compromise between the old and the new theory has been come to. The concepts of "inhibition" and "path-making" ("Hemmung," "Bahnung," in German), and the like have been employed to designate elemental conditions of the nervous system, apart from conduction, that are concerned in combined motions.

The Concepts of von Uexkuell

It seems to me that the system of elemental nervous qualities which von Uexkuell[1] has lately created may claim to be the most complete and the most original conception in this field. To state in a few words the logical value of von Uexkuell's concepts as relating to the general theory of movement, it seems to me that he has formulated what might be called the elemental "*means*" in the mutual relation of the motor parts used and con-

[1] See especially *Leitfaden in das Studium der experimentellen Biologie der Wassertiere*, Wiesbaden, 1905. Von Uexkuell's work is composed of an analytical and of an hypothetical or fictive part; we only deal here with the former, which is very valuable. This part will retain its value, it seems to me, even if the hydrodynamic and electric hypothesis of "tonus" has to be given up.

cerned in any correlated motion whatever. I should like to parallel his concepts of "tonus," "tonus - reservoir," "blocking," "latching" ("Klinkung"), etc., directly with the elemental concepts of formative stimulus, prospective potency, inner means, etc., in morphogenesis. For, in fact, all the concepts of von Uexkuell are concerned in *any* co-ordinated movement whatever, though, properly understood, *none of them, of course, says anything about the specificity of co-ordination as such.*

Now it is of great importance, that the analytical results of von Uexkuell about the elements concerned in co-ordinated motion are in a most perfect state of harmony with what Jennings discovered about simple motor acts.

Let us mention at least a few of the elemental nervous relations revealed by von Uexkuell's work. The type of any single act of a combined movement may be altered by the intensity of the stimulus, or by its quality, or by the introduction of a second simultaneous stimulus, either at the same spot or elsewhere, or by the occurrence of previous stimulations; and there may be a change in the behaviour regarding the single constituents in consecutive times of their realisation; and one reacting constituent may be stopped by any other one whatever.

There is hardly one feature in this doctrine of the constituents of combined motion that does not appear in the single motor acts as well. Combined motions thus are far from being a grouping of simple typical reflexes exclusively: most of what was believed to be truly reflex has been proved not to be so.[1]

[1] It must be understood that von Uexkuell himself (see *Zeitschrift f. Biol.* 50, 1907, p. 168) adheres to the reflex-theory of movement, and that

The Classes of Co-ordination

And now let us glance at the different types or classes of co-ordinated animal motions, always asking at each step, what would be intelligible here on the theory of a machine and what would not.

The simplest class—considered *logically*—of all co-ordinated movements is formed by the so-called "chain-reflexes," which seem to occur in several groups of Invertebrates; one typical simple reflex is combined here with a number of others in a fixed way. Either—as in Medusae or in the heart of higher animals—one simple reflex causes the simultaneous performance of many similar equal ones, or the end of the performance of one is the stimulus to the performance of the other, as in the movements of many so-called metameric animals. We may speak of "synchronic" reflexes in the first case and "metachronic" ones in the second. In the jelly-fish all the parts of the "umbrella" move together as soon as one of them has begun movement, and in the earthworm the end of the contraction of one segment always causes the next one to move. And it may happen that parts of an animal which are dissimilar in organisation may also appear as the single constituents of a metachronic chain-reflex. It is especially to J. Loeb[1] that much of our knowledge of "chain-reflexes"

both Uexkuell and Jennings are constantly at literary warfare with one another. But it seems to me that this is owing to a mutual misunderstanding. In any case von Uexkuell does not operate with the *old* concept of "reflex" exclusively; his important discrimination between *two* elemental functions of muscles and motor nerves—ordinary contraction and "Sperrung"—would by itself suffice to show that.

[1] *Comparative Physiology of the Brain and Comparative Psychology*, New York, 1900.

is due. Of course these simple phenomena would be perfectly intelligible on the machine-theory.

Unfortunately they are not so common as Loeb and others thought them to be. The next class of combined motions, first established by von Uexkuell, already forces us to introduce some other elemental nervous phenomena besides mere stimulation and nervous conduction. This type is seen in the progressive movements of many lower animals, but also, as shown by Sherrington,[1] in the movements of vertebrates, so far as they depend on the spinal cord only. The most simple scheme of the class is expressed by the fact, that every motor stimulation in "simple nerve-nets" always relates to those muscles which are not contracted but extended, whether passively or actively. This scheme of course takes no account of the stimulation, but simply states that, *if* the stimulation is *given* and if the organisation of an animal with regard to its muscles is such as it is, the kind of movement is determined in the very simple manner we have mentioned. Many of the rhythmical movements in walking are explained in this way. They depend on the antagonistic character of certain muscles: one muscle has just the opposite effect to another, so that, if the one is contracted, the other is extended; the latter therefore receives the stimulation and contracts; then the other extends, is therefore stimulated, contracts, and so on.

Of course there would be no difficulty in understanding on a purely mechanical hypothesis this simple class of combined movements, in which only one elemental

[1] *Ergebnisse d. Physiol.* 4, 1905; *The Integrative Action of the Nervous System*, New York, 1906.

nervous function, besides mere conduction, seems to be at work.

But, unfortunately again, the simple scheme fails us, as soon as the limits of mere typical progressive motions are transgressed. The sea-urchin, for instance, very properly follows our law when simply walking, but something very different happens as soon as it is put on its back and has to turn over into its normal position; all sorts of new elemental functions, relating to the dependence of the different single motor constituents on one another, are playing their part here, just as circumstances require, and the stating of a simple formula becomes an impossibility. The same holds for the turning over of the starfish, in which the successful movements of some of the arms stop the movement of the others, and, indeed, we properly can say, that almost any movement of an animal, in any way deserving the name "abnormal," shows a particular type of motor combination.

The "righting reactions" of the starfish and certain other points of interest form the subject of a recent very important memoir by Jennings (*Univ. Californ. Publ. Zool.* 4, 1907, p. 53). Jennings fully confirms the older results published by Preyer, and adds a good number of new results. Let me mention only a few topics. *Asterias* was found to avoid obstacles whilst creeping to a certain place in a known environment, but to "explore" every object in new surroundings. The "righting reaction" may show a great many very different types. In each case the *initial* movement of each single arm is determined *separately* by external stimuli or internal conditions, but as soon as the least result with regard to righting is reached a "*unified impulse*" appears; co-ordination sets in where incoordination had been, and by no means can every single motor act now be related to a single stimulus, as was the case at the very beginning of the process; on the contrary, "single" stimuli now cease to have any influence at all; we may say that the animal is not "distracted" by anything. The "unified impulse" may be based upon a great many different constellations of initial movement of the single arms. It is very important to notice well that the righting reactions are not referable to the "normal" position of the animal as such: this hypothesis is refuted by the fact that during the unified period of the reaction the single arms very often perform movements by which they come into "abnormal" positions themselves, or which are indifferent for their own righting: everything occurs in the service of the whole.

It is true, Jennings has shown that the starfish is capable of a good deal of what is popularly called "experience"; therefore the righting reaction and other movements of this animal do not properly belong to this chapter. But it seems to me that it was well worth devoting a few words to the discoveries of Preyer and Jennings at *this* place, as the movements of the starfish have often been looked upon as enormously simple. In any case the reactions of the starfish are not "reflexes," but are in the highest degree what on a later occasion will be called "individualised movements."[1]

In Vertebrates also almost all of the "reflexes"

[1] I am very glad to see that Jennings himself insists upon the *unity* of the phenomena observed. He even concedes that my entelechy would explain this unity, though he declines to see here a true "explanation." In this respect I hope that Part II. of Section B will convince him.

dependent on the spinal cord are *not* reflexes in the old sense of the word, but are motor reactions determined by the stimulus and by all that has happened and that is happening in other parts of the moving body, nay, even by the contingency of the actual general arrangement of the motor organs at a given moment (Sherrington).

The "centres," we are told, store and bind and stop stimulations, and set them free at the right time, and so on. But the word "centre" is only a name here for hypothetic anatomical places, where these processes are supposed to occur. Nothing whatever is explained by the use of this ambiguous word.

And now there are still other instances of combined motions of a far greater complexity in style than a simple turning over into the normal position. I am thinking of what is generally known under the name of "instinct." And the last and highest group of combined movements is what is called "action," in which "experience" is at work. What shall we say in the face of all these natural facts?

I regret that I am unable to give here an accurate and minute analysis of all possible sorts of co-ordinated movements; but it seems to me that some special characters at least of the most typical of the higher classes of combined animal motions ought to be subjected to a closer consideration. It may lead at least to a clear conception of the real *problems* of motor physiology, and perhaps even to somewhat more than that. In the next chapters therefore the typical form of instinct and the typical action will be analysed completely. I shall try to fix, as sharply as possible, what problems may appear in these two groups of organic movements, and what solutions may be given. Other kinds of complicated movements, which are neither instincts nor actions proper, will form a sort of appendix to one or the other of the two great fundamental groups.

2. INSTINCT

We know from our last studies that the elemental processes concerned in animal movements are not only nervous conduction, but may also consist in facts of different kinds which have forced modern authors to make use again of the old word "centre" in a purely physiological sense, after the anatomical meaning of this word had proved to be of rather dubious value for physiological analysis. It is to von Uexkuell that the most thorough analysis of organic movements into their simple components is due, and, in order to express the true logical value of such an analysis, we did not hesitate to compare its results with those furnished us by the analysis of the genesis of form.

But this comparison now has another and very important consequence. We saw that form evidently was the result of the arrangement of certain elements, and that all genesis of form could be reduced to the constellation of certain factors concerned in it; but neither was form a mere sum of those elements nor was its origin the result of a mere sum of these factors. Nothing at all is proved about a totality being a mere sum or not a mere sum by demonstrating the elements it consists of: this holds for form as well as for movements.

As we said, we cannot study here minutely all the varieties of combinations of movement which occur in the animal kingdom. For many of them, it is true, we are able to imagine a machine that would represent how they take place: for the sake of simplicity let us take it for granted that a machine actually exists here, though it is not by any means proved.

But are there not cases of combination of movements, most familiar to all of you, for which it is by no means clear from the beginning that a machine even *could* be present as their foundation? Are there not at least a few classes of animal movements which common sense daily describes by words which seem to express anything but the conviction that they are simple, mechanical, and machine-like events?

Instinct is one of these classes of animal movements, and it is with instinct that our analytical study will have to deal in this chapter.

a. INSOLUBLE PROBLEMS

The problem of instinct used to be one of the chief points in the fight between Darwinians and Lamarckians. As we cannot accept either of these theories, it follows that we shall not study instinct from the usual points of view. It may suffice to state here that the specific instincts of the worker-bees, which are excluded from propagation, would never be open to any Lamarckian explanation, as Weismann has most clearly demonstrated; and on the other hand, every Darwinian explanation fails here for the same general reasons for which it fails in every explanation of combinations that are typical units. *We do not know* what the "history" of instincts is, nor do we know the factors concerned in their history. Let us rather try to discover a little about what factors are concerned in instinctive movements as they actually come before us every day.

At this point a second problem appears, round which discussion centres nowadays. We shall be forced to decline *a limine* this problem also, but a certain justification is required for declining it, and as this justification is to rest on an epistemological basis, which is of first-rate importance for all our studies of animal movements in this chapter and the next, a short excursion into philosophy is necessary.

Are instincts "conscious" or "unconscious" movements? this is the question that is always being discussed at the present day. And yet this problem *cannot* be a scientific or philosophical problem, at least not if the words "conscious" and "consciousness" are to signify what they usually do. Let us proceed most rigorously with regard to this point.

As naturalists we study animal movements as movements of bodies in Nature, and we can do no more. But the terms "conscious" and "consciousness" do *not* belong to that part of the Given which we call Nature; they belong to the Ego, to "my" Ego, and to my Ego exclusively. It is not even possible to express with clearness what is meant by saying that there "*is*" consciousness in any being in Nature. We are faced here by a pseudo-problem of the purest type.

Other physiologists also have denied the possibility of discovering "consciousness" or "unconsciousness" in the motions of animals. But it almost always was in a practical sense that they spoke of such an impossibility. We understand it in an epistemological sense. There may be feelings quite unknown to us, such authors have said; therefore it would be better not to speak about feelings. But we say: the " being " of " feelings " in Nature is meaningless altogether. " Being " relates to bodily movements and changes, in that sense of " being " which is the only starting-point of all science, in the sense of " being given to my Ego."

It is true: the concept of " being " may be enlarged by an advanced philosophical science; we ourselves have enlarged it, and shall do so further on by introducing potentialities as " being." But even such potentialities if conceived as natural agents or factors would never be " consciousness." The word " conscious " belongs to introspective psychology exclusively.

β. THE ACTUAL PROBLEM. DEFINITIONS

But what about instincts? How are we to formulate *our* legitimate and scientific problem? It seems to me that there can be but little doubt how we are to formulate it. Are those animal movements, commonly called instincts, such that they might be founded on a machine, a physico-chemical manifoldness in space, embracing only physico-chemical elemental factors, or are there some features in instincts which forbid us to assume the existence of such a machine even hypothetically?

Let us first try to give a purely verbal definition of the instinctive motions in question. It will prove to be rather difficult to find an under limit of instinct, though it is easy to find an upper one. All instincts are separated from the next higher group of motion, which we propose to call "actions" in the widest sense of the word, by being complete in their specificity from the very first time they occur. There may be some improvement in consequence of their being repeated, but this improvement never affects their specificity as such. Perhaps it will be more correct to say that we shall not apply the term "instinct" to any animal movement that shows an improvement with regard to its specificity.

Instincts are often said to be "purposeful" with regard to their performer. We prefer to say, at present, that they possess some regulative character; that they tend to "normality" with regard to the whole life of the organism which performs them. Here the limit between instincts and other classes of motions is not always very clearly marked: almost all typically combined motions, be they pure chain-reflexes or be they of a more complicated type, are alike in possessing a regulative character. And it is impossible to draw a sharp boundary here, if one has renounced the question of "consciousness" as illegitimate. In fact, all instincts are chains of single nervous acts concerned in movements, just as are real chain-reflexes and many other combined motions: it is only the degree of chaining that comes into account.

But what is the meaning of the word "degree" in this connexion? Does it apply only to different states of complication of the same invariable general type? It is here that our analytical problems begin.

γ. THE WORK OF J. LOEB

Up to about 1890 instincts were studied almost exclusively from the historical point of view, or with regard to their relation to "consciousness." Jacques Loeb was the first to see the inadequacy of both these methods, and to put the problem of instinct on its clear physiological basis. Unfortunately in doing so Loeb was influenced by the materialistic dogmatism of his time. The single reflex was to him the prototype of all elemental factors concerned in movement, all complex or chain movements were regarded as being of the most simple additive kind, even the complications afterwards discussed by von Uexkuell were then unknown. Hence it was possible for Loeb to regard instincts also as nothing but chain-reflexes of the mere additive type. One of the elementary processes composing the instinct was regarded as being the cause of the next one, and so on. The general state of the organism was not neglected in this analysis, and it was well known to Loeb that young animals may show "chain-reflexes" different from those shown by the adult, and that a well-nourished animal may react differently from a hungry animal; but the different physiological state of the animal in these cases was *a priori* regarded as being a mere point of its organisation in the widest sense, and nervous conduction remained the only physiological element taken as proved; even so-called "inhibition" was not regarded as a nervous function *sui generis*.

Thus pseudo-psychological problems yielded to problems of mechanical dogmatism in the physiology of instincts.

But in spite of that, one point of great importance was

gained by the work of Loeb, and it is from this point that a purely analytical treatment of the theory of instincts must start. By resolving all instincts into chain-reflexes that as a whole were of the well-known character of "taxis," Loeb implicitly had stated a very important *problem* in the form of a *fact*: science in the future will have to find out whether there *is* any such fact.

δ. THE PROBLEM OF THE STIMULI OF INSTINCTS

If indeed all instincts are of the type of very simple co-ordinated motions, whether that be the most simple and merely additive type or any more complicated one—in short, if all instincts as a whole are of the character of a "taxis," it follows that it only can be the simple and elemental agents in Nature which can act as *stimuli* to instincts. The stimuli of instinctive movements may be light of different wave-lengths, or heat, or moisture, or chemical compounds, *but they never are specific typical bodies.*

It will soon appear how important this statement is. If only *simple* stimuli are concerned in instinctive life, the relation between the medium and the instinct may easily be explained on the analogy of a machine, at least in principle. But what are we to say if typical complicated stimuli, if "*individualised*" stimuli, as we shall call them, also awaken instinctive movements?

Let us first try to show, by the aid of a simple instance, what is meant by our two contrasted classes of stimuli: Lloyd Morgan [1] performed a series of very fine experiments in order to show whether chickens, just hatched from the

[1] *Habit and Instinct,* London, 1896.

egg, react to the specific bodies forming their food or not. Putting them in front of a dish which contained peas and other small bodies of the most different kinds mixed together, he saw them pick up these little bodies most accurately. But they took *all* kinds of them, and experience alone taught them to discriminate between what was food and what was not. On the other hand, it had often been pointed out that young poultry had an instinctive fear of the hawk and the hawk's cry. Lloyd Morgan showed that young poultry are frightened by *any* large body in motion and by *any* very shrill sound. Thus these fine experiments teach us two things: they teach us what simple and what individualised stimuli are, and that, as far as experimentally ascertained, only simple stimuli are the external stimuli of instincts. Indeed, all cases of instincts which have been the subject of experimental work hitherto have proved to be due to simple external stimuli exclusively. The instinctive antipathy between dog and cat is probably also the effect of chemical compounds, of a "smell," if we choose to speak a little less accurately, and not of an individualised stimulus, not of the cat or the dog as being "seen."

But the experiments about this important question are not at all numerous, and it can by no means be categorically asserted that instincts, in the true sense of the word, are *never* called forth by a specific body which psychologically would be called a "seen" one,[1] or, speaking more generally, by a stimulus of the individualised type.

[1] Elise Hanel (*Zeitschr. f. allg. Physiol.* iv. 1904) has shown, following the line of certain experiments of Ch. Darwin, that the earthworm reacts specifically to the specific form of leaves or pieces of paper, always trying to draw them into its tube-like cave by their most pointed edge; the earthworm, in fact, can be stimulated by a typical sequence of different singularities,

Now it is very important to notice that, *if an actual case of a specific individualised stimulus of an instinct should become known, the limits of the possibility of a mechanical explanation would be exceeded.* They would be exceeded, and an autonomic or vitalistic factor would be at work, because it could by no means be understood how the specifically combined or "individualised" stimulus could be *received* by the organism in such a way as to become the cause of a specific and fixed series of motions in the organism. Supposing that any organism were specifically affected in its instinctive movements by the mere *sight* of any other typical organism, say of the same species but of the other sex,[1] and that this affection were the same, whether the organism which forms the stimulus were seen from before or from behind, or from the side and at any angle whatever: what would follow from such a fact? A machine could only be fitted to receive the specific complicated stimulus in a few typical positions, but how could a machine be imaginable if an infinite variety of aspects had the same invariable instinctive effect?

We may stop our discussion at this point, as a very

which are only relatively determined, and its reaction is perfect for the very first time, that is, instinctive. New researches are required to clear up the facts that come into account here.

Chickens are well known to peck their peas or corn with a right calculation concerning the dimension of depth the very first time they do peck. Speaking psychologically: the right idea of space is innate in them not only "a priori," in the sense of Kant, but strictly "before" all experience in the temporal sense of the word "before."

Are these facts of use in our present problem?

[1] As regards sexuality the existence of "individualised" stimuli of instincts seems indeed highly probable. Male moths deprived of their wings were found by Mayer-Soule (*Journ. exp. Zool.* 3, 1906) not to be admitted to copulation by the females; but only if the females were not deprived of their sight!

similar problem will meet us in our analysis of action, and will be fully discussed on that occasion. Moreover, the whole of our present analysis rests on a *problematic* basis: for nothing is *known* at present with absolute certainty about individualised stimuli of instinctive motions. But it seems to me highly probable that future investigation will discover such cases, and the present discussion is written particularly in order to encourage research in this direction. Bees and ants especially, but vertebrates too, it seems to me, would have to be studied with respect to the question whether there are cases in which specific complicated bodies that are "seen" may be the stimuli of real instincts.[1]

If we like to give up for a moment our strictly scientific language and allow ourselves the use of the common pseudo-psychological terminology, we may say that all cases in which individualised stimuli were at work would require the assumption of a something that would be nearly related to the "innate ideas" refuted by Locke in another sense. Physiologists of the old school of the German "Naturphilosophie" often have spoken of a sort of dreaming as being the foundation of instinctive life. It would be this sort of dreaming that we should meet here, and the only difference between the old investigators and ourselves would be one of terminology: we should not speak of dreaming or of innate ideas, but, as naturalists arguing from the standpoint of critical idealism, we should say that an autonomic,

[1] In a former publication (*Die "Seele"*) I distinguished two classes of "reflexes," the fixed and the "freely combined" ones ("frei-combiniert") —the word "reflex" being used in a wider sense than in the present book. All "freely combined" reflexes, it seems to me, might present quite the same set of analytical problems as true instincts do, in *every* respect—provided they are not simple forms of "acting," as indeed the righting reactions of the starfish are (see page 31 f.).

an entelechian natural factor was found to be at work in instinctive life, as far as the reception of stimuli is concerned.

ε. THE PROBLEM OF THE REGULABILITY OF INSTINCTS

Our mention of the old physiologists may serve us as a stepping-stone to the analysis of the second chief problem which instincts offer to theoretical biology. Here also the main point must remain problematic, as facts are too scanty at present for a definite statement. But here also the analysis of possibilities may serve to give an impulse to future research.

The old physiologists, such as Treviranus and Johannes Müller, often compared morphogenesis with instinctive life, and it is to Schopenhauer that the most thorough comparison between the phenomena of instinctive movements and embryological processes is due. Instincts are regarded by this school as being in some way the *continuation of morphogenesis*, as growing upon the same ground, as governed by the same reason, viz. the vital principle.

As we have said already, we do not know at present whether such a view is fully legitimate or not; further investigation will determine that. But we can make use of the comparison between morphogenesis and instinct to raise another question, besides the problem of the nature of the instinctive stimuli, the answer to which may one day enable us either to admit the autonomic nature of instincts or to deny it.

Certainly instincts are comparable with morphogenetic phenomena for the simple and descriptive reason that they occur completely and purposefully the very first time they go on in the individual. Might not there be another point of similarity? Morphogenetic processes, as we know, are liable to be regulated on the largest scale: disturbances of the organisation or of the morphogenetic process itself are followed by atypical processes leading again to the typical result. Are there any true *regulations* known among instincts?

Regulations in instincts, of course, would hardly be accessible to observation if there were not any visible effects of the instinctive activity: but that does not happen very often. Regulation occurs, in fact, in all cases of so-called technical or artistic instincts, as known among birds, among spiders and among bees, ants, and some other insects. The instinctive activity of these animals ends in a certain specific state of the medium. Let us disturb the state, say of a nest or a bee's hive, let us change the material offered to a bird for its nest, and let us see what will happen.

Unfortunately not a single experiment except one has been carried out with the special purpose of determining the kind and degree of regulability of instinctive movements as such. Such knowledge as we have has been gained almost entirely in the field of so-called natural history, and without a full analytical discussion.

It is important to notice once more at the very beginning, that we are not dealing here with the possibility of a modification of instinctive life by so-called "experience." Our question is this: Are instinctive acts liable to regulative modifications in the same manner, complete and purposeful from the beginning, as are embryological processes?

Bees are known to repair the cells of their honeycomb

after disturbances; they, moreover, may change the style of building them, to suit the requirements of space, and they also may build their house in an abnormal direction with respect to gravity, should circumstances require it: instead of building from above to below, they may also build from below to above, and also sideways. The silkworm is said not to form its web of silk if it is cultivated in a box containing tulle, and some species of bees which normally construct tunnels do not do so if they find one ready made in the ground, they then only perform their second instinctive act: separating the tunnel into single cells.

In all of these cases, except the one relating to gravity, the state of affairs seems to be the following. What has been changed from without is either the perfect result of the full sequence of instinctive acts, or it is what might be called an embryological state somewhere in this sequence, that is, some state in the sequence that leads to the perfect result. And the artificial change of the second class may again be of two kinds: either something may be taken away from what the animal had accomplished already, or something may be added to the result of its activity, something, of course, that would occur in the process of normal construction. In all these cases the animal will adjust its instinctive movements to the *actual* state of matters, no matter whether it has to do more or less than normally—more, if parts of its own construction are taken away, less, if parts are added to it artificially.

There can be no doubt that the term " regulation " is justified in these cases. What then does this mean, and what can it teach us as to our question about the autonomic character of instincts?

Of course, the *actual* state of affairs, artificially modified from what had been performed by the organism, must be transmitted in some way to the latter, in order that its future behaviour may correspond to this actual state. It seems to me that it is from the possible or probable nature of this transmission that an analytical discussion of our problem must start. The instinctive motions concerned in all sorts of constructions form a consecutive chain of single performances, which normally seem to be called forth one by the other, but which, as experiments show, *may* also be called forth independently. So we again meet the problematic question as to the "calling forth" of instinctive motions, as to the instinctive stimulus. Normally the whole sequence of a constructive instinct *may* go on as follows. The elemental act a results in the state of construction A; the next state of construction is B; B is due to an instinctive process b; b *may* be set going only because a is finished, but it also *may* be called forth by the existence of A, which, of course, is something very different. The mere fact of regulation, as we have described it, seems to show that the second alternative meets the case: that it is the existence of A, the constructive result of the first elemental instinctive act, that is the stimulus of b, for in the case of the regulation b goes on without a or after b itself has already once taken place: without a, if the result of the instinctive act was changed by the adding, and after a previous b, if it was changed by the removing of anything. It is here that we meet the problem of how the state of A *as such* may be transmitted to the organism in order to determine what is to go on, and it is clear that this is precisely the problem of the *nature of the stimulus* calling forth b, regarded as an independent instinctive phase. *Is this stimulus simple or is it individualised*, that is to say, specifically combined of elements?

It is not very pleasant to be again obliged to leave our question unsolved, but nothing has been done in an exact manner towards answering it. It may seem, of course, as if only typically combined or "individualised" stimuli could suffice to explain the modification of the instinctive acts in exact correspondence with what is required; but this is only probable, nothing more.

I once more feel obliged to say that the evidence of the mere *fact* of regulation among instincts is very scanty at present. Indeed even what we have mentioned about observations of this kind is hardly as well established as it ought to be, and I freely confess that I have treated so-called "facts" here as if they were a little better established than they probably are, simply in order to get a basis for our analytical discussion. It remains, however, a mere discussion of possibilities. For not one of the observations which we have mentioned, regarding the regulability of instincts, has been made with the special purpose of studying that particular point.

Let us shortly mention the only experimental case in which our problem has been studied with full and careful attention. The entomologist Ch. F. Schroeder,[1] in studying the behaviour of certain caterpillars by the aid of experiments, has found that these animals are able to adapt their instinctive acts of spinning most accurately to the real state of the product formed so far; he not only saw them repairing their weaving, after it had been disturbed inten-

[1] *Verhandl. d. zool. Ges.* 1903, p. 158.

tionally, but his caterpillars also formed typical tissues by using leaves of abnormal forms intentionally prepared, or by using leaves of plants that are not normally employed.

It is to be hoped that future research will follow in the track of the one last mentioned, that is to say, that entomologists will observe the behaviour of their insects with the full appreciation of the bearing of the study upon the problems of theoretical biology, and not only in the interests of natural science proper.[1]

ζ. CONCLUSION

Here, then, we may close our discussion of instinctive movements. It has yielded some indications of vital autonomy in the field of instinctive life, but no real, absolute proofs; for the facts are too scanty at present to allow any definite answer to the chief problems appearing in this field, viz. the problem of the nature of the stimuli and of the regulability of instincts, the latter problem being reducible to the former. It is probable that both these problems will be answered some day in favour of vitalism, that, as matters stand, no machine can *in fact* be imagined capable of accounting for what happens.

Such a result would not be in conflict with the analytical

[1] Once more I call attention to the "turning over" of animals when put into an abnormal position, though we are not accustomed to speak of instincts proper in these cases (see page 31 f.). No doubt the process of turning in its single phases is exclusively made up of "regulations." Are they of such a type that the "whole" of the actual abnormal state enters in some way, or are they mere sums of single acts, purposeful only on account of their performer's general organisation? Certain experiments of Preyer's seem to me to deserve more attention with regard to our question than they have generally received (*Mitt. zool. Station Neapel*, vii., 1886. See also Jennings, *Behaviour of the Lower Organisms*).

scheme of the co-ordination of organic movements as set forth by von Uexkuell. The *elemental* physiological factors of this scheme would be found to be at work also in instincts; but there would be something else also at work, a "something" that may be said to *make use* of the factors of this scheme.

3. Action

a. PRELIMINARIES

THE way generally taken by science is from the simple to the complicated phenomena, and therefore when turning to the analysis of those organic movements which are called "actions," we might probably be expected to follow this ordinary and well-established route. But we shall not do so, and we have good reasons for so choosing our path. It might seem most natural, after having discussed the main points of the theory of reflexes and instincts, to proceed to analyse first the most simple cases of what might for any reason whatever be called "action," and, after surveying the whole series of animal organisms, to end by analysing the action of man. But there is one special point which renders a totally different arrangement of materials far more suitable and convenient. On account of a very strange feature, which, in spite of its strangeness may be pronounced the most universally known in theoretical biology, we prefer to begin our analysis of action with those cases where action is of the most complicated nature, and only to add certain remarks about its simpler forms at the very end. *The reasoning and analysing naturalist is an acting organism himself*—that is the strange though universally known fact spoken of. One of our final chapters will try to deal with the most central problem, both of philosophy and of biology proper, that is established by this fact; at present we make use of it in a purely practical manner. In observing the actions of animals and men, many more differences are revealed to us in the men than in the animals, because we *understand* the former and not the latter. Psychology thus, though not our aim, is becoming our means of investigation. Only by the aid of a truly objective psychology are we able to analyse action into its ultimate elements. We never could analyse the actions of any animal so far: we do not even see everything that there is to analyse in them.

No Pseudo-psychology

By no means, of course, do we intend by our appeal to psychology to introduce that sort of pseudo-psychology which we excluded from natural science when we were studying instincts. All acting organisms, including acting men, are to us simply *natural bodies in motion*; at least they are *immediately* presented to us as such, though analysis in its progress may introduce natural agents which would represent not motion only but also the possibility of movement. These agents or factors, however, would by no means be psychological in the introspective sense—the only sense which the word "psychological" may legitimately possess.

Our time is limited, and therefore I cannot insist more explicitly upon this methodological point; but let me beg you always to remember that in what follows we shall deal only with such phenomena as occur on *bodies in nature*, called organisms, and that it will be our purpose to discover the laws according to which the motions of these bodies occur. We may end in vitalism again in this chapter; but certainly we shall not end in pseudo-psychology.

General Definition of Action. Classes of Movements which are not Actions

A few remarks about the most general definition of action, in both a positive and a negative form, seem desirable by way of preliminary.

An "action" is every animal movement which depends for its specificity on the individual life history of its performer in such a manner that this specificity depends not only, as will be seen later on, on the specificity of the actual stimulus but also on the specificity of all stimuli in the past, and on their effect. No animal movement is to be called an action in which this criterion is not present at least in a certain degree. In the language of subjective psychology this criterion is called "experience." We shall presently introduce a more suitable name for it, but in this short survey the word "experience" may be used.

There is no experience, and therefore no "action," when the final physiological elemental process in the motor organs, *i.e.* the process of contraction, goes on better the second or third than it did the first time: we speak of "functional adaptation" of the nervous system[1] in this

[1] Functional adaptation of the muscles as such is, of course, another phenomenon, not belonging to the present discussion.

case. Nor is there "action" in the case of so-called muscular "fatigue."

But both these phenomena, especially functional adaptation, that is, an improvement of functioning by functioning itself, may be combined with real acting, and, indeed, there is one group of facts in which this combination is very important. You all know the process which is commonly called the *mechanisation* of acting; the piano-player offers a good instance of it, but any one going down a staircase is also an example. Popular psychology says that here we see complicated motions, which, though under the control of consciousness when first learned, are freed from this control later on. It would be more correct to say that one and the same action-effect, repeated very many times, may combine with functional adaptation of some unknown part of the nervous system in such a way as to acquire almost the character of a typical reflex. This process of what is called "*exercise*" is by no means identical with the process of acting as such, and we have devoted these few words to it in this place in order that we may exclude it from our studies later on.

Moreover, we are not entitled to speak of an "action," if one and the same stimulus has different motor effects according to the variation of certain physiological conditions which are not concerned in the specificity of anything motorial. Such cases are well known among lower animals, and in dealing with the directive motions and with the recent discoveries of Jennings we have already mentioned a few instances in which changes in temperature or salinity, or in the degree of hunger, also change the sense of response to external stimuli. In such cases there is nothing like an individual history of the performer, certainly nothing like history with regard to the particular stimulus then at work.

But then historical elements of *this* sort are entirely absent in another group of phenomena, where at first glance it might possibly seem that they were present. Let us begin with an instance discovered by Jennings in studying the Protozoon *Stentor*, and already shortly mentioned above. To one and the same mechanical stimulus *Stentor* first reacted by a simple turning aside, but this reaction did not bring it out of reach of the stimulus; it then reversed the direction of its ciliary movement, and after that contracted itself into its tube, but without success; the stimulus, a falling of powder, continued; then, finally, the *Stentor* swam away. We here see three or more different reactions following each other in correspondence to one stimulus. We may say, perhaps, that the following reactions occurred *because* the first one was not successful, and certainly there is something of an individual historical element in this behaviour; but, in spite of that, we should prefer not to speak of an action. It is *one series* of events that occurs here, not one reaction at one time and another reaction, modified by experience, at another; there is "trial" perhaps, but no "experience."[1]

But there is "experience," and therefore action, though

---

[1] The same holds for the movements of Ophiurids, according to von Uexkuell and Glaser (*Journ. exp. Zool.* 4, 1907). There is a great variety of reactions, but no "experience." Preyer was right in his description of facts, but not in his interpretation. But in Asterids there exists "experience," besides a great variability of reacting (see the recent memoir of Jennings cited on page 31).

in its most primordial form, when *Stentor*, the experiment with the powder being repeated after a short time, reacts from the very beginning with its fourth kind of reaction instead of with the first one. This example, besides its excluding a whole group of motor phenomena from our future discussion, may well serve at the same time to illustrate provisionally what really will be called "action" by ourselves.

The Distribution of Acting

True actions, though, as will be stated later on, of a less high degree of complication than actions in man, are most clearly exhibited in the following classes of the animal kingdom : in all, even in the lowest classes of vertebrates, in bees, ants, and some beetles, in crabs, cuttle-fishes, Actinia, and some Protozoa.

One point has always to be kept well in mind in all investigations about so-called animal "intelligence." All organisms, of course, can acquire "experience" only about what *is* "experienced" by them : in other terms, only about that which stimulates them to motor reactions. Now it is clear, that it always must remain doubtful in lower organisms what sort of sense organs—to use the common expression at this stage of our argument—they possess; their "medium" will only be the sum of the factors to which they are accessible. How, for instance, could we expect individualised stimuli to act upon organisms possessing no organ like the eye or the ear ? Perhaps it is for this one reason that so little is exactly known about real acting in Protozoa. There are many observations about them — those about their hunting, for instance — which seem to prove that a rather high degree of experience may exist in infusoria; but who can feel able to give any fairly correct answer about the stimuli—of a chemical nature perhaps—which are able to reach such minute organisms?

And, on the other hand, there may be spheres of experience—in the higher classes of the Invertebrates, for instance—which are almost unintelligible to ourselves in a subjective way. Bees seem to remember the absolute amount of their change of place in space. Even if they have been transported passively, and not on a direct line, they always reach their hive again. And similar facts occur in birds.[1]

The very important facts recently discovered by Pawlow and his followers also belong here, as it seems to me, though they do so in a different way. " Association " may relate not only to phenomena of the sensorial or motor class, generally spoken of as " conscious " ones, but to processes of secretion also. Secretion, on the part of the salivary glands, for instance, may be called forth by any stimulus that has ever been contemporary with the original stimulus of the *purely physiological* process of secretion in any way.

A few words on the distribution of experience, not in the animal kingdom, but among the parts of one organism, may close these preliminaries. A little more on the same subject is to follow in another connexion. It has been shown by the experiments of Goltz, Schrader, and

[1] Rádl (*Biol. Centralblatt*, 26, 1906, and other papers) has given a very good analysis of the behaviour of animals with relation to their orientation in space. Part of it is certainly due to sight, to keeping the eye on a fixed object; another part is due to the semicircles connected with the ear of vertebrates, or to other ''statical'' organs; a last part, it seems to me, is not yet understood at all physiologically. The behaviour of bees would belong to the last group.

others that it is not only the so-called hemispheres of the brain of vertebrates that are related to experience. Frogs and pigeons at least, and probably dogs also, may acquire new experience, or may at least make use of older experience, even after the total extirpation of those hemispheres. No doubt there is less experience shown after the extirpation than before it; but experience is by no means lost. Thus we see that other parts of the central nervous system besides the hemispheres may also be in relation to experience. This holds for all so-called lower brain centres, and perhaps for the spinal cord also.

What the real meaning of these facts is, must also be reserved for a future discussion. And now we are prepared to enter minutely into an analysis of the process of acting itself.

β. THE FIRST CRITERION OF ACTING. THE HISTORICAL BASIS OF REACTING

The phonograph is a well-known machine the reactions of which depend on its individual history in their utmost specificity: the phonograph may give forth what it has received in the past. Now we have said already provisionally that the individual history is one of the most important features concerned in the characteristics of acting. Is for this reason acting in any way comparable to the reactions of a machine such as the phonograph? With this question we may fitly begin our analysis of the process of "action."

If we at first consider the acting organism as a whole, without laying any special stress on what is called its nervous system or its brain, we may say that the specificity of every one of its actions depends on the specificity of all stimuli relating to sensation and movement which have encountered it in the past, and on all the specific effects of those stimuli. This character we have already tried to describe briefly by saying that acting depends on the "individual history" of the organism, and we shall now describe it technically by saying that an "*historical basis of reacting*" ("historische Reaktionsbasis") is one of the chief components of which the specificity of every action is a function.

Without any difficulty you will become convinced, I suppose, that this "historical basis of reacting," being one of the foundations of action, is something different from the "history" of a phonograph. Therefore the *technical* term "historical basis of reacting" requires a precise *technical* definition: it is to mean more than the mere verbal expression states. The phonograph, though determined in the specificity of its reactions by the specificity of its history, is not able to change the specificity of what it has received in any way; the organism has the faculty of profiting from the specific combinations received in order to form other combined specificities. It changes, so we may say, the specificities it has encountered into other specificities, which it forms on the foundation of their elements. Here we find what we are in search of: the historical basis of acting is "historical" only in a most general, not in a specific meaning; specificities, it is true, have made up the "history" that is commonly called "experience," but the basis of reacting, as a basis of action created historically, is not in any way specified in detail, but consists of the *elements* of the experienced specificities. The second half of our analysis of action will have to show us how new combined specificities may be formed on the foundation of the elements of the historically received ones.[1]

But a second fundamental difference between the "historical basis of reacting" of a phonograph and of an organism may at once be discovered as easily as the first difference was. The phonograph receives vibrations of the air and gives off vibrations of the air; in other terms, previous stimulus and later reaction are of the *same* nature. The organism receives impressions on its sensory organs whilst acquiring "experience," and gives off movements. That is to say, the events which have created the organism's history, and the events which occur on the basis of this history, belong to two absolutely *different* classes of phenomena.

We now must insist more fully on the analysis of our "historical basis," and shall in the first place justify a certain phrase that we have used in our definition. We have said that actions not only depend on all the stimuli received in the past but also on the *effects* of those stimuli. The word "stimuli" is to include here everything that has affected the sense organs of the acting subject in any form whatever; the word "effects" is to embrace the final consequences of any previous moving that had been caused by any stimulus. The second half of this explanation now may seem to want some further interpretation, and this interpretation may advantageously be founded upon a short discussion of a fundamental

[1] There would be a strict analogy between the "historical basis" of a phonograph and the "historical basis" of action if all human speech were like reciting a story or a poem learnt "by heart." But—a conversation, for example, is something very different from this.

problem, very often discussed by philosophical psychologists, the problem of the so-called *origin of the act of volition* in the child. It will hardly be avoidable to use a few psychological expressions in the following analysis, but we repeat that we use them only for the sake of brevity, and it would be better could every one of them possess its proper phenomenological correlate; for it is with moving bodies in nature that we are dealing.

The Origin of the Acts of Volition

Movements without any specific regularity, called forth by unknown general causes from without and within, are considered to be the real starting-point of acting in the child; a supposition that agrees very well with the recent discoveries of Jennings. The child notes the effect of every one of those movements and its share in bringing pleasure or pain—these words taken in their broadest meaning—and afterwards it "desires" and carries out certain possible effects of its movements, and others it does not "desire" and carry out. The possible effects, of course, as the age of the child advances, may relate to any change of the medium in the widest sense, as far as the medium may be the subject of experience. It belongs to Psychology to make out what elemental psychical functions are concerned in this "desiring" and "liking": of course the rudiments of judging are concerned in it, and a fuller analysis would probably reveal that volition, reasoning, and liking are at work here as a whole, inseparable in fact and separated only by analytical science. It has been neglected by some writers, but has been most clearly emphasised by Wundt and a few others, that the doctrine of the so-called origin of the act of volition relates by no means to the origin of volition as such, but only to the origin of the faculty of accomplishing what had been "willed." Volition itself, just as liking and judging, is one of the unexplainable elemental facts of psychology.

But let us turn back to our proper problem, which is a problem not of psychology but of natural science. The discussion of the genesis of the volitional act has shown us most clearly, that the *effects* of motor stimuli *may* form part of the historical basis of reacting. It was the effects of random movements that became liked by the child, and this liking of the effects enters into the historical basis of his future actions, just as do all sorts of stimulations themselves. In a certain sense we may say that the effects of motor stimuli become new stimuli on their own account, at least as far as they are a something presented to the organism and "experienced" by it, and in this way the whole analysis of the "historical basis" might seem to become more simple and uniform. But nevertheless it is worth while to maintain the distinction between two different types of historical bases of acting, and to study them as they actually occur in special cases.

The Different Types of Historical Bases

Acting based upon the experienced final effects of previous motor stimuli always starts from "chance," and it is in so-called "trying" that it gains its highest importance. Imagine you have got a new portmanteau without knowing how to open it. You first try all sorts of manipulations familiar to you from your experience about the effects of moving your hands with regard to opening other trunks, but no success attends this "trying." At last by chance you press a certain plain knob, and the opening of the box is the "effect." The second time you will press the knob at once; there is no "trying" any more, but the new experience assists you in "trials" in the future. The whole process has a great similarity to what we know already from the analysis of the first actions in the child, though, of course, differences must not be overlooked.

Experience based upon stimuli alone is no less familiar to all of you than our last instance. The learning of languages and all cases of imitation are typical instances of this class. The general scheme of this type of "historical basis of reacting" is this: you learn by experience that a certain simple secondary phenomenon always accompanies the primary one which is the proper motor stimulus of your acting, and you then, in response to that secondary or indicating phenomenon, perform the same action that at first only followed the primary stimulus. In this way you learn to identify different tramway lines by the coloured boards or coloured lights they bear.

All of you know, of course, that it is "association," as the psychologists call it, of which we have here given a rather complicated but not incorrect description.

A good popular illustration of the difference between an "historical basis" concerned with previous stimuli and effects and one concerned with stimuli alone is given by the two following instances. If in a strange town you want to reach a certain place, of which you only know the general position, you will probably go wrong very often the first time, but will "learn" to go right by the "effects" of your walking. If, however, you are accompanied the first time by a friend who knows the town and give good heed to what you "see" on your way, you may find the place the next time without any "error."

"Association"

One of the most important features, we said, of the historical basis of reacting is that its specificities may be resolved into their elements. We must not, however, forget that, in spite of this possibility of being resolved, a *certain* conservation of the combination of the specificities received is the *conditio sine qua non* in the process of acting: otherwise there would be no "association." Psychology, as you know, speaks of two kinds of "association," one dependent on contiguity, the other on similarity or contrast. Now all association by contiguity is to be regarded as in some sort the conservation of at least a part of the original specificity of combination in the stimuli forming the historical basis of acting. The mere fact on the other hand that, psychologically, association alone is quite unable to explain the totality of psychical life, shows that conservation of a portion of the specificities originally present cannot play more than a subordinate part in acting: conservation does indeed play a part, but there would be none but very primitive forms of acting, if conservation were not accompanied by separation and new combination of what had been received originally, and if there were no such thing as the remarkable phenomenon of association based upon contrast and similarity. But these processes, and in particular the process of resolving given complex peculiarities into other peculiarities, can hardly be properly understood without a discussion of the second fundamental characteristic of action.[1]

In proceeding to discuss this second characteristic we do not bid farewell to the first. On the contrary, as the first proved to be incomplete in itself without the second, so the second will prove to be inseparable from the first.

γ. THE SECOND CRITERION OF ACTING. "INDIVIDUALITY OF CORRESPONDENCE"

We have already explained, whilst dealing with the theory of instincts, what is meant by a "simple" and an "individualised" stimulus. A stimulus is individualised if it consists of a specific combination, specifically arranged, of single elements; the arrangement may be one of space as well as one of time.

Now the second of the two main characteristics of action, considered as a problem of natural science, is *that action always is a reaction corresponding to an individualised stimulus.* I need only remind you that the sight of a specific person or a specific house may influence your

[1] A psychological theory of association is not our business. Mere *passive* association certainly contributes very little to psychical life, at least when we are awake. It never accounts for the fact that among the innumerable ideas that are "similar" to one another *one* comes into consciousness at the given moment and none other. See the excellent discussion by Bergson (*Matière et Mémoire*, Paris, 1896), and compare also the concept of "apperception" as used by Wundt.

behaviour in a specific manner, and that a melody or a specific phrase you hear may do the same, in order to give you a concrete instance of what our analysis expresses more abstractly.

And then the individualised stimulus of actions has an *effect that is individualised also*. There are many cases in the inorganic world where the same thing happens, and yet in spite of that there is a great difference at the first glance between the Inorganic and the Organic in this field. A seal with specific initials may also be called an individualised stimulus or at least cause, and if it is pressed into hot sealing-wax the effect will be individualised also: but the two individualisations are of exactly the same kind in this case. That is not true in the individualisations of cause and effect appearing in action: the one is individualised in a specific manner, but the other is individualised quite differently.

In more technical language we may state the result of our provisional analysis as follows. Besides the principle of the "historical basis of reacting," there is another fundamental principle concerned in actions, when considered as bodily processes in nature; this second fundamental principle may appropriately be called the principle of "*individuality of correspondence*" between stimulus and effect.

We now in the first place have to study more fully in what the individuality of correspondence in acting really consists, and it is here that the interpenetration of our first and our second principle, spoken of already, will become apparent. For the individualisation of the acting effect, though dependent on — because corresponding to — the individuality of the cause, is at the same time found to depend on the "historical basis of reacting": in other terms, the elements of the individualised acting effect are derived from this basis.

What the theoretical consequences of this relation are will be shown hereafter; at present the minute analysis of the correspondence between the individualised stimulus and the individualised effect concerned in action is to be our chief problem. As every problem of a complicated nature is easier understood when at first demonstrated in a concrete instance, I prefer to begin our discussion with a concrete fact. It will be a fact very familiar indeed to all of you, for it is the great advantage in this department of biology dealing with action, that the facts are generally matter of common knowledge, whilst in morphogenesis even the most simple facts of a merely descriptive character have to be first explained to laymen in order to make them available for theoretical discussion.

We all experience a hundred times a day what a conversation between two human beings is. Let us try to analyse what a conversation would mean from the point of view taken by natural science. Two friends meet in the street, and one of them, A, says to the other, B, "my brother is seriously ill." There will be a very specific effect caused in B by the stimulus that went out from A. Let us imagine that the brother is in America: B then would talk about the difficulty of his coming home, or of visiting him, and very many other things, all of them of a very definite and specific character. But what would have happened if instead of the word "brother" the word "mother" had been used? Certainly something very different, and certainly something very specific also. The mother may be living in the town where the friends meet, then B might ask, whether he could do anything for her, he might remark that the illness must be attended with some danger at her age, and he would say very many other things, all very specific.

Taken as stimuli from the point of view of natural science, the phrases " my brother is seriously ill " and " my mother is seriously ill " differ only in a point of utmost unimportance: *br* is pronounced in one case where *m* is pronounced in the other. In spite of this *minute* difference the effects of the stimuli are *totally* different.

And now let us assume that the two friends are of different nationalities, the one being German, the other French, but that the town, where they are staying and where they meet, is an English town, and that both friends talk English, French and German equally well, and that they are accustomed to use all three in their conversations. Then A, instead of saying " my brother is seriously ill," might also have said " mon frère est sévèrement malade," or " mein Bruder ist ernstlich erkrankt." What would have been the effect of these variations? Certainly the same as that of the phrase spoken in English.[1]

This example shows us, that in acting the effect may remain unchanged in spite of a most fundamental change in the stimulus: this second result of our analysis is the exact counterpart to the first.

In acting then, there may be no change in the specificity

[1] It has been said that in these instances it is not the phrases "my brother is ill," etc., that constitute the real stimulus of action, but the general "mental" condition of the person addressed. But, beyond doubt, these phrases *are* real stimuli in the true physical meaning of the word, and, moreover, the general "mental" condition, *i.e.* what we call the "historical basis" in all its essentials, could never account for these particular and specific reactions at this particular place and time.

of the reaction when the stimulus is altered fundamentally, and again, there may be the most fundamental difference in the reaction when there is almost no change in the stimulus. This is a very strange result to have reached by our analysis.

Let us now try to state our result in more abstract form. This will bring us face to face with our central problem: Is acting explainable on the hypothesis of a specific physico-chemical arrangement, say a machine, or is it not?

The individualised stimulus in acting, represented in our instance by the phrase "my brother is seriously ill," may be expressed analytically as being a specific arrangement of the specific elements $a, b, c, d, e, f, g, h, i$, and so on. The specific effect which the stimulus has upon the acting person, say the friend B in our example, may be figured as being a typical combination of $a_1, b_1, c_1, d_1, e_1, f_1, g_1, h_1, i_1$, and so on. The question then is: How is the series a, b, c, etc. connected with the series a_1, b_1, c_1, etc., and is there any way of explaining a_1, b_1, c_1, etc. by a, b, c, etc., with the aid of the given organisation, with the aid of the brain in particular, or at least with the aid of *any* kind of machine, in the broadest sense of the word, in general?

Matters would be easy if to each element of the stimulus there corresponded an element of the effect, if a_1 were the effect of a, b_1 of b, c_1 of c, and so on. That is so in the phonograph, but by no means in acting. How then may our observations of what happens in ordinary conversation be formulated analytically? It seems to me that our particular result may be generalised in the following manner.

Firstly, change the stimulus from $a, b, c, d, e, f, g, h, i$

into $a, b, \gamma, d, e, f, g, h, i$, and the effect may be transformed from $a_1, b_1, c_1, d_1, e_1, f_1, g_1, h_1, i_1$ into m, n, o, p, q, r, s, t.

And secondly, change the stimulus from $a, b, c, d, e, f, g, h, i$ into $a, \beta, \gamma, \delta, \epsilon, \zeta, \eta, \theta, \iota, \kappa$, and the effect may *remain* $a_1, b_1, c_1, d_1, e_1, f_1, g_1, h_1, i_1$, in spite of that change.

There can hardly be a clearer expression of the fact that it is the *totality in its specificity*, both of the stimulus and of the effect, that comes into account in acting, and nothing else. But what is the meaning of this totality?

Here we have used the word that embraces our problem, almost unwillingly; we may say, that it came upon us unawares: the word "meaning." The totalities of stimulus and effect have a "meaning," and their meanings do not at all depend on one another piece by piece.

We meet a psychological term here, though we know that we are not allowed to enter the field of psychology: at any rate we have found something very strange.

δ. A NEW PROOF OF THE AUTONOMY OF LIFE

Preliminary Remarks

We now ask the important question: Is there anything like this in inorganic nature? If not, one of our principles concerned in acting, the principle of the *individuality of correspondence*, would form a new and independent proof of the autonomy of the phenomena of life, of vitalism.

Is it possible to imagine a machine, or rather, to conceive the brain as a machine, the reactions of which, being individualised combinations of a high degree of complexity, change correspondingly with any sort of a stimulus which is also itself individualised ? Or does it contradict the concept of a machine to assume that a typical arrangement of physico-chemical elements might respond to typically combined stimuli with always a typically combined effect, though the single elements of the one do *not* stand in causal relation to the single elements of the other ?

In a former part of our lectures, when dealing with the physiology of metabolism and of immunity in particular, we said already that the indefiniteness of correspondence between specific cause and specific effect, always following the principle of adaptive regulation, may be taken as indicating at least the autonomy of life-processes. It was of "simple" stimuli that we were then speaking; but now we have to do with "individualised" stimuli, and it seems to me that a *proof* of vitalism is now possible instead of a mere indication of it, on account of the intimate nature of the correspondence between the individualised stimulus and the individualised effect, both of which are totalities.[1]

Goltz,[2] when analysing the movements of frogs deprived of their hemispheres, introduced the term "answering reaction" ("Antwortsreaktion") in order to state what happened in his experiments. He did not altogether avoid pseudo-psychology in his discussions, but, in spite of that, his concept seems to me to be as valuable as his experiments were. Indeed we may say that it is because they are

[1] What this "totality," built up of singularities, is, can be best understood by an excursion into the field of pure psychology. The artist, a painter for example, bears within himself the complete totality of what he is to perform, and what afterwards is to be carried out by single acts of movement of his hand. In the same way the single phrases of a conversation, in spite of their consisting of single elements, form a totality that "means" something.

[2] *Beiträge zur Lehre von den Functionen der Nervencentren des Frosches*, Berlin, 1869.

answering reactions, or still better, individualised answering reactions, that actions seem to be beyond the reach of mechanical explanation.

A few words may not be out of place with regard to the different possible kinds of "individuality" that stimuli and effects in acting may acquire. The individualised effects of action, as will easily be understood, may be composed according to order in time exclusively, like a phrase in a conversation or a melody, or according to time and space, like all objects of art or handicraft. The individualised stimuli may belong to the two classes just mentioned, but there is also a third class which is composed specifically only with regard to space: the perfect object of art or handicraft as a stimulus belongs here, and so does *any* typical object, any "Gegenstand." Also this last class of stimuli possesses an individual *wholeness*, as a table or a dog, for instance. We meet here the problem we met already when dealing with the problematic stimuli of instincts. The dog, "this dog," "my dog" is "the same" stimulus, seen from any side or at any angle whatever: it always is recognised as "the same," though the actual retina image differs in every case. It is absolutely impossible to understand this fact on the assumption of any kind of preformed material recipient in the brain, corresponding to the stimulus in question,[1] even if we intentionally neglect the fact that the material recipient would have been created *by* the stimulus in the individual's life: a recipient for the dog seen from the side would not suffice for identifying the dog from behind! In fact—to speak psychologically—

[1] Such an attempt has lately been made by von Uexkuell (*Zeitschr. f. Biol.* 50, 1907).

identification or simple remembrance of sameness depends only in part on stimulation, and is in the main an active trying on the part of the Ego according to probability.[1] We shall come back to this point later on.

So much, for the present, about the "individuality of correspondence" in its bearing on vitalism.

It always is an agreeable occurrence when two investigators in the same scientific field independently arrive at almost the same results, and as some such independent but contemporaneous discoveries have been made in the subject that we are now considering, I should like to ask your permission to say a few words about them. It was in the spring of 1903 that I first published the argument forming a new and independent proof of vitalism, which I just have explained to you, and it was at about the same time that the late philosopher Busse, in his book, *Geist und Körper, Seele und Leib*, brought forward an argument against so-called psycho-physical parallelism, which is almost identical with my analysis down to the smallest details; and we knew nothing at all about one another. Busse uses a telegram as his instance, where I use a conversation, but that is the only difference. Later on we shall see that proving the autonomy of life, as revealed in acting, is indeed the same as defeating the parallelism-theory.

But there is still another case of independent argument to be mentioned. I was very glad to learn after this chapter was written that one of the most original thinkers of the present day, the French philosopher Henri Bergson, in his profound analysis of the relation between *Matière et*

---

[1] Compare Bergson, and also the paper of von Kries: *Ueber die materiellen Grundlagen der Bewusstseins-Erscheinungen*, Tübingen, 1901.

Mémoire,[1] had, as early as 1896, established what I should call the autonomy of acting, by a discussion which, though confined to Psychology, and therefore different from my own analysis *in verbis*, is very similar to it *in re*. I most strongly recommend Bergson's book to all who take a deeper interest in our subject.

Let us call those arguments in favour of the autonomy of life which were gained from the analysis of the differentiation of the harmonious-equipotential systems as concerned in morphogenesis the first proof of vitalism. Let us call the evidence obtained from the discussion of the genesis of the complex-equipotential systems, which are the foundation of heredity and of many morphological regulations, the second proof. Then we may see a *third proof of vitalism* in our analysis of the principle of the "individuality of correspondence," which is one of the chief characteristics of action. This proof is as independent and self-contained as the first two proofs; nothing but the general logical scheme is the same, viz., a machine of whatever kind or degree of complication is not imaginable.

The Union of the two Chief Criteria of Acting

But our third proof is not yet complete; we must add another half to it, and it was for this reason that we have so far dealt with it comparatively briefly.

The principle of the individuality of correspondence, as we know, does *not* mean that there is a *statical* or fixed

[1] Paris, 1896.—This excellent work was quite unknown to me when I wrote my *Seele* (1903), and is not even mentioned by Busse or by A. Klein (*Die modernen Theorien über das allgemeine Verhältnis von Leib und Seele*, Breslau, 1906).

something, the brain, through which that correspondence passes, and the real nature of which—whether machine or not—is in question. The brain, or rather the reacting something, has been created in its specificity, has been made such as it is *by* its history. The first half of our argument, therefore, though able itself, it seems to me, to prove vitalism, requires to be completed by another half, and this second half will be gained by a minute analysis of the "historical basis of reacting." Both our principles of action, we know, are united inseparably.

That which acts in action is, as we know, determined in its potential specificity by its individual history. All the stimuli it has received in the past, and all the effects of these stimuli, determine how stimuli may be answered in the future, in agreement with the principle of the individuality of correspondence.

Here, now, we are faced by the very strange fact that a something, from which reactions are to start, is determined in the specificity of its faculty of reacting almost completely from without; but not in the sense of a mere giving back of what had been received. We know, firstly, that it is solely the *elements* of the typical combinations received that form the basis of all reacting in the future, and secondly, that specificities are received in a very different field from that in which they are given off in reacting. So-called sensations, or rather typical constellations of centrifugal irritations of the central nervous system, are received; movements, or rather typical constellations of irritations of centripetal nerves, are given off. It is the latter point, as we know, that distinguishes our reacting "something" from the phonograph.

I could not imagine *any* sort of " machine " so constructed as to react in the manner the organism does, and I suppose that you also will not be able to do so. Imagine that it is the medium, in the widest meaning of the term, and the medium alone, which makes a child speak English or German or French, that the medium only makes him a reader of the Latin or the Greek, or the Cyrillian or the Arabic alphabet, and you will become convinced still better perhaps than by mere abstraction, what an impossibility it would be to assume a machine to be the foundation and basis of these facts.

Does it not contradict the very concept of a " machine," *i.e.* a typical arrangement of parts built up for special purposes, to suppose that it originates by contingencies from without ? And, in fact, the " historical basis " of acting originates in its specificity by contingencies from without, and afterwards plays its part in the " individuality of correspondence." The " individuality of correspondence," even in itself, is inconceivable on the basis of something pre-established or prepared, since stimulus and reaction are totalities. But now what might *possibly* have been prepared *a priori*, proves to be not prepared but made from without, and made from without in such a manner as to allow of resolution into its elements and transport into another scene of events.

So-called "Analogies" to Acting

Mechanistic authors occasionally have brought forward some inorganic " analogies " to " experience " or to " memory " as the potential ground of experience. I doubt whether any one of them really thought he had given even the slightest mechanical explanation of the facts in question by doing so. In fact, what they have brought forward, it seems to me, does not even deserve to be called "analogy," much less "explanation" of the historical basis of reacting as it really is.[1]

In the first place, we must notice that—speaking psychologically—mere "memory," as the faculty of simple storing and identifying, is far from being the same as the "historical basis" as it plays its part in action. In psychological terms "association" comes in here, *besides* "memory" pure and simple, and not merely association alone but association submitted to judgment. Here again the "historical basis" is inseparable from its rôle in the "individuality of correspondence."

The so-called elastic after-effect, and some similar phenomena, have occasionally been called analogies to the historical basis. In my opinion, however, they are *not even* analogies to simple "memory"; they *may* be analogies to "fatigue," but that is about the opposite to what is concerned in "experience." Certainly an elastic ball is "altered" by its "history"; but our critics must remember what *we* understand by this word in *our* definition, which is throughout of the style of a technical term. Others have objected to my argument by saying that the "reactions" of a mountain, with regard to its being slowly washed away by

---

[1] A very careful analysis of my *Seele* has been given by Becher (*Zeitschr. f. Psych.* 45, 1907, p. 401). Becher is right in saying that my two "criteria" ought always to be regarded together. But his mechanical analogy to their being at work together (p. 428) fails, since he does not consider that the historical stimuli and the reactions of my "historical basis" belong to *different* fields of events.

rains and rivers, also depend on its individual geological "history." Granite resists destruction longer than limestone, but why do my critics not say that a mountain "acts," whenever it is lowered by atmospherical agents? *In fact* they do *not* say so—and I suspect they never will. But let us formulate the distinction as strictly as possible. In the elastic after-effect one and the same process occurs the first time in a typical manner, considered as to quantity, and the second time a little differently. In dynamical geology different phases of history are followed by merely passive different effects in later days, the first differences corresponding with the second in locality. In acting, however, historical specificities (including differences) in quite a special class of occurrences, namely, sensation in the widest sense of the word, are responsible for specificities (including differences) which firstly are active and true reactions to real stimuli in the narrowest sense of the term, and which secondly occur in quite another field of happening, in the field of movements. In the face of these diversities all "analogies" between "experience" and inorganic events appear to be a mere playing with words.

Analogies like these would never have been even suggested, had it always been borne in mind that so-called experience, or rather the principle of the "historical basis of reacting" in our strict definition, not only means the mere recollection of what has happened, but means also the ability to use *freely* in another field of occurring the elements of former happening for newly combined *individualised* specificities of the future which are *wholes*. We see one of our fundamental principles of acting always united with the other, and this fact may also be well expressed by stating that the word "element," in its relation to the principle of the "historical basis," is throughout relative. "Elements" may be words, but may be the mere letters also, or whole phrases, or the mere lines of the written characters — just as you like. We understand how restricted the rôle of "association" in acting is: it is important, no doubt, but only as a *means* of acting; or, to speak psychologically, association offers the material for judging, but is not judging; and judging enters into all psychical acts that are more than association.

But as all so-called analogies of inorganic facts to experience are not really analogies, so, on the other hand, all endeavour to transfer the elemental organic or vital facts to the inorganic world are extremely misleading also. It is nonsense to speak about the stone "liking" to reach the ground, even if "liking" is only a psychological word for a natural process. There is nothing at all in the inorganic world even in the least comparable with the "individuality of correspondence." Modern monism, so-called, is unfortunately almost always a monism of mere phrases but not of ideas.

Conclusions

Let us then try to formulate in a definite manner our third proof of the autonomy of life, founded upon the analysis of acting as a phenomenon in objectified nature.

All acting is correspondence between individualised stimuli and individualised effects occurring on a basis of reaction that has been created historically from without.

Acting defies explanation of any kind on the basis of

physico-chemical tectonics of any sort, for the following reasons.

It would be very difficult, if not impossible, to imagine a machine—in the widest sense of the word—such as to allow of even the individuality of correspondence in acting, taken alone. For it can be shown that it is not the single constituents of the stimulus on which the single constituents of the effect depend, but one whole depends on the other whole, both "wholes" being conceivable in a logical sense exclusively.

But to this first general impossibility is added a second, still more important, by an analysis of the character of the historical basis. That the individualised correspondence in acting takes place upon a *historical* basis, that its basis is made from without, is a very strange feature in itself—but here we have the phonograph as an analogue. The historical basis of acting—the "prospective potency" for acting, if you care to say so by analogy—differs in two fundamental respects from the phonograph, or from *any* sort of machine imaginable in physics and chemistry. Firstly, the effects that are given off in acting occur in a field of natural events very different from that of the stimuli received historically: sensations belong to one, movements to another field. Secondly, the historical basis serves only as a general reservoir of faculties, the specific combinations of the stimuli received historically being preserved by no means in their specificity, but being resolvable into elements; these elements then—transferred, however, to another sphere of happening—are rearranged into other specificities, according to the individuality of the actual stimulus in question.

The "something" that "acts" has the innate faculty of producing some specific combination of muscular movements; the combination it produces in a special case depends on the individuality of the stimulus present in that case, and on the whole of past sensations in the widest sense.

This is the result of an analysis of action unbiased by dogmatism.

ε. THE "PSYCHOID"

This seems to be just the right place in our discussion to give a *name* to the acting something which we have discovered not to be a machine. We might speak of "entelechy" again, as we did in the theory of morphogenesis, but it appears better to distinguish also in terminology the natural agent which *forms* the body from the elemental agent which *directs* it. The words "soul," "mind," or "psyche" present themselves, but one of them would lead us into what we have so carefully avoided all along, viz., pseudo-psychology. I may speak of *my* "psyche"—which is no more than saying "Ego"—but there "are" no souls in this sense in the phenomenon called nature in space. I therefore propose the very neutral name of "Psychoid" for the elemental agent discovered in action. "Psychoid"—that is, a something which though not a "psyche" can only be described in terms analogous to those of psychology. In fact, there can be no doubt that only the processes called "abstraction," "thinking," and so on, will enable us to *understand* the correspondence of the two individualities in our important principle: and the process of so-called

" abstraction," regarded as a process occurring on bodies, cannot be performed by a machine. That is our justification of the name " Psychoid."

If the analysis of instincts should help us some day to a true proof of vitalism, instead of offering only some indications towards it, it might also be said that a "psychoid" is the basis of instinctive phenomena. The usual difference between the " Conscious " and the " Unconscious " would then have to be brought to its legitimate and truly philosophical expression by distinguishing between two different kinds of psychoids.

There certainly is a difference, expressed already by the want of experience in instincts. But there is a difference between the instinctive psychoid and morphogenetic entelechy also.

The first systematic vitalist we know, Aristotle, saw these analytical differences very clearly and gave a very adequate denomination to them. Calling the spiritual principle, which he regarded as the real foundation of life, ψυχή in general, he carefully discriminated between three kinds of it. The lowest of all is the ψυχὴ θρεπτική, the soul of metabolism, which, together with its modifications, called αὐξητική and γενητική, that is, the soul of growth and of propagation, may be said to represent our " Entelechy " as concerned in morphogenesis; it is possessed by all organisms, plants as well as animals. The next higher class of souls is represented by the ψυχὴ αἰσθητική, the soul of sensation as well as of volition; it belongs to animals only, and to some extent may properly be called the soul of instincts. It is only to men, according to Aristotle, that the highest soul, the νοῦς, is given, that is, the faculty of reasoning, corresponding to what we have called the "psychoid" as regulating action.

Indeed, it seems to me that the general classification of Aristotle may be accepted even nowadays, at least with a few modifications, if we give up his restriction of νοῦς as being only possessed by man. Certainly there is more than mere instinct in animals, at least if the word instinct is used in its original meaning, that is in the sense of purposefulness and perfection in reacting *without* any experience or anything similar to experience in any way. We do not intend to deny by this statement the great differences that exist between acting in man and acting in even the highest animals; later on we shall learn a little more about these problems. But there certainly *is* "experience" in the proper sense of the word in many animals. In this respect I cannot agree with the terminology of Wasmann, though, what is more important, I almost wholly agree with his actual analysis of the facts in question.

We now have completed the outlines of our analytical study of action as such, and have given a distinctive name to its results. But we must not yet leave our present studies: the part which the brain and nervous system play in acting is not yet clear from what we have said, and a few words about the real differences in acting between man and animals may also seem to be required.

ζ. THE "SPECIFIC ENERGY" OF THE SENSORY NERVES

According to our analytical researches so far it might seem as if the brain were almost unnecessary in acting;

but, of course, such an opinion would be very far from the truth.

Let us then try, in the first place, to connect our analysis with a physiological problem which has been discussed very often in the last century, and which can by no means be said to be solved; a problem that relates to our concept of the "individuality of correspondence," in so far as the process of the "individualisation" of the stimuli comes into account. I refer to the problem of the so-called "specific energy" of the sensory nerves, and you will easily understand that this problem is not unconnected with our analysis, if you remember that all stimulation to acting is transmitted along the sensory nerves.[1]

According to Johannes Mueller, the father of the "law" of the specific energy, the meaning of this principle was that the specificity of sensation, say of red or green, or heat or a musical tone, was in some way a "property" of the single nerve fibre under stimulation, and that it was quite indifferent by what sort of an occurrence the stimulation had happened. Later science has transferred the specificity from the nerve fibres to specific localities of the brain, but the general view has remained almost the same, and Emil du Bois-Reymond gave strange but clear expression to the doctrine when he said that after an operation which combined the ear with the optic nerve and the eye with the acoustic nerve, we should hear lightning as a crack and see the thunder as a line of sparks.

Intentionally we shall put aside the whole epistemo-

---

[1] So-called "spontaneous" actions are intentionally left out of account here, as they do not touch our most fundamental problems. No doubt something affecting the brain, in some way, is concerned in these facts also, and therefore no special discussion is required.

logical part of the question concerned here, which is by no means an easy problem, and has been treated rather improperly in almost all essays on it. Even Johannes Mueller was wrong when he paralleled his principle with the Kantian doctrine of apriorism, with which it has nothing at all to do. Intentionally we shall take up the position of naïve realism in the short discussion that is to follow, and shall not hesitate to enter for a moment into the field of pseudo-psychology.

We simply ask, is it true that the process of nervous conduction is always the same, and that specific qualities reach the brain only because specific parts of it have been stimulated without any relation to the nature of the stimulus? It seems to me, I confess, that we are quite unable to say at present whether it is true or not. Certainly there is not a single instance brought forward in favour of Mueller's principle that can be said to be above all doubt. The often discussed fact, for instance, that cutting the optic nerve gives the sensation of light proves nothing, since, as all modern authors agree, this operation is not possible without stimulating the retina to a certain extent before the nerve has been cut quite through. The electrical phenomena, on the other hand, that are exhibited equally well in any stimulation of nerves whatever, are only secondary phenomena, and prove nothing either for or against the problem of qualitative differences in nervous conduction. There remain only the facts—strange as they are—of a localised feeling of say the hand or the fingers after the amputation of the whole arm, but not a single one of these amputations has been performed on an individual who had not already received the specific sensations in question in the normal manner during his previous life. There always had been many normal stimulations before the operation, and who is able to say whether the different localities of the brain may not have become specific *by having been stimulated specifically*? We shall come back to this question on another occasion.

Now, on the other hand, the experiments made with the aid of an extirpation of parts of the brain, as carried out by Goltz and many others, have positively shown, as will also be discussed later on, that there may be a certain regulation in those parts, at least to a certain extent. Of course, there probably will be a difference in regulation according to whether the single parts of one and the same sensory sphere, or whether parts belonging to different "senses," are in question. There may be a regularity in the first case and not in the latter. But even then the principle of "specific energy" would be broken as far as the single elements of one nerve or the single parts of one so-called "centre" are concerned: one and the same element of the brain would be related to *various* qualities of sensation—at least with regard to one and the same sensory sphere—and, on the other hand, we could hardly escape the hypothetic assumption that one and the same fibre of a nerve is able to transmit stimulations that are different with regard to sensory "quality." This view is held at present by Hering,[1] while Wundt[2] seems to go still farther in assuming what might be called the original equipotentiality of the brain.

Thus the principle of Mueller might be half true, half

[1] *Zur Theorie der Nerventätigkeit*, Leipzig, 1899.
[2] *Physiologische Psychologie*, 5. Aufl., Leipzig, 1903.

false, as far as the adult is concerned, though it is perhaps quite false for the child.[1] We soon shall enter once more into these questions.

At this stage of our analysis the most important point for ourselves—strange to say—is not the question about the adequacy or inadequacy of the theory of "specific energies," but the simple fact *that this whole problem does not touch at all our principle of the " individuality of correspondence."* It was only to make this clear that our short remarks about the present state of the problem of specific energy have been made here.

In fact, if any kind of equipotentiality of the brain were positively established, a *new* and independent proof of vitalism might be gained from that fact alone. But even if Mueller's law held good, *nothing* would be affected in our *previous* discussion. For the principle of the "individuality of correspondence," one of the two foundations of our third proof of life-autonomy, only deals with the *unity* and *individuality* of a totality which is constituted by single elements, *without asking in any way by what sort of processes the elements of the external " individualised " stimulus may be offered to the "something" that is reacting.* That this something cannot be a machine remains equally true both if different processes of conduction may occur in the same nerve fibre, and if it is different localities of the brain which, when irritated, represent the different elements of the

[1] In refuting the principle of a "specific energy," in the sense of Johannes Mueller, we, of course, do not intend to deny what may be called the specificity of sensation and its incompatibility with everything like movement or energy. Whenever—to speak in the language of naïve realism—sensation occurs, there always occurs something absolutely alien to that which "caused" sensation. But to cause specific sensation is not the innate specific potential property of specific parts of the nervous system as such.

"individualised stimulus." In neither case is this stimulus a mere sum; and the fact that there *is* more than a sum proves in *any* case that there is more than a machine at work.

Thus we understand that our analysis of action is independent of the problem whether the doctrine of "specific energy" be right or wrong. The great physiological importance of this problem, of course, is by no means diminished by what we have stated; but problems must always be clearly separated.

η. SOME DATA FROM CEREBRAL PHYSIOLOGY [1]

But now let us try to ascertain positively what the part played by the brain in acting is.

We all know, of course, that the brain and the nerves actually do play a most important part in actions as in all movements; for the sake of completeness, therefore, we are forced to state at least in general terms what that part is. Otherwise our whole argument about action might seem rather unconnected with well-established facts.

At the beginning of the present part of our lectures we observed that we should study organic motions especially under the aspect of regulations, and we mentioned briefly that regulations may enter into these motions in three different ways. The specificity of movement may be determined, firstly, by the specificity of the stimuli coming

---

[1] Compare besides the text-books of Physiology: L. Asher, *Zeitschr. f. Physiol. d. Sinnesorg.* 41, 1906, p. 157; Nagel, *Handbuch d. Physiol.* iii. 1; von Monakow, *Ergebn. d. Physiol.* i. 2, 1902; Lewandowsky, *Die Functionen des centralen Nervensystems*, 1907. A very good historical and critical review of the whole subject will be found in C. Hauptmann, *Die Metaphysik in der modernen Physiologie*, 1893.

from without; secondly, by the specificity of the variable state of the motor organs; and thirdly, by the specificity of the variable state of the central organs.

Hitherto we have been studying only the first class of these regulations. Our analysis, leading to a new proof of vitalism, was based exclusively on the correspondence of the stimuli and the reactions. The brain, and in fact organisation altogether, played no part in that analysis, but it will become important as soon as we come to study the other possible kinds of motor regulation.

Let us say a few words, in the first place, about regulability of the brain functions themselves. This subject has just been touched in our remarks on the doctrine of specific energy. There exists anything but unanimity and agreement in this field of physiology, and to form a proper judgment is very difficult for one who, like myself, has no personal experience of the matters in question, and is obliged to rely on the literature. On the one hand, the parts of the brain are regarded as almost completely equal in function, whilst, on the other hand, the utmost functional specificity, even of the individual cell, has been insisted on.

As far as I am capable of judging, it seems to me, from a study of the literature, both experimental and pathological, that *two different* fundamental factors are to be distinguished relating to the organisation of the brain and of the so-called cerebral hemispheres in particular, and each accounting for different results among the experimental and pathological facts.

In fact there is an interesting parallelism between the brain and the youngest germ, inasmuch as they are constructed according to two different types of complexity. In the mature germ[1] we had the intimate structure of mere direction, more or less regulable according to the state of the protoplasm, and the true material structure showing scarcely any regulability at all. In the brain of the adult, as we shall see, we find the two features—a simple structure for conduction and then some higher sort of tectonics, and here again only one of them seems to be regulable to any great extent. The hypothetic differences between the young and the adult brain with regard to regulability are paralleled, on the other hand, by the differences of the germ before and after fertilisation and maturation.

The Connecting Function

In the first place, the brain is a system of nervous connexions of almost inconceivable complexity for the work of *conduction*. I think we shall not be very wrong in saying that not only is every part of the brain connected in some way with every other, but also almost every part of the surface of the body is by the aid of the brain connected in some way with every other part.[2] It is to these features that the functional regulability of the brain relates. It is a known fact that cerebral diseases, apoplexy in particular, diminish in their symptoms after a certain time, at least to a certain extent, and it is also known from experimental work[3] that defects in the brain, caused by a localised

---

[1] See vol. i. page 85 ff.

[2] For man this statement can be proved as follows: You are able to decide voluntarily that when a certain point of your skin is touched you will touch with your finger another certain point of it; the two points may be any you please.

[3] Experiment is always better than clinical observation: for sickness may also have affected the faculty of regulability and may overshadow it where it exists.

operation, are followed by sensorial and motorial defects, but that these defects become smaller and smaller as time advances,[1] until a certain maximum of regulation is reached. It is highly probable that this regulation, in part at least, is due to the fact that some typical nervous connexions in the brain, which had been destroyed by the apoplexy or by the operation, are restored after a while: not, of course, morphologically, for there is no actual restitution or regeneration of any sort in the brain of vertebrates, but physiologically, in the sense that the functional connexion between the parts A and B is now, after the destruction of the shortest route, accomplished by some other of the many possible routes.

It was upon these facts that our doubts respecting the doctrine of the so-called "specific energy" in its extremes were based. The same facts, when more accurately and minutely established, might furnish a sort of new and independent proof of vitalism, by showing the brain to be what might be called a "functional harmonious-equipotential system." The specificity of a motory reaction is not dependent on the specificity of the brain as such, but the organisation of the brain is only *used* in order to perform a specific reaction, and its different parts may be used differently in such a manner that harmony, *i.e.* the specificity of the individualised effect in question, is never altered.

By no means do we wish these words to be understood as if the possible harmony of the parts of the brain in use were perfect in every case. On the contrary, in spite of

[1] As a rule this diminishing of functional defects is attributed to the ceasing of the "shock." Most recent authors, however, agree that use has been made a little too freely of "shocks." There can be little doubt that this favourite term has often blinded us to the existence of true regulation.

the enormous manifoldness of cerebral connexions it can very well be imagined that *certain* apoplectical or experimental disturbances will render functional reparation impossible. In such cases there is no longer any connexion between the points A and B, and clinical or experimental defects are permanent.

Specific Functions in the Adult

But the permanency of such defects generally seems to have other reasons, and I hope we shall learn to understand them, if we now turn to study the second fundamental feature concerned in cerebral organisation. The brain is *not only* a system of connexions : it is something more. The specific differences of sensations, to speak psychologically, seem to require some specific arrangement in organisation, specifically localised, which render the brain *in*equipotential to a certain extent.

And these arrangements are really found to exist. Certain specific parts of the brain seem to have a specific functional value that is more than a mere locality of specific connexion, at least in the adult. Disturbances of these " spheres," as they are called, by disease or experiment are to a great extent irreparable. These cerebral specificities would seem to be responsible for the specificity of " sensation," and to justify as much of the old law of Johannes Mueller as will stand criticism, at least with regard to the adult. But they are not the only factors concerned in specific sensation : the specificity of the process of centripetal nervous conduction is another factor of importance. It is now granted by the first authorities in this field that at least in one and the same sensorial sphere, such as sight, for instance, one nerve element may transmit different "qualities" in their specificity; and as far as the sense of smell is concerned I do not see any possibility of escaping this conclusion. The peripheral organs, being the seat of the real stimulation of the organism, in this way become responsible for the specificity of sensation to a very high extent, though not, of course, on account of the nature of the stimulating external agent alone, but also on account of their own (chemical ?) specificity.

Thus it is by the co-operation of both parts, the specific centres as well as the specific reception organs, that specificity of sensation occurs. The specific centres are not liable to regulation.

Are there Specific Functions in the Newly Born ?

But this is only true for the adult. Bechterew[1] remarks that extirpation of the so-called motor spheres carried out in the *newly born* dog or cat has no effect whatever on its future motions. Moreover, it is a well established fact that aphasia may be almost completely cured by re-learning to speak. These facts seem to prove that "spheres" are not innate but created *during life,* and that even "spheres" are liable to regulation, at least in some cases. That would allow us to call the brain an organ which possesses originally the same functional "prospective potency" in all its parts, these parts obtaining their specific "prospective value" secondarily, and being able to modify it to a certain extent under certain conditions. Such a doctrine would be the

[1] *Bewusstsein und Hirnlocalisation,* Leipzig, 1898, p. 48.

death-blow to the doctrine of "specific energy" in *any* sense. It is true, nothing has been actually ascertained here at present, so far as *sensorial* nerves and centres are in question; no experiments have yet been made on the newly born. Might we expect that specificity of "centres" in the adult is *completely* a *product* of specificity of previous centripetal conductions?—that by interchanging the connexion of the optic and acoustic nerves to their respective sensory organs in the newly born, the optic brain centre of the adult would be transferred to the place where the acoustic centre normally is, and *vice versa*? Such ideas regarding "centres" as simply what is generally called "Einfahrung" in the single nerves, are rather revolutionary; but one must grant at present, it seems to me, that they are possible, and that, so far as only one sensorial sphere is concerned, they even are probable. If they held good to the fullest extent, all kinds of "pressure-points," "heat-points," and "pain-points" found in the skin of the adult would prove nothing at all, of course, regarding innate specificities of nerves or parts of the brain: all specificities would originally be peripheral.[1]

[1] The few "facts" relating to the specificity or non-specificity of nerves or parts of the brain, besides those mentioned above (p. 86), are the following, all relating to the adult. Stimulation of the chorda tympani, *i.e.* the nerve of taste, carried out directly by electric or mechanical agents, is always followed by a sensation of taste; this fact, of course, may be interpreted *in favour* of the specificity of "centres" in the adult, but may *also* be related to a chemical process in the nerve, set up by the irritation. Langley succeeded in transforming a vaso-contracting nerve into a vaso-dilating one, and a motor nerve into one that stimulated peripheral ganglia; a connexion of the central part of nerve A with the peripheral part of nerve B, and *vice versa*, had been effected here; the experiment proves the possibility of centrifugal conductions leading to different results in one and the same nerve, it does not immediately relate to "centres."

I myself have laid stress upon the fact that in many of the transplantation experiments in young amphibial larvae, as carried out by Born, the brain has to accomplish quite abnormal duties, which it does in perfect harmony. See

But enough of such hypothetic discussions: the cerebral physiology of the *adult* certainly *does* reveal specificities in the brain which are not liable to regulation.

The " Centre " in General

This is the right place to say a few words on that very ambiguous word, " brain-centre." At first the " centre " was conceived purely anatomically as a so-called ganglion, but this view has been abandoned, especially under the influence of Loeb and Bethe. Loeb[1] then regarded the centre as nothing more than a typical locality of typical intracerebral connexions. It seems to me that this view is a little too restricted. As we have said, there may be specific functions in the brain, related to sensation, and these functions might be specifically localised, at least in the adult. Of course, the word " centre " would be a very suitable name for these localities.

The Brain and the Psychoid in General

But, most important of all, the very factor that determines the specificity of any cerebral or rather motor reaction is not a " centre " in any sense; we have proved that this factor is not physico-chemical in character at all. So we may say, there is something more concerned in reactions starting from the brain or passing through the brain than mere localities of connexion, and something more also than

my *Scele*, p. 42 ; also Braus, *Anat. Anz.* 26, 1905. The transplantation experiments performed on the earthworm, by Korschelt, Joest, and Ruttloff, seem only to prove the possibility of nervous conduction going on in a direction opposite to the normal (*Arch. Entw. Mech.* 25, 1908).

[1] *Comparative Physiology of the Brain*, New York, 1900.

localities of specific function; but this "more" is not a "centre" in the sense of something *in* the brain. This "more," our Psychoid or Entelechy, *uses* the conductive and specific faculties of the brain as a piano-player uses the piano.

In these words is included what we are *not* entitled to attribute to brain-functions proper.

The Brain's Part in "Association"

Another very important topic now requires some further elucidation. The "historical basis of reacting" is created in its specificity from without; it therefore must be marked in a certain *bodily* manner in the central nervous system. Let us try to show what this manner is. The immediate functions of the historical basis are of two kinds. It is an elemental fact, to speak psychologically, that a sensorial impression occurring the second time is known to be "the same" as the first impression; this character, "sameness," may be called the first immediate function of the historical basis of reacting. Its second function is "association by contiguity," or the fact that any sensation is not only regarded as the "same" or "different," but that it also awakens the remembrance of other sensations of the past, which were connected with it in time or space on a former occasion.

It is in the brain that the possibility of the origin of these two kinds of elemental functions of the historical basis must lie in some way; experiments indeed show that they are present in it in a sort of specifically localised distribution.

But by no means, it must be repeated, is the primary

factor in acting identical with these bodily prerequisites of acting, or with their distribution: the brain is a sort of warehouse, a place of storing, and some day indeed we may understand its physiology. But the acting factor is not identical with the warehouse: it *uses* it, just as it uses the brain as a system of connexions.[1] The brain, as a specifically organised body, possesses nothing but the faculty of storing all the impressions that have occurred to it in any way *just as they are given*, and, by doing so, it is able to become *differently* stimulated the second time by the same stimulus: the "having been stimulated" by it alters the type of its future effects. Borrowing a very convenient name from a book of Semon's,[2] we may say that the brain possesses the faculty of storing "engrammata." But it *only* can store engrammata in the sense of given combinations of given elements, and therefore nothing but the psychical phenomena of simple recognition and of association by contiguity is immediately related to cerebral processes: it is absolutely inconceivable how the brain *qua* bodily brain could accomplish the new and free and "logical" rearrangement of the elements of the engrammata, following the lines of individuality.[3] The storing of en-

[1] It cannot be our task here to develop a theory of insanity, and so we may content ourselves with saying that in all "mental" diseases it is not the "mind" which is ill but the brain: on account of abnormalities in the brain the mind receives what might be called an "abnormal reality."

The theory of hypnotism is also beyond the province of this book. Of course all hypnotising agents, though "psychical" in themselves, must affect the brain somehow. The same holds for the phenomenon of so-called "double consciousness." What is generally called "subconsciousness" in psychology—a very bad term indeed—would be a psychoid of inferior order, according to our terminology.

[2] *Die Mneme*, Leipzig, 2nd ed., 1908.

[3] Von Uexkuell's "schemata" promoting "iconoreception" and "motoreception" can be nothing except engrammata in the sense defined. Of

grammata may be compared in some way, as already said on another occasion, with the elastic after-effect or even with the faculty of a phonograph, but the faculty of rearranging, nay, even the faculty of "association" by identity and contrast, has no relationship with any performance of any combination of physico-chemical agents whatever.[1]

By a psychological analogy we shall understand still more easily and more fully what happens. It is the difference between association and apperception we are thinking of, or the difference between idea and judgment. The ideas come as they like, but I judge about their being right or wrong in each case. The first has real cerebral processes as its starting-point, the second has not; it has been shown in our third proof of vitalism that the second cannot be a mechanical process of any sort. To summarise the most important points of this proof: the "historical basis of reacting" *might* be understood mechanically, if this basis revealed itself as it does in the phonograph; but it reveals itself by *free* combination of its elements. Therefore a factor that is by no means like anything inorganic in any sense is concerned in

course these "schemata" are acquired, as far as action comes into account. They *only* can be *means* for acting and are in no sense whatever the acting or reacting factor itself. (See *Zeitschr. f. Biol.* 50, 1907.) It must be mentioned that von Uexkuell himself regards his "schemata" simply as "Erkennungs*mittel*."

[1] Our argument burdens the brain with a certain, though limited, rôle to be played in relation to "memory."

Bergson would not even go so far: to him "souvenir pur" has no relation whatever to matter, except so far as "perceptions purs" come into account. See his excellent analysis of "attention" and "reconnaissance." Association (except in sleep) is a very *active* process, according to him (see *Matière et Mémoire*, Paris, 1896; compare also page 66, note 1).

acting, and the "historical basis of reacting" can only be said to have been created by physico-chemical processes, that is, by the stimuli affecting the brain, as regards its elements; these elements stand at the disposal of an agent that is autonomic.

θ. REGULABILITY OF MOVEMENT WITH REGARD TO THE MOTOR ORGANS

We have finished our discussion of the regulations occurring in the brain and of all that is connected with them, and therewith have closed at the same time the study of the second type of the possible regulations concerned in movement, those relating to the intermediate organs, at least as far as the "hemispheres" come into account. Before adding a few words about regulation among the so-called "lower" brain-centres certain remarks seem to be required about the third possible kind of regulation of movement, that is, about regulations regarding the motor organs as such. This may be done rather shortly, for facts may suitably be reduced here to the two other types of regulation.

The dog who is wounded in one of his legs, and therefore is forced to walk on three legs only, is a good instance of what we mean: regulations are going on here in the use of the three legs left; these three legs are used otherwise than they would have been used if there were still all four of them. It seems to me that all instances of this kind may without difficulty be subsumed under our first class of regulations in motion, those dealing with the correspondence between stimuli and reactions, and therefore a full discussion is not required. Indeed the fact that there are but three sound legs is an item in the sum of the motor stimuli and conditions just as a carriage crossing the path of our dog would be; it forms part of the "individualised stimulus," according to which the individuality of the action is determined. But any one who prefers it might also gain an independent proof of autonomy from this kind of motor regulation, by saying that, besides the individual correspondence between the stimulus proper and the action, a correspondence of an individualised type is also going on between the specified state of the motor organs and the specified use of them. In some way, of course, it is to the brain again that this regulation relates; other centrifugal nerves are used for one and the same action, according to what kind of abnormal state the motor organs are in.[1]

A very interesting clinical experiment, carried out by Vulpius, deserves mention in this connexion. The tendon of a flexor muscle of the foot was split and one of its halves was made to heal in such a way that it could perform the function of stretching—the extensor muscle being paralysed. After a certain time, in fact, the flexor muscle was "split" also physiologically: part of it was used for bending, part for stretching, as circumstances required. In a very strange and perfect manner the "acting principle" had succeeded here in using quite an abnormal centrifugal nerve, and, of course, quite

[1] Ophiurids deprived of one or more arms also show good instances of this class of regulability in movement. Compare Preyer's experiments, which I have most completely confirmed myself.

abnormal central parts also, in the service of certain "individualised" reactions that were needed. One could hardly imagine a better illustration of the rôle of the nervous system as a mere instrument for acting; of course, in the light of this discovery the so-called "motor spheres" also appear as anything but absolutely fixed;[1] in any case the organism may learn to use *abnormal* centripetal nerves for its *normal* performances.

ι. THE LOWER BRAIN CENTRES IN VERTEBRATES

To the whole of our discussion about the rôle of the brain in acting in general a few remarks must be added concerning

[1] Flourens knew as early as 1842 that fowls use their wings in the right way, if the two main nerves of the plexus brachialis are crossed by a complicated operation. See also Spitzy, *Zeitschr f. orthopäd. Chir.*, 1904, vol. xiii. ; and Bethe, *Münchner med. Wochenschrift*, 1905, No. 25. Most physiologists at present are strongly under the influence of materialistic doctrines, and therefore try to conceive all complicated animal movement as a mere sum of reflexes as far as possible. To such authors the formula which von Uexkuell has given for *certain* very *primitive* motions (page 30) was very welcome, and they sometimes have tried to found a general theory on it. According to von Uexkuell's formula, in animals with "simple nervenets" the state of the *terminal* (motor) organ determines the path of motor stimulation, the "centres" work almost passively here as mere "reservoirs" of "tonus." How absolutely impossible it is thus to understand Vulpius's case, or the case of the dog walking on three legs, cannot be better shown, it seems to me, than by simply alluding to the *fact* that all the movements in question are notoriously under the influence of so-called "will," and certainly do not take their origin from the periphery. (See also Giardina's discovery, page 105, note 2.) Von Uexkuell's formula only holds good, as he concedes himself, for rhythmical movements once set going, but never for the origin or stopping or alteration of such movements. I can walk almost mechanically and unconsciously, but I can also "will" to walk or not! In other words : Uexkuell's formula may explain a good deal of the movements of an animal as far as these movements depend on the spinal cord exclusively (see pages 30 and 103). But it never explains how *abnormal regulatory* movements tending to a *normal end* are first *established*. When once established, of course, these movements may again obey Uexkuell's law, as far as their mere going on—not their origin or stopping—is concerned.

the physiological importance of the so-called lower brain-centres in vertebrates. Pflüger was the first to speak of a "Rückenmarksseele," that is, of the faculty of the spinal cord of frogs that had been deprived of their whole brain to react to stimuli in a manner which resembles action. But later researches have left it doubtful whether these reactions of the spinal cord really deserve the name of acting, it being perhaps more probable that there occurs nothing but a consecutive line of different single motions in correspondence to a permanent stimulation which has not been removed by the first or second of them. We have seen already that Jennings has found such a sort of behaviour—besides real acting—in the infusorium *Stentor*, and that there is no reason for speaking of actions in such cases.

It was Goltz who showed for the first time that frogs deprived of the hemispheres, but possessing more of their central system than the mere spinal cord, are capable of reactions which—to speak in our own terminology—show most clearly the two fundamental characters of action: the "historical basis" and the "individuality of correspondence." Schrader afterwards proved the same to hold for the nervous system of birds, and finally we have the experiments carried out by Goltz on a dog with no hemispheres at all.[1]

What these animals performed, was indeed much less than what they would have done with the use of the parts removed. But, after all, they *did* "act" in the true sense of the word: obstacles were avoided, even if one of the legs was made helpless; there were reactions to specific optic

---

[1] Pflüger, *Die sensorischen Funktionen des Rückenmarks*, 1853; Goltz, *Beiträge zur Lehre von den Funktionen der Nervencentren des Frosches*, 1869 and Pflüger's *Archiv*, 51, 1892. Schrader, *ibid.* 41, 1887, and 44, 1889.

sensations; dogs (but not pigeons) ate and drank spontaneously, frogs caught flies, pigeons flew with an absolutely right calculation of distance. The "memory" of these animals, it is true, for the greater part related to experience gained before the operation, but to a certain extent they also were able to acquire new experience even in their defective state. In other words, on the basis of a general "prospective potency" the lower parts of the brain acquired a definite "prospective value," which otherwise they would not have acquired.[1] It therefore cannot be denied that acting in some measure is possible even without the main part of the brain, though the degree of this acting is of a much lower kind.

The term "Antwortsreaktion," which we have already made use of elsewhere, was invented by Goltz to describe what he had discovered in his frog deprived of the hemispheres. He himself speaks of the impossibility of imagining a machine as the basis of the phenomena, and then tries to introduce a psychological terminology. It is strange that he did not notice that it was vitalism, the autonomy of vital processes, that had been proved by his discoveries. But Goltz does not stand alone here: many authors agree that the so-called "soul" plays a positive and causal rôle in acting, without noticing that a natural factor which is neither chemical nor physical is thus introduced into the argument.

That real acting may go on in animals deprived of the hemispheres, is of great importance, of course, for the theory

[1] Therefore, as Lewandowsky also well observes, operative experiments are not able to teach us the "normal" performances of the parts left by them. But they demonstrate what I call the "prospective potency," and that is more valuable. All experiments about electric irritability of parts of the brain, of course, relate to their "prospective *value*" only. Compare our hypothetical remarks on the newly born in the text.

of life-autonomy in general: it shows that the "psychoid" is not only related to the cerebrum, but may also use the lower parts of the brain. One might say that a higher sort of psychoid governs the main brain, a lower one the thalamus opticus, the cerebellum, the medulla, and so on, and this would correspond, in some way, with the discrimination between consciousness and "subconsciousness" that is made by some modern psychologists or rather pseudo-psychologists. But it may well be true, in spite of our statement, that all motor entelechy is *one* and the same in one individual, and that it is only on account of the primitive state of their organisation that it can do less with the lower parts of the brain than with the hemispheres. In any case there must remain an open question.

Regulability in a vicarious sense [1] among the parts of the lower brain themselves is beautifully shown by some experiments of Luciani carried out on the cerebellum, whose function it is to maintain the equilibrium of the body during movement. All disturbances of its functions caused by partial extirpation were regulated after a short time. Even the extirpation of a whole half was followed by ataxy only for a while, and then regulation set in, and swimming and walking went on as well and symmetrically as before.[2]

---

[1] Compare our analysis of the "potencies" of the hemispheres.
[2] Recent discoveries of Giardina's (*Arch. Entw.-mech.* 23, 1907) seem to belong here also. Pieces of the tail of tadpoles, if taken from very young animals, move in co-ordination, but if they are taken from animals of a certain age co-ordination is established only after a while. In the latter case the lumbar spinal cord *had* already exercised a certain influence in the sense of a general governing, and the co-ordination "centres" had to be established secondarily in the nervous system of the tail, whilst they were arranged *ab origine* in the very young pieces. So-called "shock" was excluded experimentally. All this is directed in the first place against Loeb's so-called "segmental theory" of nervous physiology, and is, in fact, well able to

κ. DIFFERENT DEGREES OF ACTING IN DIFFERENT ANIMALS [1]

Human acting was the starting-point and centre of our analysis of acting; but our discussion would be incomplete if we said nothing about the different kinds and degrees of acting in the other parts of the animal kingdom.

Man and the Highest Animals Contrasted

Darwinism and phylogeny laid stress on man's affinity to animals, and with justice in respect to most details of his organisation; that was all right so far, though there was always a difficulty with regard to the hemispheres of the brain. In agreement with this particular the experiments of the last few years, carried out by English and American authors (Lloyd Morgan, Thorndike, Hobhouse, Kinnamann), have shown that as far as the *degree* of acting is the point of comparison, there is a difference between man and even the highest ape which is simply enormous: man after all remains the only "reasoning" organism, in spite of the theory of descent.

We have said more than once that motions of animals are the only subject we are studying in this chapter, motions and nothing else. But to describe them at all satisfactorily

disprove it. Giardina claims to have proved by his experiments an "indipendenza iniziale o virtuale," but not an "indipendenza effectiva"; these concepts seem to signify about the same as the terms "prospective potency" and "prospective value," as applied to brain physiology.

[1] A fuller reference to the subject will be found in the following works: Thorndike, *Animal Intelligence*, 1898. Lloyd Morgan, *Introduction to Comparative Psychology*, 1903. Wasmann, *Instinkt und Intelligenz im Tierreich*, 3. Auflage, 1905. Here the full literature may be found. The recent literature on the subject is well discussed in the articles of the "Comparative Psychology number" of the *Psychological Bulletin* (vol. v. No. 6), and in the article "Animal Behaviour" in *The American Naturalist*, vol. xlii. p. 207.

we hardly can avoid psychological terminology, and in fact nobody would blame us for applying it, after we have stated emphatically that we make use of it only in the sense of a descriptive analogy.

Apes and dogs, it is true, learn a good deal; there is an "historical basis" to their acting of a very complicated character indeed, but their acting lacks all that we call "abstraction." This would seem to be the chief reason why they invent nothing, and have nothing resembling language except quite superficially. Wundt has well said somewhere that animals have no language not for any reason of their organisation, but because they have nothing to talk about. It is very strange indeed how absolute the lack of a real inventive or imitative faculty is even in the highest apes. Thorndike observed some apes kept in a sort of stable with several doors that might easily be opened; he opened a door several times very carefully and distinctly in order to show the apes the mechanism of opening, but not one of them followed his manipulations. Only after one of the animals had succeeded in opening the door by chance did it notice what opening was, and thus "learn" opening. Even then his fellows did not profit by their companion's experience: each animal had to learn by personal experience, realising absolutely by chance what opening was.

Certainly there exists even in apes that which our term "historical basis of reacting" expresses. The specificity of their behaviour is determined by their individual history, *i.e.* by the specificity of the stimuli that occurred to them, and by the effects of these stimuli. But the individual combination of the elements of their experience is far less complicated and far less variable than it is in man. Some authors, like Wasmann, for instance, have said aptly that animals may possess a "sensorial memory" ("sinnliches Gedächtnis") but nothing more.[1]

It seems to me that analysis must keep especially to one point of the characteristics of acting in order to state well in what the differences in behaviour between man and higher animals have their foundations. We have said on another occasion that the term "element" as a part of the analysis of action means something relative. Everything in the stimuli and effects concerned in the creation of the historical basis *may* be regarded as an "element" in some way. Single words *or* letters may be the elements of a phrase; in a landscape the elements may be whole parts of it, or the individual bodies in it, or some parts of the individual bodies, or anything else. Now I think a fair description of the behaviour even of higher animals would be, that they are far less capable than man of resolving data into elements. They cling to the combinations in the form in which they have occurred, at any rate they do not go farther than to resolve what is given into individual bodies; a stick and a bone are as it were the very letters of a dog's alphabet.

And from all this follows the comparatively small range of their power of combination: for it follows that their association is only by contiguity, be it in space or in time, but never by similarity or contrast in the real sense, and therefore the material to be combined in acting, according to individualised circumstances, is very small.

[1] But I do not agree with Wasmann when he tries to regard this "sinnliches Gedächtnis" as akin to instinct; for it is the chief criterion of instinct that it does *not* rest upon a "historical basis."

Thus the lack of the power of resolving data seems to be the reason of the rather low mental state of animals; all the other differences between the acting of men and the acting of animals are consequences of this fundamental diversity.

But we should not learn very much more for our philosophical purposes by entering more deeply into this subject, and I therefore must leave the further study of the differences in the acting of the highest animals and of man to your personal meditation.

Higher Invertebrates

Acting of the type found in apes and in dogs seems by no means restricted to the higher vertebrates only: many insects, not only ants and bees but also beetles, seem to be capable of actions of almost the same degree of complexity. Many of you know, I suppose, that Sir John Lubbock, now Lord Avebury, has carried out numerous beautiful experiments about the experience of ants. I need only remind you of his "bridge-experiment," for instance. He found what modern students of the behaviour of dogs and apes have found also: there is acting, but so-called abstraction is almost completely lacking.

We can now assert with perfect confidence that the old view was very mistaken which regarded the behaviour of ants and bees as quite like the behaviour of a human society. Acting is of a far less high degree in these creatures than it is in man, but their instinctive life is developed in a much higher degree, as we know; in a degree in fact that is almost inconceivable to us. We of course take the word instinct here in its strictest meaning, as signifying a complicated reaction that is perfect the very first time, and I take this opportunity to remind you once more of the fundamental problems of the doctrine of instincts, relating to the possibility of their regulability and to their being called forth by individualised stimuli.

Experience in insects, of course, though of a far less high degree if compared with human experience, may in spite of that be of a very different character, and may relate to very different occurrences that are experienced. Thus it might be possible, as we have said already, that bees are able to remember the absolute amount and direction of a change of their localisation in space; that in fact would be something of which man can be said to have only a very shadowy idea.

The Lowest Forms of Acting

Let us close our present discussions with a few words about the most inferior kinds of experience.

Psychologically, as we know, the most simple case of remembering occurs by the mere observation of "sameness," that is, in noticing that a certain stimulus is the same as a former one. It would hardly be possible to prove objectively the existence of this sort of experience in organisms; there may very likely be something of this sort when an animal reacts quicker to a certain stimulus the second time than the first.[1]

The second step, or rather the second foundation of

[1] Compare the experiment on Daphnids, carried out by Davenport and Cannon, *Journ. of Physiol.* 21, 1897.

remembering in the psychological sense, is constituted by the mere act of association by contiguity: a stimulus not only recalls the idea of sameness but also recalls other stimuli (and effects) which had been combined with it the first time. Memory of this sort, of course, is only *concerned in* acting, but is not acting; it even is better kept separate from true "experience" altogether, the word "experience" being reserved for something about acting as an actuality.

"Experience" in this sense is seen in its most simple type, if one of the elements concerned in associative memory is a certain behaviour of the motor organs, able to call forth liking or to overcome disliking. It is from this kind of experience that the acting of man takes its origin, as we have discussed already, when dealing with the so-called origin of the act of volition; but it is this kind of experience, too, which fully deserves the name of a basis of "acting," even if almost no resolution of the given "historical basis of reacting" into its remoter elements occurs.

American authors [1] especially have studied the most simple types of acting in lower animals, in particular in Infusoria, Actiniae, worms, and crayfishes. We have stated on another occasion already, when trying to define the concept of acting in its contrast to other kinds of changeable motor reactions, that a mere consecutive line of changes of reactions in response to one and the same often repeated stimulus, as discovered by Jennings in the Protozoon *Stentor* and in the earthworm, never deserves the name of real acting, but may be due either to fatigue or to some

---

[1] For literature see the work of Jennings referred to at page 17, note 1.

unknown conditions of the physiological state of the organism. But there is acting, if the first time the reactions A, B, and C have answered to the stimulus *a* one after the other, and if the second time C answers to it without any delay, it being understood of course that it was C that had produced a "liking" or had overcome a "disliking" on the part of the organism: that is what actually happens in *Stentor*, and is very important as being a case of experience in a *simple* motor act. Primitive forms of experience relating to motorial *combinations* can be studied most advantageously in Crustacea. In Yerkes's "labyrinth" experiment a crab was placed in a box containing two different tracks, only one of which led to the water. The crab ran at random for a while, until at the end of many "trials" it found the entrance to the water; the second time the path to the water was taken with much fewer mistakes, and at the end of a set of experiments the crab ran to the water directly without going wrong. Here we have a most typical case of "experience" in which the "effect" of previous motor stimuli is concerned, and it hardly matters at all, whether we assume that the crab was guided by sight or that it was guided by some spatial memory, unknown to us, such as we have supposed to exist in some insects. Experience here consisted in the omission of a set of previous reactions in favour of the last effective one occurring in a series of consecutive stimulations. In another set of experiments carried out by Spaulding the facts lay a little differently. A hermit crab was fed with pieces of fish placed under a green screen, and after a certain number of experiments it ran beneath the green screen even if no piece was there. Similar experiments have been carried out by the pupils of the Russian physiologist Pawlow with dogs.[1] In all these cases a certain reaction, originally caused by the stimulus A, is in the end called forth by a stimulus B that always was united with A. Whilst in the instance with the crab shortening its way to the water there was a very clear kind of trial, there is not trial in the second experiment. Both experiments offer good instances of the two fundamental characters of our historical basis: in the first it is not only former stimuli but former effects also that are responsible for the specificity of the reaction, in the second it is former stimuli only.

But the scheme is always the same.[2]

A fine instance of real "training" by means of "lessons" has been demonstrated by Jennings in his excellent paper on the movements of the starfish, already referred to. "Training" relates to the righting movements in this case; former stimuli, former reactions, and former effects are equally concerned here.

And now let us close our long discussions of animal motions with some remarks of a most general character.

[1] But here the process influenced by association is not movement but secretion of the salivary glands. Compare in particular, besides the writings of Pawlow himself, the good article by Boldyreff in *Zeitschr. f. d. Ausbau d. Entw.-lehre*, vol. i., 1907, Hefte 5 and 6.

[2] Compare our general discussion on pages 63-65. In the experiment described by Yerkes the term "trial and error" as used by Jennings is quite appropriate: what was at first the effect of a series of trials including errors will become the immediate reaction when the stimulus appears a second time. But it seems to me unjustified to speak of trial and error when there is no objectified experience, and when a series of consecutive various reactions only ceases if a certain state is reached: this state *may* be a "liked" one, but there is no criterion to discover this in lower animals. What Jennings calls the "resolution of the physiological states one into another" expresses about the same as does my "historical basis of reaction." But Jennings is wrong when he says that this "resolution" only becomes "easier and

λ. "PSYCHO-PHYSICAL PARALLELISM" REFUTED

In analysing acting we have become convinced that, on account of the individualised correspondence between cause and effect, founded on a basis historically created, we are not able to explain what is going on by the aid of physics and chemistry, or of mechanics, if you prefer to say so. There is a new and autonomic natural factor concerned in action, a factor unknown to the inorganic world.

Now it is very important to notice well, that by stating the autonomy of natural events as occurring in action we are in fundamental contradiction with a wide-spread theory that is at present very much in vogue among psychologists. I refer to the theory of "psycho-physical parallelism."[1] At least we are in a fundamental contradiction with one side of this theory. All of you know, I suppose, what that theory claims, and I can dismiss it the more briefly since Professor James Ward, a few years ago, gave a splendid sketch of the different aspects of the theory of psycho-physical parallelism in this very place.

The theory of parallelism may start from a metaphysical basis by saying that the psychical and the physical facts are but different aspects of one unknown absolute reality, standing in permanent correspondence with each other, as was the opinion of Spinoza and his followers, though sometimes stated in a more materialistic form. Or the

more rapid" with each repetition : there are links left out of the chain, and that is most important.

[1] Compare the general critical discussions in Busse, *Geist und Körper, Seele und Leib*, Leipzig, 1903. See also H. Bergson, "Le paralogisme psycho-physiologique," *Rev. métaph. et mor.* 12, No. 6, 1904, and the book *Matière et Mémoire* (1896), by the same author.

parallelistic theory may be put upon an idealistic [1] and phenomenological basis, stating that the " Given," as being objectified in space on the one hand, and as being immediate self-experience on the other, shows a complete correspondence of the elements of its two sides, there being not a single element of the one side without a correlated element on the other. In either case the advocates of the theory of parallelism have held *that the physical side of their duality forms a continuous chain of strictly physico-chemical or mechanical events without any gap in it.* That has by no means been proved by the defenders of the parallelistic theory, but it generally has been regarded as self-evident without any further reflection.

There can be no doubt that we *cannot agree* with these statements regarding the physical part of the parallelistic theory in any of its usual forms: we have shown that there is not at all an unbroken mechanical chain of events in action as a phenomenon of motion, that there is a mutual relation between factors which are mechanical or physico-chemical and factors which are of quite another elemental character.

But it must be well kept in mind: we do not speak of " psycho "-physical interactions in spite of that; our funda-

[1] In one of the next chapters it will be shown that parallelism on an idealistic basis is a simple absurdity. We wish to say in passing that even metaphysically parallelism has always proved and always will prove to be quite an impossible statement in our opinion. How could a mere sum or addition, as the physical side of the supposed reality is maintained to be, appear "from its other side" as a something that is quite certainly *not* such a mere addition? Parallelism nowadays seems to be almost wholly driven out of the field. Even Wundt is no longer a convinced parallelist. That Kant never was a parallelist is proved in my book *Der Vitalismus als Geschichte und als Lehre.* See in particular the additions made to the Italian translation.

mental point of view, which is critical idealism, forbids us to say so, at least as long as we are not metaphysicians. Our statements regarding action refer to natural events in space and to such events only: there are factors contrary to mechanics in these natural events, but these factors are "natural" factors too; they belong to "physics" in the sense of the ancients, though not to physics in the modern sense. Our "psychoid" in this sense is a factor of τὰ φυσικά, an agent or factor of nature, looked upon as part of Givenness.

From our idealistic standpoint, as long as it is non-metaphysical, "psychology" and the "psychical" belong exclusively among the self-experiences of the Ego.

The question now arises, if from such a point of view there might not be room for a parallelism of quite a new type, very strange perhaps at the first glance: a parallelism of "my Ego" and "my psychoid" as a natural factor at work in *my* body. Perhaps that would only be a parallelism of a methodological sort that might be called doctrinaire. Let us only note for the present that, for the sake of analytical clearness, my Ego and my psychoid, as my object of reflection, may in fact be regarded as being in activity "parallel" with respect to one another. A special chapter of our future lectures will be devoted to the deeper elucidation of the relations between idealistic philosophy and vitalism in its most general sense.

At any rate we must deny the claim of parallelism that there is an unbroken mechanical chain of events in acting, and we must deny "psycho"-physical interaction also, if we wish not to become metaphysicians. By our non-metaphysical point of view we avoid, of course, all the difficulties of how there ever could be an "interaction" between two entities of such absolutely different kinds as the "psyche" and the physical reality in space. It is well known that it was especially these difficulties which led Spinoza to his dogmatic parallelism, Leibniz to his doctrine of monads, and Berkeley and Kant to their idealistic theories of different styles. From our present point of view we only recognise "interactions" between physico - chemical and non - physico - chemical agents of nature.

μ. THE SUPRA-PERSONAL FACTOR OF ACTING IN HISTORY

These short remarks form one of the ends of our discussion of acting, and at the same time one of the ends of our long discussion of problems of analytical natural science altogether. The next lecture will bring us into the realm of the real philosophy of nature.

But still another end must be given to our theory of action: let us say a few words about the rôle of acting in history, and about what may follow therefrom.

That human history is throughout based on acting needs no further explanation, and indeed finds its proper expression in the concept of the "historical" basis of reacting, as being one of the foundations of action: the individual history of the acting man is responsible for the specificity of what he will do. That speaking and writing are the most fundamental factors, upon which the history of generations builds itself up, also needs only to be shortly mentioned.

But another problem arises, one related with the problem

of human history in general, as discussed in the last lecture of last summer.

No Supra-personal Factor known in History Proper

Does history teach us that there are concerned in true historical states and events any elemental agents or factors or laws which are *additional* to what is said in the fundamental formula of individual acting, resting upon its two familiar principles?

The answer to this question is given by our analysis of history: by proving that the history of mankind seems to be a mere process of *cumulation* only, a process by which one complication is simply added to the other without there being, as far as we know, the "evolution" of a real unity. By proving this we express at the same time that in the State, in religion, in science, in law, in economics we only meet cumulations of acting and their results, but no new elementalities. So-called "philosophies" of the State or of law, as created most profoundly by Hegel, therefore, are philosophical branches of the second order; they stand to the philosophy of action in the same relation as geology stands to chemistry and physics. State and law are no "entities," as far as we know, to speak in an ontological terminology. The *State* is *not* an "organism"—strange to say, for so very often in modern literature the real biological organism was pretended to be "explained" on the analogy of the State! Even the so-called "States" of bees and ants are real organisms only to a very small degree and not in detail.

In order that any form of human society *might* properly

be called an organism in itself, it would be required that disturbances of this organism should be repaired by force of the whole. But nothing of this sort exists: there *are* "regulations" in social life, as, for instance, when a business that needs workers attracts them by offering better payment, whilst an overcrowded business readily parts with workpeople: but all this happens for the sake of the *individual's* liking and happiness, and for *no* other reason, as far as we know. There certainly is a little more of real organisation in the "State" of Hymenoptera.

Morality as a Supra-personal Factor

But now let us ask another more general question: Does anything *new* appear in nature besides mere acting, when there is not one single acting human being, but a community, or at least two human beings on the scene? Such a new factor, of course, would play its part in social life, though not in a properly "historical" sense.

We may also ask like this: Is a really complete philosophy of acting already created or at least prepared by the analysis we have given of it? It seems to me that one chief thing is wanting still for such a preparation, and that this chief thing is the elemental entity that is concerned *in* historical and social becoming, besides the two principles of acting we have analysed.

Entelechy in morphogenesis, metabolism, and instinctive life tends to guarantee the specificity of form and function; entelechy in acting, our psychoid, guarantees the realisation of what is "liked"—to speak a little incorrectly, but quite intelligibly—by the performer of the action. In both cases it is for the sake of the *bearer* of the entelechy that everything goes on.

But if there is acting between two or more human beings there *may* be—I do not say that there always is—a very strange exception to this retortion on the performer himself: there may occur acting which tends not to the liking of the agent but to the normal state or the "liking" of *another* being. This kind of acting may even lead to the sacrifice of the agent's life in order that "the other" may be saved.

What occurs here is as contrary to entelechy as was entelechy to mechanics, though in *some* way it shows a certain similarity to instinct.

In these few words we have sketched the characteristics of *morality*—of morality, that is, considered as a phenomenon of bodily nature by a naturalist;[1] and at the same time, it seems to me, we have given account of the second elemental entity, besides acting for oneself, that was still wanted in order to complete the truly elemental facts upon which the history and social life of mankind are built up. History and its results, taken by themselves, are mere cumulations, but cumulations grown up by the permanent interaction of entelechial life in all its forms *and morality*.

It is not unimportant to notice that the rôle which general morality plays, or rather which moral acting individuals play in history, might have an enormous effect even if history were proved some day to contain certain evolutionary elements. Morality in fact, as the general law regulating the actions among at least two human

[1] Morality, of course, from such a point of view belongs to "nature," and is not alien to it, as is often asserted by philosophers. We shall come back to this point at the end of the book.

beings, could possibly counteract evolution and stop it. It would do so whenever "evolution" led through immoral phases. Suppose that an evolutionary process of any kind could only be effected by war or revolution, and that the majority of a people objected to war and revolution for moral reasons: then evolution would be stopped in favour of morality. We have spoken of the possibility that history might contain *certain* evolutionary elements. If it were evolution throughout, all "morality," of course, would be only apparent: there would in reality be no such thing as the relation between two "individuals" in this case, there would be *one* "super-individuum" using the biological individuals as its "means."[1]

CONCLUSIONS OF SECTION A

Our survey of the most important theoretical results of biology as a natural science is ended; discussion of these results as such may begin and, indeed, is to occupy us for the rest of these lectures.

Nobody can blame us, I suppose, for having understood the concept of biology in too narrow a sense; on the contrary, some people might say perhaps that too many problems have been brought by us to the court of biological natural science, such as the history and culture and morality of mankind. But biology, I think, must be taken as the natural science of *all* that is living and of all the phenomena

[1] In this case moral feeling itself would be subjected to evolution—which, personally, I do not believe. That, otherwise, all sorts of cumulations are able to be stopped by morality is too obvious to require further analysis. The problem of the content of morality as such lies beyond the limits of this book.

offered in any way during life, as far as they can be defined as states and changes of bodies in space; and all the facts we have discussed could be defined in this manner.

It follows from the great variety of biological subjects that biology, if understood in its full sense, comes face to face with many special sciences, borrowing something from each of them; only then can biology be said to be complete,[1] and to be a material that is well prepared for the philosophy of organic nature.

[1] Only one field of problematic biological phenomena has not been taken into account altogether, as I feel quite unable to judge here personally in any way. I refer to the so-called spiritualistic phenomena. The reader may refer for this subject to the critical publications of the "Society for Psychical Research," Frank Podmore's *Studies in Psychical Research* (London, 1897) giving an excellent survey of the same. The *only* thing that seems to be established beyond all doubt is "telepathy"; and even telepathy *might* perhaps some day be understood as being a phenomenon of radiation comparable with wireless telegraphy. The only new thing in it would then be the faculty of man to put special parts of his brain into a special state voluntarily, as he can do with his muscles. That at least would be the most simple theory. Of course, there *might* be at work also something absolutely different (see the end of Podmore's book). What we have called (with Semon) engrammata would in some way be comparable with what possibly is transmitted in telepathy (see page 98).

SECTION B
THE PHILOSOPHY OF THE ORGANISM

INTRODUCTORY DISCUSSIONS

1. Philosophy of Nature in General

Philosophy of nature is the demonstration of the general scheme of nature based upon the character or essence of reason. It received its modern foundation from the analytical work of Kant and his followers, though Kant himself, in his conception of the categories and the *a priori*, went only as far as to show by what means such a philosophy might be built up. In answering one of his fundamental questions: "*Wie ist reine Naturwissenschaft möglich?*" ("How is pure natural science possible?"), he proved that it really is possible on account of some faculties of reason referring to concepts and principles of relation in Givenness. These concepts and principles are *a priori* or self-evident, in other words, they cannot be denied when once understood in their meaning, albeit they do *not* rest solely on the logical principle of contradiction.

It was the school of Schelling and Hegel, and to some extent Schopenhauer also, that tried to develop the ideas of Kant; but, unfortunately, the two first-named philosophers at least were not very critical in their deduction, the whole subject of a philosophy of nature becoming more or less fantastic under their hands. That has done the utmost harm to the philosophical conception of nature in our times. Philosophy of nature, in its true sense, has been discredited altogether: a period of mere empiricism followed the period of the natural philosophers; more than that, there was not only the strong endeavour to get empirical knowledge—which might have been very useful indeed—but there was the conviction that there *never could be* anything more than mere empirical experience at all.

Such an opinion is still predominant in our times, and I need only mention the names of Mach, Clifford, Pearson, and Ostwald to remind you of this state of affairs, and to remind you, at the same time, that the men of science who hold the empirical view sketched above are in fact among the best representatives of *science* in our days.

Nevertheless, it is my strongest conviction that such a conception of natural sciences is wrong and incomplete, and that the work of Schelling and Hegel was certainly true and valuable so far as its *aim* went. There *can* be a philosophy of nature resting on the foundations of criticism, and evolving a real system of nature from reason without the use of uncontrolled imagination; and there *will* be such a system some day, there *will* be a *system* that really deserves to be called philosophy of nature in the old sense of this term.

In this country the term "natural philosophy" has been restricted to mathematical physics, and that is certainly justified in so far as a great part of theoretical physics does in fact rest on principles that are part of a real philosophy of nature, even though physicists might not agree with this statement. But the use of the word "natural philosophy" as identical with mathematical physics must be said to be misleading in so far as there are many purely empirical principles in mathematical physics also, only the consequences of which are explained mathematically. Of course, there is nothing of a real philosophy of nature in explanations of this kind.

We shall deal in the remainder of this work with the philosophy of the organism. But do not expect a complete philosophical system of life from my future discussion. You would be very disappointed if you did so.

In fact, I *shall* try to show you in this section of my lectures that the laws of life *must* be what they are, that reasoning forbids us to accept any other law, and that it forces us to acknowledge the actual laws, when once their meaning is understood. But I shall do so only at the end of a rather long discussion which will move, so to speak, half-way between mere systematic philosophy and theoretical science.

The time is not ripe for offering you a real complete philosophical system of the organism without a great number of preliminary discussions. At least I myself feel unable to offer you such a system without a certain amount of preparation. Therefore I shall begin with the discussion of certain fragments of a future complete system of philosophical biology, or rather with certain considerations relating to it; and not till that has been done shall I try to sketch the outlines of what will really deserve the name of a pure philosophy of life and the organism.

Our first task is a limited one; we must first bring the general concepts we have gained from the analysis of biological facts into connexion with parts of the philosophical system of the Inorganic, at least with some special concepts and laws concerned in that system. Of course, we have not time ourselves to formulate a real system of the Inorganic here; let us imagine that it is ready and perfect; the parts of it which we shall use are such that all of you will easily understand what is being spoken about, even though you may regard as singularities what in truth are parts of a great unity and totality.

2. The Concept of Teleology

We begin our philosophical analysis by summarising the most general results of the scientific part of these lectures in a new form and terminology. This will lead us to the discussion of a concept which plays a very important rôle in the usual logic and ontology, a concept which is regarded as a real category by some and as of a mere regulative and heuristic character by others.

Many of you, I suppose, will have noticed that in the whole of our previous discussions, this year and last, we have strictly avoided making use of a certain term, though almost all our analysis related to the meaning of that term.

"Teleology" is the concept I am thinking of; the words "teleology" and "teleological" have not been used a single time; and in spite of that we have almost always dealt with phenomena which were teleological or "purposeful" in the highest sense.

TELEOLOGY IN GENERAL

Let us begin our studies with a few analytical words about teleology, without discussing at present the true logical or ontological nature of this concept.

In ordinary language and also in science, as long as science remains purely descriptive, the word "purposeful" might be applied to relations of very great variety. The feet of men are very "purposeful" for walking, and so are the wings of birds for flying; the process of regeneration in the earthworm is purposeful, as is also the formation of an antitoxin after a snake's bite; the insect *Phyllum* has a very purposeful form and colour for being protected against enemies. But the modern railway system is very purposeful too; the lift is a very purposeful instrument; and of a man who triples his fortune in three years it might be said that he acted purposefully on some occasion, while the physician also acts purposefully when by an operation he saves his patient from death.

There is not the slightest doubt that the word purposeful cannot be used scientifically without thoroughly sifting its meaning.

Let us, in the first place, avoid applying the word purposeful to mere arrangements or states: an engine of any kind is not purposeful but is "useful"; in a certain sense it may be called "a purpose," and it is useful if it allows some *events* to go on which are "purposeful" in any sense. Only events, then, are "purposeful."

But when is an event to be called purposeful and when is it not?

To comprehend the proper meaning of the term "purposeful" let us start by considering my own actions, to which this term is originally applicable. We shall here pursue a line of thought which later on is to lead us to very important consequences, but which at present is merely used for the sake of a clear terminology. *My* acting is "purposeful" whenever it serves to bring about what I like or to do away with what I dislike. The "purpose" of my acting always is a certain state of the medium that "ought to exist"—an engine, for instance; it is always *external* with respect to myself, and therefore the concept of a "self-purpose" may be declined *a limine*. All my acting towards a purpose is based upon knowledge of the "means" by which the purpose may be attained, and upon judgment of the "suitability" of those means.

From this it is but one step to call *another* man's acting purposeful: he acts purposefully, whenever I see him acting in such a manner that I can imagine myself acting like him under similar conditions, that is, if I can imagine that, under the circumstances in which the other human being is placed, I should have some liking or disliking, and should act in some way in order to gratify or to obviate it. It follows from this that purposefulness in the acting of other men is always judged of by analogy alone. This is true, if we pass from man to the higher animals: even the actions of an ape or a dog may be said to be intelligible in some degree.

But things become more difficult as soon as we pass to the lowest organisms, still regarded as acting, and to processes of morphogenesis and metabolism: in what cases have we the right to claim certain such processes as purposeful or teleological and others not?

Mere analogy would fail here to justify the application of the term, for, in fact, we cannot imagine ourselves in the situation of a newt repairing its foot: we are certainly unable to regenerate our own foot if it is lost in an accident, and even if our body could repair it, the process would probably go on in a so-called unconscious manner. We must then seek for a somewhat different criterion of teleology without leaving the analogy with our own acting quite out of sight.

Now it seems to me that it would not meet the point to say that physiological and morphogenetic processes are teleological simply because they serve to form and to preserve the organism; for this argument, taken by itself, would not imply that there is something that *ought* to be formed and preserved. We gain a deeper insight into the nature of the individual organism, if we remember that the organism is of the type of a specific constellation of simple elements, and that it is realised in its actual constellation in *innumerable exemplars*. And these exemplars, as was pointed out by Kant, are mutually "cause and effect" to one another. It was for this reason that Kant called the organisms "Naturzwecke" ("purposes of nature"). We shall not make use of Kant's terminology, but the argument it is based upon is important. Every organic process indeed, morphogenetic or physiological, is "purposeful" for the reason that it serves to form and to preserve a specific constellation which occurs in indefinite exemplars, and whose specificity has no other reason than the existence of a previous specificity of the same type; for this reason and for no other is an organic process "teleological." For *only on this basis* is there an analogy with phenomena to which the predicate teleological *has already been given by our previous analysis*, viz., the phenomena leading to indefinite exemplars of specific constellations called machines, or objects of art and industry in general, that is the phenomena of human *acting*.

The organisms, to a certain extent at least, appear as

purposes, just as do the effects of acting, and *therefore* the processes leading to them are purposeful. Thus by regarding certain bodies in nature as purposes we return to the analogy of our own acting: in doing so we indeed merely state that we could imagine ourselves wishing or liking those bodies to exist, and liking their existence in the state of normality. It is of no consequence to these preliminary discussions that works of art or handicraft are most markedly brought to their typical constellation by occurrences external to them in the spatial sense, whilst organisms are certainly not built up by external events in space. On a later occasion this distinction will receive the analysis which it undoubtedly deserves; at present we are only seeking a useful terminology.

You might reply to our discussion by saying that nobody speaks of volcanoes or of crystals as "purposes," though both of them exist in indefinite exemplars. Volcanoes, however, are not derived one from the other, but are due most clearly to a cumulation of physico-chemical acts from without in every single case, and crystals are not typically composed bodies, as will be pointed out more fully on another occasion. Therefore processes leading to the formation of these two groups of natural bodies are by no means "teleological." Indefinitely repeated bodies must possess a specifically complex character, and must originate from their own kind, if the processes leading to them or restoring them are to be called "teleological."

We have said that we could imagine ourselves wishing the bodies called by Kant "purposes of nature" not only to exist in their innumerable exemplars but also to exist in the state of normality; this discrimination requires a further analysis. You might say perhaps that only the processes of régulation ought to be called "teleological," *i.e.* only the processes leading from abnormal states to normality; but would it not be quite unjustified to refuse the name to the processes of normal embryology, which indeed on account of the different kinds of harmony existing between them seem to promote the existence of the organic bodies in the highest degree? Their existence *as such* therefore is to be regarded as nature's purpose—existence here to include all regulation of disturbances of normality.

And now let us make the last step in our application of the term "teleological" in its relation to processes occurring in natural bodies. All processes contributing to the construction of any kind of engines and machines made by man are purposeful, for they are actions of men. The machines themselves we have called merely "useful," but all the different processes that occur in such engines or machines when they are "working" are also purposeful. There is no difficulty, I believe, in understanding this sort of teleology, which appears in inorganic bodies belonging to the class of so-called artefacts, for it simply is part of the *definition* of a machine that it shall by its working serve some purpose of man. Thus purposefulness of machines is in the last resort the mere outcome of the teleology of acting. But it is important that the concept "teleological" has been thus transferred to inorganic events.

Let us not lose sight of the real character of the present discussion. We have only tried to answer the question: What sort of natural processes may be denoted by the predicate teleological? We have done nothing but this work of terminological description. There was nothing laid down as to what teleology might *signify*.

THE TWO CLASSES OF TELEOLOGY

But now a more important analysis is to follow: to a certain extent we now shall pass from mere denomination to what may be called ontological problems.

Whilst studying the teleological processes going on in an engine constructed by man, we understand with absolute clearness and distinctness that a process in nature may be teleological or purposeful, and that it may be *at the same time* of a purely mechanical or physico-chemical order; indeed all processes going on in human-built machines are of that class, no matter what the machine. We know that in these cases every single process of the whole of the engine's function goes on in its singularity, and that its purposefulness or teleology is due only to its place and combination in the whole: it only is purposeful *because* it stands in this special *relation* to other single processes, and for no other reason at all.

Let us speak of a *statical teleology* in such cases, or of a *teleology of constellation*.

Now at once the question arises: Are all teleological processes in nature of the statical type, and what would follow if they were not? Of course, the name *dynamical teleology* might be given to all kinds of natural processes which are purposeful without being the mere outcome of the constellation of a machine.

We have proved by three independent lines of argument that such processes exist in organisms. From our analysis of the differentiation of harmonious-equipotential systems, and of the genesis of complex-equipotential systems, and from our intimate study of the process of acting, going on upon an historically created basis and with the criterion of an individualised correspondence between cause and effect, we have learnt that no machine, of whatever kind and whatever degree of combination, can afford us the means of understanding what happens here in the organism. There was a natural factor at work, *autonomic* and *not* resulting from a combination of other agents, but elemental in itself; this factor acted teleologically: it therefore may be called a factor of dynamical teleology.

It might seem that we ought to have been able to accomplish our proof more easily: might we not have said simply that the single processes going on *in* a machine are of course of the statical-teleological type, but that the act of *constructing* this machine is of course a dynamical-teleological one, being due to my will? That argument would have been simple indeed, but it would have been also wrong: for psychological terms were excluded from our discussion, which was purely one of natural science. We had to prove exclusively by natural science that there was no possibility of a statical-teleological explanation, and this, I trust, we have succeeded in doing.

After this terminological work we shall now begin to study what that impossibility means.

Let us begin with a descriptive enumeration of the important characteristics of our entelechy.

3. The Characteristics of Entelechy

Extensive and Intensive Manifoldness

Entelechy either underlies the origin of an organic body, typically built up of typical elements, or it underlies an action, *i.e.* a typical combination of typical movements. Thus we see: entelechy always results in a manifoldness of a typical kind, the single elements of which are beside each other in space, or one after the other in time, or both, always in a typical order. Let us call such a manifoldness as is the result of the manifestation of entelechy an *extensive manifoldness*, and let us not forget to notice that all sorts of engines or machines are also extensive manifoldnesses in this meaning of the word.

Now we believe we have proved that entelechy, *i.e.* the foundation of the extensive manifoldnesses just mentioned, whether organisms or machines, is not in its turn an extensive manifoldness of the type of any machine whatever. In other words, the actual organism, as it offers itself to observation, is certainly a combination of singularities, each of which may be described in terms of physics and chemistry, like a machine, and also all changes in these singularities lead to results which may be so described, but the reason of the *origin* of the combination and of all its changes is not a law or any combination of laws taught us by physics and chemistry, but rests upon entelechy, as does the reason of the origin of any kind of machine that results from acting. We therefore propose to give the name *intensive manifoldness* to all kinds of entelechies or psychoids: there is, in fact, something "manifold" in them, but the elements of the manifoldness are neither one beside the other in space nor one after the other in time. We may say that entelechy is manifold in thought but simple as a natural agent.

As being an intensive manifoldness entelechy belongs to the general sphere of *dynamic* teleology: there is something teleological *in* its very work, whether this work be directed towards the normality of an organic individual, with regard to form or function—existence in space being included in the meaning of the term "normality"—or whether, as in real acting, the boundaries of mere normality are broken. Acting, in fact—the work of the "artist" in the widest sense of that term,—not only "is" but *creates*, and entelechy creates through the artist.

Here we meet again the difference between a product of entelechy that is itself the point of manifestation of entelechy—the organism—and a product of entelechy that is a machine and is unable to perform further entelechian acts itself: "acting has gone over into its product" ("Die Tätigkeit ist in ihr Produkt übergegangen"), to use a phrase applied by Hegel. We shall have to say more about this later on.

Once more we say that entelechy or the psychoid has nothing of a "psychical" nature: in the psychical sphere there is only my Ego, at least for the critical and idealistic philosopher. "I" have sensations and likings and judgments and volitions, but nature as the object of my perceiving and judging and wishing only has agents or factors relating to its structure and type of change; entelechies and psychoids are some of these factors.

It is true, we occasionally have taken analytical expressions from psychology in order to describe these agents by analogy, and we shall do so again. But our object in doing so was, and will be, exclusively to analyse the kind and degree of manifoldness concerned in entelechy; for this kind and degree of manifoldness resembles to a great extent the manifoldness of the whole of the psychical phenomenon. In this way psychology simply becomes a method in our studies.

For a more intimate study of the nature of the manifoldness embraced in entelechy, I think it advisable to separate the different kinds of entelechies, according to whether so-called "experience" plays a part in them or not: the entelechies of morphogenesis and of instinct [1] are wanting in the criterion of the "historical basis of reacting," psychoids are endowed with it.

SECONDARY AND PRIMARY KNOWING AND WILLING

It is by no means difficult to get a good idea of part of the manifoldness concerned in "psychoids" by a psychological analysis. In fact, we have merely to apply such concepts as perceiving, liking, judging, willing to a psychoid in a metaphorical manner in order to have a good *picture*

[1] Provided entelechy *is* concerned in instinctive life. See page 50.

of what is happening in every natural event where psychoids come into play—of course a picture only, in the merely descriptive meaning of the word.

Let us speak of *secondary* "knowing and willing" in the case of those acts of a psychoid which go on upon its historical basis, its "experience." These two psychological terms seem to be sufficient to describe adequately what happens, as it is well known from pure psychological analysis that liking and judging—judging about the most "suitable" means among those which are known to promote the end—are never wanting whenever the act of knowing and volition occurs; psychical elemental functions are inseparable in fact and only separable in thought; to name a few of them therefore is, for the purposes of our analogy, to name them all.

The word "secondary," as applied to certain characters of the manifoldness of one type of entelechy, the psychoid, seems to imply that there are also some "primary" characteristics of a similar kind; in studying the *primary* features of entelechies our analysis will become far more difficult.

It is worth while to notice, in the first place, that primary characters are not only possessed by the entelechy of morphogenesis, metabolism, and instinct, but in some measure by psychoids also. That they are possessed by morphogenetic, physiological, and instinctive entelechies is clear without any further deliberation. The manifestations of these entelechies are "primary": they occur either not at all or *perfectly* the very first time; all sorts of restitutions and of instincts are instances of this primariness. But how could "secondary" faculties appear in the other class of entelechies, the psychoids, endowed with the historical basis of reacting, if there were not also primary faculties in them?

We are here faced by a very fundamental problem of the theory of knowledge in its biological form. "How is experience possible?" was the epistemological question of Kant; "how are the secondary faculties of pyschoids possible?" is the biological question. Here again, of course, analogies only are possible.[1] We may say that in order to judge or to know, the general type of judging and of knowing must be given. And the same holds about the analogy to volition: what is willed rests on experience, but willing itself is primary. And, moreover, the effect that is "consciously" willed in the "secondary" form, depending upon "experience," is always a certain state of the external world. This is accomplished by no means immediately; it is accomplished by muscular motions, and these, on their part, depend on specific innervations. Now of "innervations" the unscientific mind knows nothing at all; and it by no means "wills" innervations. But they *are* performed (in an "unconscious" way), and this fact alone, it seems to me, proves beyond all doubt that primary

---

[1] I should like to take this opportunity of pointing out that Jennings is mistaken if he thinks that in the case of the righting reactions of the starfish entelechy would in any case not be "final" and "ultimate," since these reactions in their specificity rest upon the "past history" of the individual. He does not clearly enough separate here the "primary" and the "secondary" characteristics of a special entelechian factor, or rather "psychoid." If the righting reactions were instinctive, then only primary "knowing and willing" would come into account; now Jennings has proved that they rest upon "experience," and *therefore* he believes that entelechy is not an elementality. But the *possibility* of being influenced by the "past history" *implies* the existence of a new and final natural agent. "Secondary knowing and willing" (*i.e.* "experience" or the specific "historical basis") implies "primary knowing and willing" (*i.e.* the *possibility* of acquiring a specific "historical basis").

knowing and willing is concerned in any kind of acting: the faculty of innervation is "primary."

So far there would hardly seem to exist any serious analytical difficulty; but the problem becomes very complicated as soon as we turn from the facts to the "how," as soon as we inquire the meaning of the primary faculties of those entelechies in which an historical basis does *not* play *any part at all*. We indeed are in a rather desperate condition with regard to the real analysis of the fundamental properties of morphogenetic, adaptive, and instinctive entelechies: for there *must* be a something in them that has an analogy not to knowing and willing in general—as it may be supposed to exist in the primary faculties of pyschoids—*but to the willing of specific unexperienced realities*, and to knowing the specific means of attaining them. And we are by no means able to understand such a specified primary knowing and willing in even the slightest degree.[1]

It is here that the difference between the "conscious" and the "unconscious" enters the field, if we choose for a moment to adopt Eduard von Hartmann's terminology. We do not accept this terminology definitively, but the differences expressed by it are real differences.

Without doubt it is at this point that vitalism encounters its greatest difficulties. It is here that so many make up their minds that they cannot accept vitalism as a theory at all. They would be inclined to accept the autonomy of life as far as psychoids are concerned, as far as the historical

---

[1] To speak of an "inherited experience" here would only be to state the problem in another form. Besides that there is no good reason at present for assuming such an inheritance. Compare vol. i. pp. 278 ff.

basis of reacting, *i.e.* secondary knowing and willing, comes into account, but they feel unable to accept autonomical teleological agents unpossessed of these secondary faculties. Schneider, Pauly, Strecker and many others among modern authors take this view; Kant, it seems to me, thought similarly, for he left open the question of vitalism proper, and only advocated formal teleology in morphogenesis and metabolism, though he was not opposed to the theory of so-called " psycho-physical " interaction.[1]

But it is my firm conviction that we cannot avoid the admission of vitalistic autonomic agents possessing no experience, *i.e.* no " secondary " faculties, and yet endowed with *specific* knowing and willing: indeed, as far as morphogenesis and physiological adaptation and instinctive reactions are concerned, there *must* be a something comparable metaphorically with specified knowing and willing, but without experience. Of course, we must be careful about *what* has to be "known" and "judged" and "willed." This problem seems rather easy to answer in the light of morphological restitutions. Here the end to be attained is the normal organisation; that "means" towards this end are known and *found* may seem very strange, but it is a *fact*; and it is a fact also, in the case of what we have called "equifinal regulations," that different means leading to one and the same final state may be known and adopted.

As to the primary faculties concerned in adaptation great theoretical caution seems to be advisable. We have already urged on a former occasion that it is quite

[1] Compare my book, *Der Vitalismus als Geschichte und als Lehre*, Leipzig, 1905.

impossible to imagine even by analogy how the organism could "know" that any substance when taken in either by the intestine or by the skin *will* poison it. But it *is* possible to imagine that the organism knows how to act, whenever the functional state of its life is on the point of becoming disturbed, and that it then does something to repair the disturbance. In fact we have noticed that "antibodies" are not formed till *after* poisons have entered the organism, and we have noticed changes in the permeability of surfaces that do not occur until *after* the abnormal specific exchange of material between the medium and the fluid of the organism had gone on for some time.[1]

[1] The concept of "function" may seem to require a little further logical sifting in this place beyond what was said about it in the first volume (pp. 168 ff.). In the strict meaning of the term a part of an organism is "functioning" when it performs that kind of specific metabolism which is normal to it; the totality of all the normal metabolic performances of the parts of the organism is its "normal functional state." If this state is disturbed from without, "adaptation" may restore it; this adaptation consists in a specific change of the functioning of a specific part. So far everything, it seems to me, is quite clear, and so far the concept of "functioning" was discussed at great length in the first volume of this work. But the word "functioning" may also be applied in a certain other sense: not relating to the performance of a certain organ as such, but to the relation or effect of this performance with regard to other parts of the same organism, or even the *whole* organism. It is the "function" of the cells of the pancreas to secrete trypsin; let us call this their "proper function." But by secreting trypsin the pancreatic cells prepare material for assimilation by all the other organs of the individual: that is the "harmonious function" of the pancreas. And in the same way it is the "proper" function of the cells of the bones to secrete salts, whilst it is their "harmonious" function to support the organism mechanically. We now see what "adaptation" of the disturbed "functional state" of the organism, carried out by a change of functioning in a certain part of it, really means teleologically. The *harmonious* function of a certain part—its rôle in the total unity of the living individual, in other words—had been disturbed by disturbing the "functional state" from without: and this disturbance of harmonious functioning, or the harmony of functioning, is rectified by adaptation. Indeed, only *because* it leads to the restoration of this harmony, is the change of the "proper" functioning of the organ in question *adaptive*.

In this way, regarding it only as a kind of description, I see no fundamental difficulty in speaking of entelechy's *primary* "knowing and willing"; at least no other description of what happens seems to be derivable from any species of analogy.

ENTELECHY AND THE "INDIVIDUUM"

We shall now regard entelechy from yet another point of view, necessitating a comparison between organisms and crystals.

From ancient times the organism has been called an individuum, *i.e.* a something that cannot be divided without ceasing to be what it was. "Individua" in this meaning are the atoms of the Organic, the words "individuum" and ἄτομον indeed expressing the same thing. If this view is held, entelechy must be said to represent the individuum, to be itself individualising. But it is only with some restriction that modern science can make use of the concept of the individuum. We know from experimental work that the organism, both adult and embryo, can be divided *without* change of its nature, since it restores its parts to new wholes. The term individuum, therefore, if applied to bodily forms, is incorrect, at least in very many cases: parts of an original individuum may be individua too, at least potentially. Perhaps it would be more successful to apply the term individuum to entelechies only and not to bodily forms:. but if we do so the fundamental problems of the divisibility of entelechy and its relation to matter at once present themselves. The discussion of these very central problems of biology must be reserved for a future chapter.

Let us rather restrict ourselves at present, and let us ask: In what sort of natural bodies are entelechies manifested, and in what relations do these bodies stand to other bodies in nature?

THE CLASSES OF BODIES

All bodies [1] may be classified according to two general views: they are either homogeneous or combined, and their form is either accidental or essential. Homogeneous-accidental bodies are called amorphous; they are without any interest for our present discussion. Combined-accidental bodies play a great rôle in geology: islands and mountains belong to this class; their form is given to them from without by processes which are parts of a cumulation, as studied in a chapter of our first volume. Homogeneous-essential bodies are crystals, all typical arrangements of crystals, such as so-called dendrites, and all other varieties of form capable of being assumed by homogeneous matter, such as figures produced by the shrinking of gelatin or albumen or some other material. Combined - essential bodies are organisms and artificial products exclusively.

One of the great differences between crystals and organisms is that crystals are of the same material nature throughout, while organisms are not. The other fundamental difference relates to their manner of origin. Organisms

[1] We shall not insist here on the problem of what is meant by "being a body." This question—the subject of a theory of matter—is not a proper problem of theoretical biology.

originate from a starting-point which exhibits less visible manifoldness than does the end; crystals are always themselves, and might almost be said to show nothing but mere increase of size. A third difference might be found in the fact that crystals during their growth use the specificity of their medium in its very specificity, whilst to organisms the medium is only a means of growth, their specificity resting in themselves; but I shall not lay much stress upon this point in our present analysis.

It may be objected to the second of our definitions that researches of the last few years, especially those of Rauber and Przibram,[1] have shown a very high faculty of restitution in crystals. Broken crystals, in fact, are not only capable of restoring the parts that are wanting, a process resembling regeneration, but are also able in some cases to transform themselves into a new and smaller whole, by changing all their proportions—a process which resembles the differentiation of an harmonious-equipotential system. How could I say in the face of such facts that crystals are always themselves, and show nothing but mere growth? I could say so, because in spite of their so-called "restitution," crystals go through their formative processes *only* with the aid of the forces which also determine their growth, and with no other help whatever. These forces show different intensities in the different directions of space, embracing a typical arrangement of the relative maxima of these intensities, and this character of their formative forces, taken together with some relations of tension between the solid material of the crystal and the solution surrounding it, is sufficient to

[1] *Arch. f. Entw.-mech.* 22, 1906. The full literature will be found there.

explain normal growth as well as so-called restitution: the same thing happens all the time. In this respect crystallisation is a mere process of addition, in spite of so-called restitution: the material of growth always comes from the solution in its specificity, and the typical form is completely determined by the directed forces of all the minute particles of the crystal. Knowing the forces of one particle and knowing the physical conditions existing, we know that this sort of growth must occur. Ultimately everything may be reduced to some sort of molecular arrangement: the specificity of the arrangement gives the specificity of the distribution of forces of different intensity. A crystal thus can be said to be "whole" in each of its parts, not only "potentia" but "actu," and all processes of restitution in it only relate to a change in the arrangement of such "wholes," the result of it being *not* a proper "totality" in itself.[1]

I have said a little more about crystallisation than might seem to be necessary, because nowadays the analogies between crystallisation and morphogenesis are being unduly pressed.[2] It is my opinion that there *are* analogies, nay more—

[1] I have shown elsewhere (*Arch. f. Entw.-mech.* 23, 1907, p. 174) that Przibram was wrong in saying that crystals are harmonious-equipotential systems, according to my definition, because in some cases they are capable of changing their exterior form after disturbances and producing a new smaller proportionate whole. There is nothing whatever like a "prospective potency" concerned in this process, as there is in organic harmonious restitution: there is only a change of *place* going on among equal parts. Even this change of place is not one single process, but the result of two independent processes: something is taken away in one locality by the forces of the medium, and something is added in another locality by the forces of the crystal. I have never said that the mere fact of regeneration proves vitalism; but the special nature of the "systems" that form the basis of organic regeneration does prove it (see vol. i. page 241 f.).

[2] Compare also the article by Hofmann in *Annalen der Naturphilosophie*, 7, 1908, p. 63. It seems to me that Hofmann's argument cannot stand against the analysis given in the text and in the preceding note.

identities; but only in so far as crystallisation is one of the means of inorganic nature employed by entelechy for its purposes. Morphogenesis, however, only *uses* some features of crystallisation, which, taken by itself, has nothing to do with any organic phenomenon.

The combined essential bodies called organisms originate, like crystals, with materials delivered from without in the form of oxygen and nourishment. But the starting-point of an organism does not use these substances directly; it first forms out of them what is to be used, and its manner of employing them is anything but a mere addition: it is a consecutive series of typical differentiations typically placed.

To build up the organism as a combined body of a typical style is the task of entelechy: entelechy means the faculty of achieving a "forma essentialis"; being and becoming are united here in a most remarkable manner: time enters into the Timeless, *i.e.* into the "idea" in the sense of Plato.

Even elementary physiology teaches its student that the organic form is "forma essentialis" in yet another sense of the word. The form of the organism is not only built up typically, but is also kept in its normal state, in spite of a permanent change of material, by metabolism in the widest sense. Some authors have spoken of this feature as "dynamical equilibrium." The expression is a harmless one, if it is to denote nothing but the mere permanency of form in spite of material changes; but nothing is "explained" at all by such terminology, and still less does it reduce anything to the inorganic sphere, as uncritical physiologists have sometimes asserted.

THE ORDER OF ENTELECHIES. ENTELECHY AND MACHINE-WORK

We know already that not every event that takes place during morphogenesis and metabolism is the direct outcome of entelechian acts, and it seems worth while to say a few more words about this point. And first let us remark once more that different kinds of entelechies may be said to be at work in the organism. There is first the entelechia morphogenetica, and after that the entelechia psychoidea, and the latter may be discriminated as governing instincts and actions separately. Furthermore, the different parts of the brain, such as the hemispheres and the cerebellum in vertebrates, may be said to possess their different kinds of entelechy. In fact, we may speak of an order concerning the rank or dignity of entelechies, comparable with the order of ranks or dignities in an army or administration. But all entelechies have originated from the primordial one, and in *this* respect may be said to be one altogether.

Now the primordial entelechy of the egg not only creates derived entelechies but also builds up all sorts of arrangements of a truly mechanical character: the eye, in a great part of its functioning, is nothing but a camera obscura, and the skeleton obeys the laws of inorganic statics. Every part of these organic systems has been placed by entelechy where it must be placed to act well in the service of the whole, but the part itself acts like a part of a machine.

So we see finally that the different forms of harmony in the origin and function of parts that are not immediately dependent on one another,[1] are in the last resort the consequence of entelechian acts. The entelechy that created them all was harmonious in its intensive manifoldness: the extensive structures which are produced by it are *therefore* harmonious too. In other words, there are many processes in the organism which are of the statical-teleological type, which go on teleologically or purposefully on a fixed machine-like basis; but entelechy has created this basis, and so statical teleology has its source in dynamical teleology.

We now see the full meaning of the statement that entelechy is an " intensive manifoldness " realising itself extensively; in other words, we know what it means to say that a body in nature is a living organism; we have given a full descriptive definition of this concept.

CONCLUSIONS AND NEW PROBLEMS

But how can an " intensive manifoldness " be an elemental factor in nature ? The answer to this question will depend, of course, on what is understood by the expression " elemental factor in nature." In other words, a detailed analysis of this concept will serve to show us the circumstances under which it is legitimate or illegitimate to speak of a factor of nature as elemental.

Materialistic dogmatism would reply here that the concepts of mechanics or energetics are the only legitimate elementalities of all science—but we have nothing to do with dogmatism of *any* kind.

The principle of so-called " economics of thinking," as prevalent nowadays, might say, on the other hand, that

[1] See vol. i. p. 107.

every elemental natural factor is legitimate by being necessary. Whenever analysis shows that there is something hitherto unrecognised in nature that is not to be expressed in terms of natural factors already known to science, then— and then only—"economy" would allow us to create a new elementality, and would only want to find out whether this new factor is to be regarded as a "constant," or a "force," or a sort of "energy," or what not. To the epistemological "economist," whose *summum jus* is to be "practical," science is mere experience, and for him there is no such thing as real philosophy—nothing higher than science. Of course, any new factors, created in this style, would by no means "explain" but merely "describe" in a shortened way: but the economists say there *cannot* be anything except description in this sense.

We are by no means partisans of modern empiristic "economism," and therefore the question as to the epistemological *justification* of our newly created natural factor is to us an important problem.

We shall begin this justification forthwith.

PART I

THE INDIRECT JUSTIFICATION OF ENTELECHY

A. ENTELECHY AND UNIVOCAL DETERMINATION

A COMPLETE system of ontology has to develop the sum of aprioristic concepts and principles regarding nature on the principles of reasoning. It cannot be our task to do so here, and it would not even be necessary for our immediate purposes. Our endeavour is, in the first place, to show how our concept of entelechy as an elemental natural factor is related to those concepts of general ontology which play any part in the science of inorganic nature. On a later occasion a few words on the theory of categories will be added.

The concept of the *univocal determination* of being and becoming may be called the very starting-point of a philosophy of nature. No states and no events in nature are without a sufficient reason for their being such as they are at such a place and time, and the same thing always is or happens under the same conditions. These are the most general expressions of the principle of univocality. Of course, nothing in the doctrine of entelechy is opposed to them; given certain circumstances, and given a certain entelechy in a certain state of manifestation, there will always be or go on only one specifically determined event and no other.

I do *not* give the name of "causality" to this principle of natural necessity or determination. Causality relates to a particular kind of changes exclusively, and the relation entelechy bears to it will be discussed later on. Our principle of necessity or univocal determination relates to *everything* that may be or happen in the universe, without any reference to the character and nature of the changes in the case of things that happen. Of course, this principle holds, whether entelechy plays its part in a series of events or not. The facts in the universe that originate in entelechy will be univocally determined as such whenever entelechy is such as it is, and entelechy is either of this or of that determined kind. And, moreover, any *single* spatial occurrence induced or modified by entelechy has its previous *single* correlate in a certain *single* feature of entelechy, as far as it is an intensive manifoldness. It would be quite inconceivable to assume anything else, though our assumption leads to the consequence—strange as it is—that nothing really new can happen anywhere in the universe. *All happening is " evolutio," in the deepest meaning of the word.*

We repeat once more that even when dealing with those entelechies which govern action, we never have to do with true psychical facts, but only with natural events. But we must now refer to a certain most remarkable relation which is generally expressed in psychological terms. In the philosophy of nature we are not allowed to speak of any "freedom" of acting, in the real and strict sense of the word, in the sense that is contrary to univocal determination. It is quite impossible to imagine that, with given

THE INDIRECT JUSTIFICATION OF ENTELECHY 155

circumstances and a given psychoidal entelechy, there ought to be or to happen *either* A *or* B. On the contrary, what is to happen is quite fixed, and a supreme mind, conversant with all the inorganic facts of nature and knowing all the intensive manifoldness of all entelechies and psychoids, including the individual history of the latter, would be able at once to predict the actions of any psychoid with absolute certainty. Such prediction is just as possible as it would be in pure mechanics, as stated in the fiction of the " Laplacian mind." It is interesting to note that almost all philosophers and theologians who go really into the depth of analysis are unanimous in rejecting indetermination in nature. In Christianity the word " grace " is a short expression indicating the impossibility of indetermination in nature, placing " freedom " in the metaphysical sphere : I am not even free to believe or not to believe, but to be able to believe is a gift of grace.

For the present we have to follow the course prescribed by a phenomenological philosophy of nature; there will be another occasion to deal with the problem of " freedom " from a very different point of view.

We now approach the realm of real " causality," that is, of univocality with regard to changes in space exclusively.

How does entelechy stand to this concept, now that we have learnt that it does not contradict univocal determination in general ?

B. ENTELECHY AND CAUSALITY

GENERAL INTRODUCTION

ENTELECHY may be aroused to manifestation by a change in bodily nature, such as is effected by fertilisation or by some operation, or by some motor stimulus; and, on the other hand, entelechy may on its own part lead to changes in bodily nature.

All this is very general; it asserts that entelechy may be *related to* causality, *i.e.* to the principle of connexion of changes in spatial nature. But it does not make the smallest assertion about the most important question: " Is entelechy by itself a specific form of causal connexion, or is it not ? " This question must, however, be answered.

DIFFICULTIES

Now let us recollect that not every single event in space resulting from the manifestation of entelechy has its own single *external* cause. It was precisely on account of the impossibility of this being the case that our concept of entelechy was created. We should not need this concept if there were to be found a single external cause of every single step in the differentiation of an harmonious-equipotential system, and we should not need the psychoid were it not that action is a whole and not a sum. The single steps in the manifestation of entelechy are, as we know, univocally determined, but they are so by their being united in the intensive manifoldness of their realiser: thus they seem to be *acausal* with regard to real " causes " which are not embraced in this manifoldness, but are single changes in space. In other words, it is the essence of an entelechy to manifest itself in an extensive manifoldness: all the details of this extensive manifoldness depend upon the intensive manifoldness of the entelechy, but not upon different spatial " causes." With regard to morphogenesis we thus may speak of an immediate correlation of parts that is non-causal, as indeed Rádl has done in a somewhat different connexion. There are combinations of single diversities always interchanging with one another, but each *singly* independent of the other; their common ground is the specific intensive manifoldness of the entelechy that realises them. Thus the problem of the relation between causality and entelechy seems by no means simple, and therefore we shall best approach our subject by a rather lengthy series of analytical considerations.

First let us analyse a little more deeply the pure concept of causality,[1] as understood in inorganic sciences.

[1] A general discussion of "energetics" will be found in my *Naturbegriffe und Natururteile*, 1904. I fully maintain what is said in that book about energetics itself; but as to the relation between entelechy and energy the following discussion will be found to differ from that of 1904 not inconsiderably. I hope that this change of my opinion will be found accompanied by improvement.

DIFFERENT FORMS OF THE PRINCIPLE OF CAUSALITY

A complete system of natural ontology, whilst dealing with causality, would have to develop more specified principles regarding it. Some such principles have indeed been found by naturalists, but, strange to say, they are generally regarded nowadays as being of an empirical and inductive nature, while in reality they are quite otherwise. The principle of "phases" and the principle of the "least action" are cases in point. We shall not make use of these principles in our discussion; but we shall apply and therefore shall insist more fully upon the analysis of two specific aprioristic causal principles which have played a great rôle in the history of inorganic sciences: I refer to the two so-called "principles of energy."

It seems to me that these principles, generally spoken of as the "conservation of energy" and the "augmentation of entropy," have their logical sources in the different aspects which causality offers to a thorough analysis.

The "cause" of an effect in spatial nature is that change in spatial nature which is invariably and "necessarily" followed by the effect. We now may consider this relation of "causality" in a more general and more specified manner.

We first imagine the totality of a "system," that is, a limited part of space including all the natural realities embraced in it. We study the states of the system as a whole at the different moments t_1 and t_2, all causal relation between it and its surroundings being excluded. Then we assure ourselves that the causality of the system with

THE INDIRECT JUSTIFICATION OF ENTELECHY 159

regard to its surroundings has remained unaltered in amount in spite of all internal changes. The system's state at t_1 as a whole has been the "cause" of its state at t_2; but as a causal system with regard to its surroundings it has remained the same.

Let us now study two systems in the sense described, and let us assume that there are causal processes going on between these two systems, but in no other way or direction. Then we call the whole of the change of the totality of the one the cause of the whole of the change of the other, and are convinced that both changes are equal in amount.

It is upon these two fictions that the principle of the conservation of energy rests, and from these two fictions it derives its two fundamental modern formulations: "the energy of an isolated[1] system is constant,"[2] and, "any loss of energy in one isolated system corresponds to an equivalent gain in another one," and *vice versa*. Robert Mayer was well aware that his principle was based upon an aprioristic foundation, and he did well to place in the beginning of his discussion the two phrases: "causa aequat effectum" and "nihil fit ex nihilo aut ad nihilum." In fact, it is upon a combination of the categories of *causality* and of *quantity* that the aprioristic part of the principle of the conservation of energy rests: energy is causality quantitatively determined.

---

[1] It is meaningless to speak of the energetic constancy of the universe, as long as the problem of its material finiteness or infiniteness is unsolved. In the case of its infiniteness, of course, to speak of "constancy" would be altogether meaningless.

[2] An important but secondary formulation of the principle in question is the following: the amount of energy of an isolated system is univocally determined in every movement, and the total causal effect due to such a system—the "work" done by it—if its "energy" is reduced to zero, is independent of the way of transformation.

But causality may also be conceived in a very different fashion, which enables thus the foundations of the second so-called principle of energetics to be laid. In this case we may speak of specified causality. We imagine a limited system again, but it is the singular diversity of all sorts of physical and chemical agents concerned in it that we consider. We then find that diversities in the different single parts of the system are the necessary condition that anything may happen in it at all; that nothing can happen unless there are original diversities. For the sufficient reason of happening would be wanting in a system which was uniform throughout, wanting at least so far as the system was uniform. Only if an element or any part of a system is different from others can something happen on that particular element or part. Such, at least, is the most general ontological source of the second principle of energetics: it relates to specificities in causation, just as the first principle related to generalities.

But we shall postpone all further discussion of the second principle of energetics to its proper time, and shall first try to establish a little more about the principle of conservation and its relation to entelechy.

OUR THEME

With this discussion we enter a part of our philosophical studies which, though not final, is to rank among the most important considerations of this whole course of lectures.

We have shown that there are classes of phenomena in living nature which do not allow of any resolving into elements known from the study of the inorganic world.

THE INDIRECT JUSTIFICATION OF ENTELECHY 161

But we have shown nothing more. The important question now inevitably arises: What are the ultimate relations between the inorganic and our autonomous entelechy? What is the meaning of saying that inorganic factors are not sufficient for explanation? In what way are inorganic factors, so to speak, counteracted in the organic world?

That the closest relations exist between the organic and the inorganic is most clearly shown, for instance, by our studies of the "means" of morphogenesis; moreover, it is evident from the mere fact that every organisation exhibits as many different systems of organs as it is able to perform functions, in other words, as it shows mutual relations to the inorganic. In fact, knowing what it means to be an organism, and what the different agents of the medium are, one could really deduce what systems of organs an organism must possess.

Thus our important question is inevitable. We are simply obliged to attack the problem as to what the most intimate relation between inorganic nature and entelechy implies.

We shall try to get a solution by degrees, studying one by one the general scientific conceptions of the inorganic world, and always bringing entelechy into relation to it. We shall begin with so-called energetics; pure mechanical physics is to follow.

What then does it mean to assert, as we do, that the Organic crosses the border of the Inorganic? What does it mean in terms of energetics and of mechanics?

And what is to follow ultimately from this discussion about the problem of "entelechy and causality"?

1. Entelechy and the Principle of the Conservation of Energy

a. THE PRINCIPLE

"Energy" is a measurement and nothing else; it measures the amount of causality given off or received by a limited system in no other sense than the kilogramme or the pound measures the amount of gravitating matter. The unit of this measurement, the "erg," is of the nature of "work," in the terminology of mechanics.

"Conservation" of energy means that there is a *something* in all truly causal processes, as defined above, which retains its quantity, though it may change in its character[1] from body to body, or rather from place to place. So far the principle of conservation is purely aprioristic; it becomes empirical as soon as its application to the special realms of natural sciences begins. Only mechanics must be regarded as an exceptional field of knowledge in this respect, for, as ontology teaches, the principles of pure rational mechanics, and among these the general equations of motion containing the principle of the conservation of energy in its mechanical form, are aprioristic *throughout*. It is—almost unconsciously—for this reason

[1] I intentionally avoid the term "quality" in this connexion.

that "work," that is to say the amount of one of the two kinds of energy in mechanics, has been accepted as a standard measurement of energy in general. But that in thermodynamics the so-called quantity of heat must be measured by "ergs" and not temperature, is a real empirical fact. In general terms we may say that the general form of the principle of conservation is aprioristic, though its special content, regarding the kind of quantity to be measured by ergs, is empirical, pure mechanics excepted.

All these relations seem to be very simple. In short: a body in motion endowed with the kinetic energy $\frac{m}{2}v^2$ may perform a specific amount of work pl, that is to say, may overcome the force p along the distance l, and, on the other hand, the force p affecting the body along the distance l will impart to it the kinetic energy $\frac{m}{2}v^2$ again; and one so-called calorie is always "equivalent" to 424 kilogrammetres.

But things are far from being as simple as they seem at the first glance. The law of the conservation of energy is far from being empirically true if only those natural agents which are actually measurable as performing work are taken into consideration. But the truth of our principle is postulated by reason, and therefore the empirical incorrectness of the principle is corrected in a very interesting way. Whenever the principle fails to hold, so-called "potential energies" are postulated, into which actual energy may disappear or from which it may originate. Such potential energies play their rôle in the theories of gravitation, of electricity, elasticity, and some other branches of physics, and also in chemistry. There is nothing actually stated or measured in the case of all these potential energies: it is simply assumed that there *must* be a something representative of quite a definite amount of "ergs" in order that actual energy may not seem to arise out of nothing. We therefore may properly call all sorts of potential energies *subsidiary*: they are "real," so far as possibilities can be regarded as real in ontology, but they never are immediately real in any sense.[1] In this meaning there "is" a certain amount of potential energy whenever a pendulum reaches one of its highest points. This amount is regarded as equal in quantity to the "work" performed by the pendulum whilst overcoming gravity, which "work" again is equal to the kinetic energy of the pendulum at its lowest point. Quite the same holds with regard to all the other natural agents mentioned above, the concept "work" having a more or less figurative meaning in these cases.

β. THE PRINCIPLE IN ITS RELATION TO ENTELECHY

After these preparatory discussions we now may ask: firstly, how stands entelechy to the principle of the conservation of energy, and secondly, how stands entelechy to the concept of energy itself?

It is clear from the beginning that contradiction to

---

[1] Empiricists often claim that potential energies are really proved to "exist" by the fact that it always is the same amount of measurable energy which enters into the potential forms, and which is able to arise from them. But it is clear that this "fact" rests simply upon the general principle of the univocality of nature, and that, if it should not prove to be empirically true, we by no means should abandon the conservation principle, but should invent as many more supplementary energies as were necessary.

THE INDIRECT JUSTIFICATION OF ENTELECHY 165

an aprioristic principle is absolutely impossible. The question, therefore, is not, "is the doctrine of entelechy in harmony with the first principle of energetics?" but, "how is harmony to be established here?" In other words, the principle of conservation is unimpugnable as an aprioristic principle, but the type of its inorganic realisation may be changed or enlarged without hesitation.

Let us remember once more that the principle of conservation is merely quantitative, that it says nothing at all about the quality or direction of events. What *could* this principle mean in its relation to processes of life in which entelechy is at work? It seems to me that two different answers to this question are *a priori* possible. Take an organism in the midst of a given limited medium, and imagine that we know, on the one side, the energetic value of any possible event leading from the medium to the organism, and, on the other side, the energetic value of any possible event leading from the organism to the medium. Then it is possible that the sum of the energetic values of both kinds of events is the same, or that there is a difference, either in one sense or in the other. In the first case, we should say that in passing through processes of life energy is not changed in its quantity at all; in the latter case energy would seem to be changed by passing through an organism; it would either be partly stored in some unknown form, or be awaked into actuality from some unknown form of storage. Whatever might happen, we should find a way to unite it with the general principle. The unknown energy spoken of in the case of a difference of the amounts of energy entering and leaving the organism, would be of the potential or subsidiary kind; and we should know nothing more about it, except that it must exist in some form—though not in any form known from the Inorganic; but nothing would be established about its rôle in the processes of life.

Certain Facts

Before going on in our analysis, let us appeal to certain facts regarding the actual relation between the inorganic forms of energy and vitality. The latest researches, carried out most carefully, especially by Rubner and Atwater, have shown that there is no difference at all between the sums of energy leaving and entering the organism, as far as the adult organism is considered, in which metabolism is almost completely functional and not morphogenetic. Considering the heat of combustion of the food, and comparing it with the heat of combustion of all excreta, added to the thermodynamical equivalent of the actual work performed, the two values are found to be equal within the limits of error.[1] Such a result greatly simplifies the problem of energy: subsidiary energies are unnecessary for understanding functioning energetically. The results would be different, probably, if in the place of the adult the developing organism were the subject of study: but it seems to me that even in this case a real equation between the energy taken in and the energy given out might be gained, if all substances which are chemically stored during ontogeny, or rather, which are stored as chemical ones, were considered

[1] A good summary is given by Zwaardemaker, *Ergebnisse d. Physiol.* 5, 1906.

as given out, and were measured according to their heat of combustion also.

Thus we see that the principle of the conservation of energy is actually or probably demonstrated by the organism in the clearest form ; but, what is still more important, we also have seen that it would " hold " for the organism, even if the forms of energy known to us should not appear sufficient to form a complete equation of the organism's economy.

On a Supposed Vital Energy

But what about the rôle of entelechy, and what about its relation to energy ? Ostwald, the present head of the energetical school, and many others following him, have admitted that, in cases of morphogenesis, and probably in nervous phenomena too, some unknown potential forms of energy may be at work ; and, in fact, a few such authors, as Bechterew, for instance, claim to be real " vitalists " at the same time, stating that the specificity of vital phenomena and their autonomy is due to the peculiarities which that unknown energy possesses, just as mechanical energy has its peculiarities regarding direction in space, and radiating energy regarding periodicity.

In order not to complicate our problem we say nothing in this place about the general question whether it may seem advisable altogether to deal with the concept of energy in this manner, regarding it as elemental, and speaking of " properties " and peculiarities of energy. Elsewhere [1] I have fully explained that I should not like to adopt such

[1] *Naturbegriffe und Natururteile*, Leipzig, 1904.

a view, which seems to me very artificial and unnatural. At this place we have only to ask, Is it possible in *any*, even an artificial and unnatural way, to speak of a sort of subsidiary or potential *energy* as being the natural agent called by ourselves entelechy ?

That the energy in question would be a subsidiary one, would not in itself be an objection to such a view. So-called chemical energy is of that kind : it is always the mere difference between two amounts of thermic energy that is *called* chemical potential energy—that is all. But, it is true, the " vitalistic energy " would be a rather strange sort of energy in one respect. It would be absolutely indiscoverable, since there would not even be any difference between two discoverable energies. At least in all cases where the economic equation is fulfilled there would seem to be no place for a " new " energy. Vitalistic energy, therefore, would mark nothing but a point of passage or transformation of known energies, and would not be storable in any way. But, it seems to me, not even this difficulty could be said to be absolute.

Entelechy not Energy

There exists, however, one objection to regarding entelechy as being of the type of an energy that seems to me to be absolute. All " energies," actually known to exist or invented to complete the general energetical scheme, are quantities, and relate to phenomena which have quantity among their characteristics. In asserting these phenomena to be of the energetical order, we state that there can be a *more or less* of them, and that this more or less possesses most distinctly

THE INDIRECT JUSTIFICATION OF ENTELECHY 169

the faculty of being *measurable*, as being equivalent to a more or less of actual " work."

But entelechy lacks all the characteristics of quantity: entelechy *is order* of relation and absolutely *nothing* else; all the quantities concerned in its manifestation in every case being due to means which are used by entelechy, or to conditions which cannot be avoided.

It therefore seems to me that it is not only rather imaginative to speak of a vital kind of energy, just as it is rather imaginative to speak of all other sorts of " potential " energies, but that it is absolutely wrong and contrary to the fundamental principles of definition and terminology. It is not legitimate to subsume a something under a general concept as one of its species, if this something differs from the general term just in that property which is the most important and essential. Science does better *not* to classify after the principle " lucus a non lucendo."

Therefore entelechy is *not* a kind of energy, but in spite of that it *does not disturb* the validity of the first principle of energetics.[1] This principle would hold in life, even if an equation of economy were impossible. New subsidiary energies would then have to be created in fact; but these new subsidiary energies would have nothing to do with entelechy and vitalism. Whether they exist or not is a

---

[1] Short formula of the relation between entelechy and the first principle of energetics :—In a given limited system the sum of energy remains $\Sigma (E) =$ Const., whether entelechies are concerned in the system or not.—I do not lay much stress upon the often-quoted fact that so-called "mental work" done by a man has never been found to affect the general economy of the body, including the consumption of energy, though, of course, this fact might seem to be favourable to my views. On the other hand, the fact that, if a person imagines that he is performing movements, the circulation in the brain vessels is increased, allows of no univocal conclusions.

question by itself, which certainly cannot be answered without actual empirical research.

Thus I decline, even more decidedly than in my former publications,[1] any kind of "energetical" vitalism whatever.

What, then, "is" entelechy if it is not a special kind of energy? More preparatory considerations are required to decide this most important question.

[1] See in particular my *Naturbegriffe und Natururteile*, Leipzig, 1904.

2. Entelechy and the "Principle of Becoming"

The study of the second principle of energetics is to be our next problem. It will bring us to the intimate relation between the non-energetical entelechy and the energetical factors of the Inorganic.

a. THE "SECOND" PRINCIPLE OF ENERGETICS

It has often been said that the "first" principle of energetics says nothing at all about becoming, as such, but only deals with something connected with becoming. But, as we have seen, there is another most general causal principle easily to be developed by pure reasoning: the principle that there never can be any becoming where no diversities exist.

It was in the limited field of thermodynamics that a correlate of this general principle was first established. Clausius and Lord Kelvin independently found a short expression for the relations between heat and the work actually done by it; both of them started from an old but very ingenious analysis of the motive force of the steam-engine, due to the French engineer Sadi Carnot.

The expression mentioned has assumed very different forms. Lord Kelvin speaks of the "dissipation" of heat, whilst Clausius begins his analysis with the principle that heat cannot pass by itself ("von selbst") from a cooler to a warmer body. He ends with the phrase "the entropy of the universe tends to a maximum," the concept "entropy" signifying a special mathematical function which belongs to the specific characteristics of any thermodynamical process. There are many other formulations of the same principle.

The True Principle of Becoming

Helm was the first to cross the boundaries of thermodynamics with regard to the principle here in question, and Ostwald was his chief follower. Helm formulated a general "principle of becoming" ("Satz des Geschehens"), stating that differences in the factors of so-called "intensity" must be present in order that becoming may be possible, and that the raising of one intensity is only possible by the decreasing of another. It should be mentioned here that modern energetists regard every sort of energy as composed of a factor of "capacity," such as mass, specific heat, electric quantity, and of a factor of "intensity," such as velocity, temperature, electric or chemical potential, and so on.

I have tried to show on another occasion [1] that there are *two* constituents of a very different logical character in what is usually called the "second" principle of energetics. The *proper* principle of becoming is but a specified formulation of the aprioristic phrase, belonging to the realm of general ontology, that nothing can happen without diversities, and that the originating of diversities demands pre-existing

[1] See my *Naturbegriffe*, chap. C. 2.

diversities. This principle is of an equal logical value with the principle of conservation; like the latter, it is empirical only as far as it applies to real nature. That the *intensities*, and these only, must be different, and that an *intensity* can only be raised by another *intensity* falling and becoming able to "do work," is the empirical part of it; but that a "something" must be different was prior to all experience. As an illustration of this *true second* principle of energetics we may remark that in the very largest quantity of water, say the ocean, nothing at all would happen "by itself" if the temperature were the same throughout, or if the surface level were the same everywhere, though the absolute amount of "energy" contained in the water is enormous. There would be no differences of the intensity either of thermic or of potential mechanical energy in these cases. And on the other hand, it is on account of such differences alone that a steam-engine does mechanical work, or that a waterfall can produce electric potentials.

Let us notice, by the way, that this fact of non-becoming in the absence of diversities in intensity might lend countenance to the proposal to call the real second principle of energetics the "first," the law of conservation the "second" principle. The intensity-principle is "first" far more immediately. Moreover, the conservation-principle is only ideally true; only with reference to a zero-point for, *all* energy could *all* energy practically be measured; but such a zero-point can never be attained. This shows once more that the conservation-principle rests far more on reasoning than on facts.

But let us return to the principle of Carnot in its enlarged form.

"*Dissipation*" as a "*Third*" *Principle*

Besides the aprioristic principle of becoming there is a purely empirical statement concerned in almost all of the formulations of the so-called "second" principle: "dissipation" or "augmentation of entropy," as it is called. This is a mere *fact* that is encountered in almost all fields of physics. Its importance may be realised by trying to think of a case where it is *not* found. In *abstract* mechanics a pendulum may go on possessing kinetic energy and potential energy alternately *ad infinitum*, it may swing for ever. But a *real* pendulum will soon cease to swing, on account of friction. "Dissipation," in the form of heat-conduction, here occurs by friction. We speak of the law of dissipation as the *third* or "empirical" principle of energetics.

It is clear from our statement that what really gives a certain *sense* to natural phenomena is not the true aprioristic second principle dealing with the necessity of diversities of intensity for becoming, but the empirical principle of dissipation. Without dissipation all events in nature might behave like the ideal pendulum, there would be a permanent change of diversities, but diversities would never disappear. *Experience* shows that that is not the case. Of course, it is not meant by this doctrine of dissipation that all becoming which results from different intensities leads immediately to an average value of intensity, and thus to an end of becoming, as all purely thermic becoming does. In all cases where *transformations* of energy occur, where one kind of energy appears at the cost of another, on account of another energy "doing work," there is an *increase* with regard to the energy which appears. But this increase is not only due to the *decrease* of the intensity of the other kind,[1] but it is always of a *smaller amount* than the corresponding decrease had been: the difference between decrease and increase has been "dissipated," and has thus been lost for future changes in nature.

On Catenation of Energy

By our last remarks we have been led to the important problem of the "catenation" or "chaining" of different kinds of energy, and by this we shall be led back to biology. There exists a specific equivalence between the factors of intensity of different energies, just as there was such an equivalence between the amounts of energy as such. The increasing of the intensity of any one energy stands in fixed relations to the decreasing of the intensity of the others, in such a manner that there is fixed not only what has been called the "coupling" of one energy A to the energies B, C, and so on, but also the amount of this coupling. By this fact of coupling the concept of the diversity of intensities is enlarged in a very important way: it becomes relative. There may be "equilibrium" if there is so much of the intensity of one energy and so much of the intensity of the other, and there may be a disturbance of equilibrium if the relation of the two intensities is changed.

It is at this point that potentialities regarded as realities enter the field of the second principle of energetics in the

[1] This is the language of dogmatic energetics. As a matter of fact, in chemical becoming for instance, the decreasing intensity probably always causes the increase of another intensity by means of heat. The increase is smaller than the corresponding decrease, because part of that heat is "dissipated."

same manner as they did that of the first. Intensities can be actually measured only in very few cases, in all other cases they are imaginary and subsidiary. All reasoning proceeds in a circle here. If, for instance, nothing is happening in a system of chemical compounds or of different states of aggregation, we say that "equilibrium" exists; if anything happens then there were "diversities of potentials." But all this is known only *post factum*; in other words, the potentials and their diversities are created only *after* we know what happens, and in what amount. And the leading principle of such creations is always the aprioristic conviction that there *must* have been diversities—of intensities—in order that anything *could* happen.

β. THE PRINCIPLE OF BECOMING IN ITS RELATION TO ENTELECHY

Let us now study the relation of vital phenomena to the true second aprioristic principle of energetics; the third empirical principle is to enter into our discussions only occasionally. Empirical as it is, it of course offers no special ontological problem with regard to entelechy.

That an "equilibrium" of some sort must have been disturbed if, for instance, a process of regeneration is going on, is absolutely self-evident, and does not throw any light on the problem whatever. To say "there is no equilibrium," and to say "there is happening," are identical phrases in the logical sense. Strange to say, there have been certain biological authors[1] who have thought they were

---

[1] The word "equilibrium" has been misused in biology in the most terrible manner, especially by certain physiologists (Verworn, Jensen, etc.).

THE INDIRECT JUSTIFICATION OF ENTELECHY 177

uttering profoundest wisdom in saying that vital phenomena, such as restitution, are due to a "disturbance of equilibrium"!

The true problem is: "*by what single acts* does the restoration of 'equilibrium' take place here, especially in those cases in which it is proved that entelechy is at work, and that physico-chemical diversities and potentials of themselves are not able to offer a sufficient explanation of what happens?"

Again : *Entelechy not Energy*

Any one who felt able to assume some kind of vital energy would have little difficulty in solving this problem. The "intensity" of his vital energy would have to come into "catenation" with the intensities of the inorganic energies, either causing them to increase or making them decrease by increasing itself. But hitherto a vital energy has appeared to us to be a simple impossibility, and it becomes even more so at this point. For, though always one and the same "kind" of subsidiary energy, the "entelechian energy" of an individual would have to be endowed with *variable* intensities with regard to *one and the same* inorganic intensity, in exact correspondence to different states of disturbance of the organism. In other

---

An argument often employed by these authors is this :—All organic events are the consequence of a disturbance of equilibrium, all inorganic events are the consequence of a disturbance of equilibrium, *therefore* organic events are inorganic (mechanical). This argument rests upon the "logical" formula : —All A are C, all B are C, therefore all A are B ; or in words :—All men are bipeds, all birds are bipeds, "therefore" all men are birds. I am sorry to say so, but it is true that this sort of "logic" really has been employed in biology.

words, it would be an energy *with differences in itself*, which is contradictory to the concept of energy.

Therefore we cannot speak of intensities of a subsidiary "entelechian energy" in any sense.

The Relation of Entelechy to the Intensities of Energies

But in spite of that our study of the true second principle of energetics has been of some use to us. Even though it be not comparable to an energy in any sense, entelechy, as far as it comes into connexion with the energies of inorganic nature, can do so only through the aid of those factors which are concerned in any kind of connexion of the inorganic energies with one another. The *intensities* of inorganic energies, therefore, are the point at which any possible relation between the living and the non-living must be set up, for upon the intensities depends all spatial becoming exclusively.

Now intensities of inorganic energies, as we know, if standing in any sort of possible exchange at all, stand either in the relative state of equilibrium or compensation, or in the state of mutual appearing and disappearing. It is clear from what we have said that entelechy also can act only upon the state of compensation or non-compensation of the inorganic intensities.

Let us try to fix this fundamental relation in a more concrete manner, which will illustrate at the same time, in the clearest manner, how we wish the differences between the vital and the inorganic to be understood. Imagine a non-living system of a specific number of specific chemical compounds in specific states of aggregation and in a specific arrangement; then it is absolutely determined, by the so-called "potential" and by the mass of each of these constituents, what is to happen until equilibrium is reached. We have chosen a chemical and aggregative system as our instance, because in the organism the *single* phenomena of becoming that can actually be observed are such as to consist in chemical and aggregative specificities. Let us now study the behaviour of a system consisting of chemical and aggregative constituents, as before, but forming at the same time part of a living organism. Our doctrine of entelechy teaches us that the behaviour of this system is *not* exclusively dependent on the potential and mass of the constituents, but on something further. In what possible relation is this something able to stand with regard to the potentials of the constituents of the system? *It is of the greatest importance to find an adequate answer to this question*, and I hope to be able to give at least the beginning of such an answer in what follows.

The Action of Entelechy in "suspending" possible Becoming

Entelechy is *not* able to change the chemical potentials of the elemental constituents of the system in a qualitative way: at least we have no grounds for such an assumption, which would imply, for instance, that entelechy could make sulphuric acid (H_2SO_4) if it had only the chlorides of sodium and potassium at its disposal. Entelechy, as far as we know, at least, is limited in its acting by many specificities of inorganic nature, among which are the specificities included under the phrase "chemical element."

Entelechy is also *unable* to cause reactions between chemical compounds which never are known to react in the inorganic world. In short, entelechy is altogether *unable* to create differences of intensity of any kind.

But entelechy *is* able, so far as we know from the facts concerned in restitution and adaptation, to *suspend* for as long a period as it wants any one of all the reactions which are *possible* with such compounds as are present, and which would happen without entelechy. And entelechy may *regulate* this suspending of reactions now in one direction and now in the other, suspending and permitting possible becoming whenever required for its purposes. Now, after all we have said, this suspending of affinity, so to say, is to be considered as a *temporary compensation* of factors of "intensity" which would otherwise be uncompensated, and would lead to immediate becoming. This faculty of a temporary suspension of inorganic becoming is to be regarded as the most essential ontological characteristic of entelechy. Because it possesses this faculty *without* being of the nature of an energy at the same time, entelechy is *the* non-physico-chemical agent.

Let it be well understood: we do *not* admit that entelechy may transform potentials into actual happening by means of a so-called "Auslösung" in any sense. Entelechy, according to our view, is quite unable to remove any kind of an "obstacle" to happening, such as is removed in catalysis; for such a removal would require energy, and entelechy is non-energetical. We only admit that entelechy may set free into actuality what it has *itself* prevented from actuality, what it has suspended hitherto.

The Rôle of Entelechy in the Continuity of Life

This statement implies a very important consequence. If entelechy always must *have done* something in order that it may do anything in the present and future, there can, of course, never be any real beginning of its acting, but this acting must be continuous. And this is what the fact of inheritance teaches us. Life *is* indeed continuous: a certain portion of matter that stands under the control of entelechy is handed down from generation to generation. And thus entelechy always *has* already [1] acted!

Unfortunately, as will be seen later on, we are unable to escape this *regressus ad infinitum* in any way; at least we know nothing about a "first" and really primordial act of suspension of inorganic becoming on the part of entelechy.

Entelechy and Chemism

Of course we can only affirm the possibility of a temporary suspending of reactions on the part of entelechy in those cases where there is an empirical reason for doing so; and that is only the case at present in the spheres of chemical and of aggregative events.

---

[1] It might be objected here that the continuity of entelechian control would imply a decrease of the amount of possible becoming, according to the principle of dissipation; and that for this reason life, *i.e.* the suspending action of entelechy, would soon come to an end. But the principle of dissipation is a purely empirical principle of inorganic science, and nobody is able to say *a priori* that the regulating acts of entelechy in relaxing suspension must be subject to it. Decrease and increase between coupled intensities therefore may amount to the same value in the sphere of vitalistic happening.

In these spheres there is indeed a sort of "overcoming" of inorganic nature by the Organic, an overcoming that is no more strange, of course, than is, for instance, the overcoming of gravity by electricity when small balls of elder pith are attracted by a rubbed glass rod—though, of course, in the latter case two real "energetical" intensities are in action against each other.

If spiritualistic facts should prove to be true—a matter about which I have no personal experience at all—or if it were really true that Indian fâkirs are able to overcome gravitation and to rise from the ground, there would be a far larger field of inorganic intensities where becoming, on the basis of diversities of intensity, might be temporarily suspended by entelechy.

An explanation of the Limits of Regulability and of Life in General

If we understand that the action of entelechy is only an action of suspending that which, but for this, would happen — an action of regulating by suspending — we at once understand two very important features which appear in all phenomena of life: the dependence of life on the conditions of the medium, and the *limits of its regulability*.

We know that life is impossible without food and oxygen, without a certain amount of heat and without a specific composition of the medium—all within rather narrow limits. We have frequently remarked, moreover, in our purely biological discussions that there exist great differences in the faculty both of restitution and of adaptation. One plant is able to live in water as well as in the open air, whilst another one is killed if submerged under the surface of water; the newt regenerates the foot with the utmost perfection, whilst mammals are only capable of healing up their wounds.

Even these facts, it seems to me, are understood without difficulty, if we assume that entelechy can only suspend the compensation of differences of energetical intensities or potentials which *exist* already, but that it is not able to create such differences. The acting of entelechy thus becomes dependent on the potentials of the single parts of the body, which are themselves of an inorganic character, and on the potentials of the surrounding medium.

Now somebody might say that the medium always contains potentials of the highest possible value, as exhibited, for instance, in the temperature of the medium and in the intensity of the rays emanating from the sun. These potentials certainly are of the greatest importance for the permanence of life, because, thanks to them, life is not exclusively dependent on the internal potentials of the material the organisms consist of. But we know, on the other hand, that there must be not only " differences " of potentials as such, in order that becoming may be possible, but also differences in potentials of energy which are " coupled " with each other, which may be transformed one into the other. It is, moreover, a well-known fact that most chemical and aggregative processes are almost absolutely beyond the influence of radiant energy of even the strongest intensity.

Entelechy then is limited in its operation to the differences of potentials already existing, so far as the organism is at the same time an inorganic system surrounded by an energetical medium. This limitation [1] will explain not only the limits of regulability, but also disease and death,[2] at least in principle. The limits of regulability may be founded upon some rather insignificant feature, and may be in spite of that very marked in their effects. The fragmental development of the isolated blastomeres of some sorts of eggs is a good example of what I have said. It may depend on some very unimportant peculiarity in the consistency of the protoplasm that the isolated blastomere of the Ctenophore egg is not able to restitute its simple intimate protoplasmatic structure into a small new whole. From the impossibility of performing this rather simple regulation it follows that not a whole but a half animal develops from the isolated cell.

Entelechy burdened with as Little as Possible

We have tried to formulate the relation between entelechy and inorganic elemental agents in such a manner that nothing may seem to be postulated which is not founded on experimental facts, and that at the same time the amount of specific performance burdened upon entelechy may appear as small as possible. Our *personal* belief is

[1] The discontinuity of physical phenomena upon which the so-called "theories of matter" are based, is, of course, also one of the conditions that entelechy is limited by. Maxwell, MacKendrick, and Erréra have discussed the lowest possible size of an organism from this point of view. Compare Erréra, *Bull. soc. roy. sc. méd. et nat.*, Bruxelles, janvier 1903; other references will be found in this paper.

[2] It will be understood from our discussion of morphogenetic teleology (page 134) that death, though practically the *end* of the individual's life, is by no means its τέλος—at least not from the point of view of a philosophy of nature.

THE INDIRECT JUSTIFICATION OF ENTELECHY 185

that we have charged it with *too little*, that future experience will enlarge the sphere of its acting. But it always is the best scientific method not to assume more of the new than is absolutely necessary.

In attributing to entelechy the suspending of possible becoming exclusively, though in a changeable and regulable way, we at the same time, I believe, have avoided one very bad mistake that has been very often a reproach to vitalists. We have not imputed any action to entelechy that might seem to represent any amount of energy in itself, and in fact we could not do so, as we had most strictly refuted any kind of theory regarding entelechy itself as a sort of energy. Suspending the compensation of uncompensated differences of intensities among coupled kinds of energies and relaxing that suspension are in fact not acts that would require any amount of energy. For, we repeat, our hypothetic act of suspending and setting free actually uncompensated potentials by no means relates to a removal of obstacles, such as occurs in catalysis,[1] for example.

We must always very carefully discriminate between creating differences of potential and suspending the compensation of existing differences. The former can only happen by an actual transfer of energy, whereas for suspending and for relaxing of suspension no transfer of energy is required, but simply a transformation of energy from actuality into a potential form, and *vice versa*.

[1] On the theory of "intermediate reactions" the part played by the catalyser would also require no extra amount of energy.

Entelechy and " Catalysis "

A few words seem desirable about the specific nature of the potentials of the Inorganic with which entelechy is especially connected. We have said already several times that the field of chemistry and of the states of aggregation is the proper sphere for the activity of entelechy, and it is for this reason that all researches on the chemical and aggregative nature of so-called "living matter" are of so much scientific interest. But I think we can attain still greater certainty as to the exact point where entelechy is chiefly at work. We already know that the process of *catalysis* plays a leading rôle not only in normal but also in regulative life processes. Now it is of no import to our present purpose which theory of catalytical processes is right, though personally we believe that catalysers not only accelerate reactions but that without them the reactions in question would never take place.[1] Let us also grant that the effect of the ready made ferment or enzyme is inorganic, just like that of the inorganic ferments studied by Bredig[2] and others. In *any* case the *formation* of catalysers or their so-called "activation" is the chief process concerned in regulation and adaptation phenomena, "activation" of ferments out of the state of "proferments"

---

[1] The difference between the two theories would practically disappear, if all processes "accelerated" by catalysers were regarded as happening "infinitely slowly" without them. In this form their occurring without the ferments would only be assumed in deference to a certain innate property of the mind, namely, its inability to conceive beginning. All the applications of the infinitesimal calculus to physics rest upon this property of the mind.

[2] Bredig himself is by no means a dogmatic enemy of vitalism (see *Biochem. Zeitschr.* vi., 1907, p. 326 ; and *Centralblatt f. Bakter.* xix., 1907, p. 493).

being also, of course, a formation in the sense that ferments definitively become by this very process what they actually are.

In the formation or activation of ferments we hypothetically see the fundamental rôle played by entelechy. Our theory of the mere suspending action of entelechy, of course, forbids us to regard entelechy as really creating catalytic materials. We think it right to assume that on the basis of the chemical system actually present in the organism an indefinite though not strictly infinite variety of reactions regarding the production of ferments is possible. It is this sum of possible reactions that entelechy takes part in, suspending and relaxing suspension according to its purposes of regulation.

Conclusions

We now have said, it seems to me, all that can be said at present about the relations of entelechy to the true second principle of energetics, which deals with diversities of intensities and the coupling of them, and which is aprioristic in its foundations. This principle is *fully observed* in life processes, and because it is observed we see that life depends on inorganic processes. Indeed, to some extent there *cannot* be any contradiction between the second principle and the doctrine of entelechy on account of the partly aprioristic character of the former. In this sense we can say that the principle was bound to hold and that it was only the special form of reconciling the doctrine of entelechy with it that was the problem.

Our problem then was not to state whether the true

second principle holds for the organism or not, but to make out *in what sense* it holds, its purely inorganic form being insufficient for the explanation of life.

But what entelechy really "is" has not yet been made out at all by these rather complicated considerations.

3. Entelechy in its Relation to the Distribution of Given Elements

a. SOME APPARENT CONTRADICTIONS BETWEEN ENTELECHY AND THE TRUE SECOND AND THE THIRD EMPIRICAL PRINCIPLE OF ENERGETICS

The Problem

Individual organic development in general, and the differentiation of the harmonious-equipotential systems in particular, seem to contradict the second and the third principle of energetics at the first glance, and some features which at least *may* be connected with acting seem to contradict these principles also. Therefore the problem of the relation of entelechy to the second and the third principle of energetics requires yet further consideration.[1]

An harmonious-equipotential system, before differentiation occurs, consists of elements which are equal to each other in actuality, and equal in potentiality also, and out of the sum of these elements there is formed by differentiation another system, which shows an enormous diversity of its constituents in actuality and perhaps in potentiality

[1] The fundamental problem to be discussed in this chapter was first *seen* in my *Naturbegriffe*, p. 180. But I only found a very unsatisfactory solution when I wrote that book.

too. There are, as we know, no specified and localised external causes that could be responsible for every single one of the resulting diversities. Entelechy, on the other hand, as we have seen, cannot be regarded as being of the nature of an energy, though it is able to suspend energetical processes.

What does that mean ? Does it not seem as if, in the differentiation of harmonious-equipotential systems, a state of diversity were created out of the homogeneous state of a system by the sole agency of this system itself ? Indeed, as far as the originating of diversities as such is concerned that seems to be the case, even though energetical potentials between the medium and the system play their part in this process; for these potentials only relate to becoming in general, but not to becoming which leads to diversity in the different parts of the system.

Such a state of things seems to contradict the second and the third principle of energetics at the same time.

A Partial Solution

Now, of course, it must well be kept in mind that an harmonious-equipotential system is far from being homogeneous in the strictest sense of the word. It is composed of cells, and each of these cells is probably composed of an enormous sum of chemical and aggregative constituents, both in its protoplasm and its nucleus. Part of the problem propounded here may be said to have been solved by this statement, but part of it remains.

For, granted even that there are not more different single elements—taken as *truly* homogeneous constituents of the system, as so-called "phases"—at the end of the differentiation than there were before it began, there certainly is *a greater amount or degree of diversity in the distribution of different single elements* at the end than at the beginning, and this greater amount of diversity with regard to distribution is created by the sole agency of the system itself. What about this very striking fact?

A mixture of oil and water, which afterwards separates into a layer of oil and a layer of water, shows also a greater degree of diversity or heterogeneity in the distribution of its elements at the end than at the beginning, and such a phenomenon becomes still clearer if three substances are mixed which are of different specific gravity, and will remain individual phases for themselves. But all such events go on under the influence of an external factor,—gravitation. Such an external factor that could be responsible for the increase of the amount of diversity in distribution is wanting in the case of the differentiation of harmonious-equipotential systems.

β. THE ELEMENTAL RÔLE OF ENTELECHY IN CREATING "DIVERSITIES OF DISTRIBUTION"

The Rôle of Entelechy in Morphogenesis

Now we know that an harmonious-equipotential system is endowed with entelechy, and that the function of entelechy is to suspend and to set free, in a regulatory manner, pre-existing potentials, *i.e.* pre-existing faculties of inorganic interaction.

What does that imply with regard to the origin of differentiation?

An harmonious-equipotential system is, as we know, of such a kind that out of *any one* of its cells *any* part of the organism may originate. But, as morphogenesis depends in the main on chemical and aggregative transformations, this means that in each cell of a harmonious system the same number and kind of chemical-aggregative reactions are *possible*.[1] Only part of these possible reactions become actual in each cell, and these actual reactions are different according to the relative position of the cells. This transformation from possibility into actuality is the fundamental work done by entelechy, based upon its elemental action in suspending possible becoming and relaxing the suspension when required.

What does this imply?

It seems to me that it is a phenomenon of quite fundamental importance.

If we agree to distinguish between a "*diversity of elemental composition*" of a system and a "*diversity of distribution*," we may say—

Entelechy, though not capable of enlarging the amount of the diversity of composition of a given system, is capable of augmenting its diversity of distribution in a regulatory manner, and it does so by transforming a system of *equally* distributed *potentialities* into a system of *actualities* which are *unequally* distributed.

Thus, what first appeared as a mere description of "differentiation" now appears as the immediate effect of

[1] The word "possible," of course, is *not* to be understood here in the sense of "infinitely actual" (see page 186, note 1), as in a certain theory of catalysis. It is entelechy that suspends actuality in the present case; without entelechy there would at once happen all sorts of chemical reactions until "physico-chemical equilibrium" was reached.

THE INDIRECT JUSTIFICATION OF ENTELECHY

entelechy, and as the "*definitio realis*" of "differentiation" at the same time. "Differentiation," in fact, passes the limits of inorganic events.

It is worth while to illustrate the differences between the diversity of elemental composition and the diversity of distribution in a still more concrete though schematic form. A harmonious-equipotential system may consist of n cells, each of them composed of m different (chemical) constituents. In each cell every constituent is *able* to react with every other; in other words, there exist chemical potentials or affinities between each possible pair of constituents in each cell. So far the given "diversity of elemental composition," kept in mere potentiality by the suspending action of entelechy. But now entelechy proceeds to actuality, and it does so by enlarging the amount of "diversity of distribution" in the system in question: *actually*, out of *all* the *possible* reactions in each cell, only *one* is allowed to *happen*, and this actual reaction which determines the "prospective value" of the cell, *is different in each*. The specificity in each cell is regulatorily determined by entelechy, and thus entelechy transforms a "*homogeneous*" *distribution of given different elements and given possible reactions into a* "*heterogeneous*" *distribution of effects*.

The Rôle of Entelechy in Acting

Now that the study of entelechies which govern typical order in space has given us such an important result, let us glance at some features connected with action, *i.e.* with the work of entelechies related to typical order in time.

There is a workman and there is a heap of bricks, and

the workman is building a small house with the bricks. It is clear, without any deeper consideration, that the system represented by the bricks is passing from a state of almost equal distribution into a state of distribution showing a very marked degree of diversity. But you answer me that each single brick is brought to its place by a single external factor, namely, by a single act of moving, on the part of the workman. That is true, certainly. But if you consider the workman plus the heap of bricks, and, of course, plus the medium, as the "system" to be studied, the whole problem acquires a very different aspect. Certainly there *were* many diversities in one part of the system, that is, in the man, at the beginning of the process; but at the end of it there is a very much higher degree of diversity in the whole system, as regards the distribution of elements at least: for the heap of bricks has greatly augmented its amount of diversity, *and the man has lost none of his.* Thus we see that the "system" has enlarged its amount of diversity of distribution by factors which lay exclusively in itself.[1] It is the same result as we got from the study of the harmonious morphogenetical systems, regarding this very point of the "diversity of distribution."

There is only a difference in so far as in morphogenesis the "suspending" act of entelechy relates to the material elements of the body exclusively, while in action it relates immediately to the material elements of the brain, and

[1] The energetical factors of the medium, of course, can only claim to be necessary for becoming in general, but have nothing to do with the originating of diversities in our system. By the aid of *one and the same* amount of oxygen, food, etc., the workman may *either* transform the original homogeneous heap of bricks into another homogeneous heap, *or* construct any kind of small house he likes.

THE INDIRECT JUSTIFICATION OF ENTELECHY 195

through the brain—and the muscular system—affects a certain external material also. But this difference does *not* touch the chief point in question.

γ. THE RÔLE OF ENTELECHY DOES NOT CONTRADICT THE PRINCIPLES OF THE INORGANIC AS THEY ARE, BUT AS THEY MIGHT BE FORMULATED

At the first glance our analytical results seem to contradict the second—and also, of course, the empirical third—principle of energetics. For, if diversities can be created without pre-existing diversities, the absolute amount of diversity in a given system is not only not diminished, as the third principle postulates, but is most decidedly increased, and this without any external event. And yet there is no contradiction to the usual second and third energetical principle, but something quite different, for we have *not* admitted any augmentation of the number of elemental diversities by what we have said, nor have we allowed any increase of diversity with regard to differences of "intensity." We only have stated that an increase of diversity with regard to the distribution of elements has occurred from within, a diversity with regard to tectonics,[1] so to say. *But about this point nothing is affirmed by any of the energetical principles*, either

---

[1] A very good instance of the augmenting of diversity regarding distribution but not elemental composition is offered by the process of printing. Take the compositor and the types as forming our "system": by the action of printing, which is a real "action" in our analytical sense, new types, of course, are not created in any way, but the types present, which at the beginning showed a fairly simple order of distribution, say in about fifty-two boxes, will at the end show a state of distribution of the highest imaginable complexity.

positively or negatively; the energetical principles relate to the diversity of potentials or intensities exclusively.

Now it would be wrong to conclude from this fact that there is no opposition between inorganic and vital phenomena. But the opposition does not relate to the true second principle of energetics, but relates to a certain more general ontological principle that *might* have been established with regard to inorganic events, to a principle that in fact is realised in a certain form in the Inorganic and in a certain *other* form in the Organic,[1] but that, so to say, has been *forgotten* by physics and chemistry.

This principle may most generally be expressed as follows:—

"It is impossible to transform any system that possesses a certain state of diversity among its actual and potential constituents into a more heterogeneous state by the sole agency of the system."

Our principle becomes limited to the Inorganic if the words "constituents" and "agency" are understood energetically, and in this form, of course, implies the true second energetical principle as a sub-class; but even then it speaks of *any* kind of diversity, even of mere diversity of spatial arrangement, and not only of diversity with regard to intensities, as the latter does.

What is done by entelechy now contradicts or rather *exceeds our principle in its general inorganic form*, and here

[1] It is very strange to note, that from this point of view the most remarkable biological phenomenon of "retro-differentiation" (as it occurs in *Clavellina* and *Tubularia*, compare vol. i. page 163), in spite of its biological exceptionality, appears more similar to inorganic phenomena than ordinary differentiation does: there is a *decrease* of "diversity of distribution" in retro-differentiation.

THE INDIRECT JUSTIFICATION OF ENTELECHY 197

lies the contrast between inorganic and vital becoming: organic systems *may* acquire a higher degree of diversity of *distribution without* reference to other than their own energetical agents. But—the agents of organic systems are not energetical agents exclusively: one of their agents is entelechy.

δ. BUT THE RÔLE OF ENTELECHY AGREES WITH A CERTAIN GENERAL ONTOLOGICAL PRINCIPLE

Therefore our principle, in its *most* general, strictly ontological form, can be shown not to be contradicted or exceeded by vital facts—otherwise it would not be a strictly ontological principle; nay, otherwise the principle of univocal determination would be violated. The principle of univocal determination postulates that nothing happens but what is related in only one way to the rest of the Given. Formulated with special reference to the origin of diversities of *any* kind, the principle would demand that any increase with regard to any kind of diversity must be referable in but one way to pre-existing diversities, corresponding to the increase that is studied; in other words, that every newly originating singularity is referable to a pre-existing singularity.

Our analysis taught us that a certain general ontological principle of becoming diverse is exceeded by vital facts if expressed in limited inorganic terms, but that entelechy plays a part in vital facts. *But entelechy is an intensive manifoldness*, embracing a real system of pre-existing diversities in itself: thence it follows that by our argument the principle of univocality is as well observed as ever, and that our principle of diversity in its *most* general form is observed as well. Also in organic systems diversities are only created on the basis of pre-existing diversities, even if external agents are excluded, for organic systems are governed by entelechy, and therefore contain all possible future perceptible diversities in an imperceptible latent form, but *qua* diversities ;[1] in short, differentiation is "evolutio" in the ontological sense of the word.

Of course the principle of univocality does not appear here in the form of real spatial causality, as will be seen later on.

ε. THE "DEMONS" OF MAXWELL

Physicists, particularly in this country, have very often contrasted vital with physical principles. As far as these statements relate to pure mechanics we shall have to deal with them later on. But there is one famous instance of an assertion that organic processes may contradict the true second energetical principle, at least in thermodynamics. The principle of Clausius, that heat cannot pass from the cooler to the warmer body unless an equivalent amount of work is performed, has been said to be possibly contradicted by something like an organism. The famous instance we refer to starts from so-called mechanical physics, but as it does not touch the

---

[1] We have not said a single word in our discussion on the so-called vital "self-motion" of a particle of matter, and, in fact, should reject this "concept" most emphatically. "Self-motion" is self-contradictory, if applied to a particle of matter alone. We do not even admit the creation of motion by entelechy, but merely the regulation of existing motion, as will become still clearer in a later chapter.

THE INDIRECT JUSTIFICATION OF ENTELECHY 199

mechanical principles as such, it may be mentioned at this place.

Maxwell imagines two boxes of different temperature, communicating by a small hole, which may be closed and opened as you please. Now, he says, let us assume that there is a sort of "demon," who is able to move the door of the hole at his pleasure, and who only opens it when a molecule of great velocity is passing from the box A to the box B, but in no other case, the temperature of B being the higher one. The result of doing so will be, that the temperature of B, in spite of being the higher one, will be raised at the expense of the temperature of A; and this contradicts the second principle of thermodynamics.

It seems to me that in Maxwell's fiction things stand just as they did in our instance of the workman and the bricks, where only an increase of diversity of distribution was accomplished by the vital agent. Let us not forget that "temperature" as such does not exist for Maxwell from his mechanical point of view: molecules in motion are his elements to be studied, each of them endowed with a specific velocity. His "demon" deals with these molecules as our workman with his bricks; he does not create diversities of velocity, he only increases the amount of diversity in the *distribution* of differently moving molecules. In this sense there is *no* contradiction in Maxwell's statements to the general principle of the rôle of diversities in *general becoming*; there only is a contradiction to the second principle of mere thermodynamics: but "heat" and "temperature" are nothing elemental to the mechanical physicist. Of course, the empirical law of the dissipation of energy would be contradicted by Maxwell's fiction.[1]

Let it be well understood: Maxwell's argument rests upon a fiction, and does not *assert* that life contradicts any energetical law. But it is important, since now, after *our own* analytical discussions, it may really be applied to life as to a natural autonomous reality.

---

[1] It has often been said that the "second principle" of energetics does not hold for mechanics, but the "true second" and the "empirical third" principle have always been confused in such an analysis. It seems to me that the *true* second principle ("principle of becoming") finds its mechanical expression in the simple phrase that a system of bodies all moving in the same direction with the same velocity is unable to change its individual velocities. The law of dissipation, our "third empirical" principle, has been applied to mechanics by Boltzmann on the basis of calculations on probability. To express the chief point in our terminology: a homogeneous distribution in any system of moving bodies, endowed with different velocities, is more "probable" than a heterogeneous distribution.

4. Provisional Remarks on Entelechy and the Classes of Natural Agents

On "Phenomenalism"

Are we now at length prepared to decide what sort of a factor or agent or elemental value entelechy may be in nature regarded as a whole?

First of all it may be not quite out of place to say a few more words on so-called "phenomenalism" as the basis of natural science. So-called *pure* phenomenalism, so much in vogue nowadays, never is what it calls itself in the strict sense of the word, even if it rejects the concept of *a priori*. Even then it is not based upon "phenomena" exclusively, and ought rather to be called empirical idealism. For phenomena *alone*—that is, the mere sum of what is *immediately* "given" in the form of so-called sensations—would never allow science of *any* sort to be formed. The Ego is not only receiving but is also producing, and what is generally regarded as the "world," even by unscientific people, is for the greatest part a product of the producing Ego. Now, the "Given," as conceived in space of three dimensions, as regarded to "exist" even when it is not directly perceived, as subjected to causality in its different forms, may well be called "phenomenological," so far as it is *not* regarded as something absolute, *i.e.* metaphysically—and science is possible without regarding the Given in this way. But the Given in this sense, though existing with respect to the Ego exclusively without further analysis, has already been made a "conceptum," and is no mere "perceptum"; it is not immediate, but "*enlarged*" *givenness*. So much for the present on this important point, and on our manner of using the term "phenomenological." *Our* "phenomenalism" is identical with critical non-metaphysical idealism; in this form it is the only basis of science that is quite free from prepossessions of any kind, and therefore all science should *start* from this idealism, even if metaphysics is to form its *end*.

The "Constants"

The question as to the logical or ontological nature of any factor or agent in the realm of the Given, in the sense explained, is simply the question with what kinds of general categories, concerned in the creation of the *mundus conceptus*, these factors or agents may be co-ordinated.

We know already that energies and the intensities of energies are among the factors constituting the "world" in the sense of a phenomenon conceptually enlarged. Most of you, I believe, will also know that there is another class of such factors, commonly called "constants." Intensities and constants are both *properties* of bodies; intensities are variable or temporary properties, constants, as their name implies, are permanent properties. These constants show very clearly the conceived character of natural factors in its contrast to mere perception. Specific heat, conductivity,

THE INDIRECT JUSTIFICATION OF ENTELECHY

mass, etc., are instances of constants; but so are also, in a more complicated degree, the terms expressing the transformability of one sort of energy into another, and as constants must also be regarded the relations of affinity between chemical elements and the specificity of the direction of the attractive forces that appear in crystallisation.[1]

None of these constants, in fact, gives us any information about anything that is immediately observed or perceived; all of them deal with possibilities only, with possibilities of immediate becoming, which "exist" as realities in the most general meaning which this word *can* have in true idealism. Constants are expressions for possible immediate experiences of different but elemental kinds, they are concepts created in order to simplify the survey of the whole of possible experience. Their creation, however, is not only a matter of our own choice, but has to go on according to the fundamental characters of the organisation of mind.

It follows from what we have said that a sort of order of complication exists among all the different classes of constants conceived by phenomenological philosophy. The simplest class relates to simple physical properties only. Specific heat is a good instance of this class: it is an expression of the degree in which a substance is accessible to heat. The physical constants combining two fields of energy, dealing with the transformation of one into the other, form the next higher class, whilst chemical and crystallographic constants, the one dealing with the mutual relations of constants of the physical order, the other dealing with the specificity of directed forces, form the two species of the highest class.

[1] Compare my *Naturbegriffe*, Part A.

Negative Characteristics of Entelechy

What sort of natural factor then is entelechy?

We know already that it is not energy and not intensity, since quantity is not one of its characteristics. For the same reason it cannot be a "force" in any of the very ambiguous meanings of that word. Could it be called a "constant"? I thought so once myself;[1] I thought it possible to speak of the entelechy of an organic system as its "constant" in the sense of its permanent property; the word property meaning the same as it does in the Inorganic, where it is to signify nothing but the possibility of becoming that would be actual with regard to immediate perception. But it now seems to me that the word "constant" can be applied to an entelechian system only in a very metaphorical meaning, if at all: for a constant always is the property of a *body*, always is a something that is really possessed by the body. Only by help of the categories of substance and inherence can the real relation of a constant to its bearer be properly understood. Our next lecture will show that we are not at all able thus to regard the relation of entelechies to the material systems upon which they act. So then it must be sufficient to state it here in a more provisionary and apodictic way: *entelechy is not a constant.* We may only say that in this specific harmonious system or in this acting system we are studying there is something which is constant, viz., its prospective potency, which comes into all its reactions in the same manner. But this something which is constant is not "a constant."

[1] *Die organischen Regulationen*, Leipzig, 1901.

What then is our elemental vital factor in nature?

Let us only say in this place that entelechies remain "elemental" also with regard to their true ontological character, just as they were elemental with regard to the law they obey. Entelechies are *not* energies, *not* forces, *not* intensities, and *not* constants, but—entelechies.

Entelechy, as we know, is a factor in nature which acts teleologically. It is an intensive manifoldness, and on account of its inherent diversities it is able to augment the amount of diversity in the inorganic world as far as distribution is concerned. It acts by suspending and setting free reactions based upon potential differences regulatively. There is nothing like it in inorganic nature.

A Gap in the Scale of Natural Factors

We have learnt that there is a sort of scale of constants in the Inorganic, leading from simple physical constants to the constants of chemistry and crystallography. As far as what happens is regarded exclusively in relation to univocal becoming in general, we could say that this scale is continued in the Organic, and that entelechy is the next degree of it. Morality, considered as a phenomenon in nature, might perhaps be said to form the highest degree of all. But there is a gap between the constant factors of the Inorganic and the factors concerned in the phenomena of life that is not to be filled, as far as the relation of these factors to matter is taken into consideration. Owing to this gap the scale of factors of becoming, if taken as a whole, possesses only a certain descriptive value.

Once more we remark here that nothing "psychical," in the *proper* meaning of the word, is introduced by our entelechy: entelechy is an elemental factor of *nature*, conceived to explain a certain class of natural phenomena.

A Few Words on "Explaining"

I well know that the word "explaining" is very ambiguous, and that in all "explanation" there is a good deal of moving in a circle. Constants are said to explain, and so are entelechies and specific kinds of forces and energies. What is actually done here is nothing but a kind of subsuming the single phenomena under certain classes of generalities derived from the singularities themselves, and the question must *remain* at this very unsatisfactory point in "pure" phenomenalism or "empirical idealism," as advocated by Mach, Ostwald, Pearson, and others. On the basis of our critically idealistic philosophy, we may look a little more optimistically upon "explaining." According to this doctrine, the generalities which are considered to "explain" are formulated according to the immanent and categorical principles of reasoning *a priori*, and what empiricism adds to them only consists in the coordination of some truly inductive general terms with the categorical generalities. In other words, the general type of all so-called natural laws is known independently of the amount of experience, and is only brought to consciousness by experience, and it is only the empirical addenda to these laws that are first "abstracted" from empirical singularities, and after that serve to "explain" these singularities. Not only constants in their different specificities but also *specific* entelechies are instances of these empirical addenda. There is no difference in this respect with regard to the sciences of the Organic and the Inorganic. Later on we shall see that with regard to apriorism also inorganic and organic natural factors are on equal terms.

5. Entelechy and Mechanics

a. THE FOUNDATIONS OF MECHANICAL PHYSICS

On a possible Qualitative Science that is Complete

We now leave the realm of energetics, with all its consequences, and turn our attention to another possible interpretation of nature.

Ordinary qualitative energetics is by no means a complete system, even of inorganic nature: the problem of matter, in other words, the problem of the "being material," of the "being a body," is almost forgotten. But the problem, though neglected, is still there. Now it must be granted that a science of inorganic nature seems possible which should not put aside the problem of materiality and should yet remain qualitative. Such a possible science would have to deal not only with qualitative energies and intensities, but also with the concept of qualitative forces, defined on the analogy of "force" in mechanics, and would regard ultimately the inorganic universe as a system of geometrical points, from which lines of different kinds of qualitative forces proceed—representing heat, electricity, chemical affinities, and the different characteristics of the states of aggregation. The word "quality" would have two very different meanings in such a scientific view: it firstly would be used in the simple sense of a property, such as warmth or redness, but secondly, there would be qualities with regard to "bodiness," so to speak, and this second class of qualities would relate to the problems of materiality, especially to the problem of continuity or discontinuity, which is almost wholly neglected by common energetics.

As a complete qualitative science of the Inorganic, as sketched here, does not exist, it is enough to have mentioned its possible existence. We pass on to a more commonly known scientific point of view.

The Epistemological Character of Universal Mechanics

It is very difficult to introduce in a really legitimate way the possibility of so-called *mechanical physics*, that is, the interpretation of nature as a pure mechanical system, and the reduction of all quality in nature to mere constellation of elements.

Mechanical physics has been called a "metaphysical hypothesis," *i.e.* an assumption which relates to something absolute, and might some day prove to be true; but such a view without further explanation is not compatible with an idealistic philosophy. Others have called the theories of mechanical physics "fictions" or "pictures," adequate to describe by analogy the relations of natural phenomena with regard to their quantity only, but possessing no value beyond that of mere "economy of thinking," which might even be reached better in some other way. It was this point of view in particular that led science to its qualitative period,[1] for it was quite a natural result of regarding mechanical theories as mere fictions to reject them completely as mere ballast, superfluous for a pure description of phenomenalities. But in spite of these attacks mechanical physics still lives in our days, and, more than that, in the theory of electrons it is undergoing a remarkable renaissance.

That seems to prove that there is a great vitality in these theories, and indeed it seems to me that they are much more than mere fictions, though, on the other hand, they by no means relate to anything absolute. It is owing to innate necessities of the human mind that they arise again and again. They always arise whenever science tries to reach the final problem of "the Material" as such, and when science tries to explain the varieties of material states and of ordinary qualities *on the same basis*. A system of nature that is complete and at the same time free from logical and real contradictions needs mechanical physics of a certain form, and cannot be satisfied until it has succeeded in demonstrating the variety of the "Given" as being due to a mere arrangement or constellation of some elements, the law of whose behaviour is known aprioristically, at least as to its general scheme. To modern "purely" phenomenological science the combination of properties, of constants in particular, in one and the same "thing" is a mere given state, a something that is merely

[1] It is not the place here to deal with the elimination of causality as advocated by some modern empiristic phenomenalists. As may easily be conceived, this elimination is based upon a philosophical doctrine that is altogether *incomplete*, and so too is the mathematical form of this "functional" phenomenalism. The philosophy of nature cannot be satisfied by the mere statement of necessary dependence; it asks for *causality* in its strict ontological form.

THE INDIRECT JUSTIFICATION OF ENTELECHY 211

to be acknowledged. But that is by no means satisfactory. Mechanical physics offers a real explanation of the problem of the combination of properties, and at the same time it allows us to understand another important problem, which is insoluble in any other way: the problem which may be called the systematics of natural events and properties in the Inorganic.

In fact, mechanical physics in its *ultimate* aim tries to prove all combinations of properties in one thing on the one hand, and the totality of possible properties (and events) as such, on the other, to be the mere outcome of the possible kinds of equilibrium or causality of elemental matter. To mention only one class of phenomena that may be thus explained: mechanical physics shows us firstly why there may be so many kinds of typical atoms, it shows us secondly why there may be so many kinds of molecules, and it shows us thirdly why there may be so many kinds of crystalline systems. In order to do so it only has to solve certain problems about the possible types of equilibria in space, first of electrons, and then of atoms, and finally of molecules. Thus all its problems, to some extent, become mere problems of geometry.

All that we have said is absolutely independent of the present state of mechanical physics; it is true whether classical mechanics holds the field, operating with one kind of material elements ("mass"-elements) and two kinds of primary forces, or whether we shall have to reduce mass to electrons, and to consider space as a sort of activity in the form of "ether."

Future mechanical science, then, will have altogether

to abandon the *metaphysical* view of the older mechanics; in this respect it may learn from modern energetical phenomenalism. But mechanical physics is not a system of "fictions." Mechanical physics *is* "phenomenalism" in the enlarged meaning of the term as we have defined it, it deals with the "mundus conceptus" as presented to the mind; but it is a *thorough-going*, a truly ontological phenomenalism.[1] Its general scheme is aprioristic or ontological, its specific form at a given time is truly "hypothetic," with reference to what "existence" means in enlarged phenomenalism; in this sense molecules may be found to exist some day, just as do the nucleus and the chromosomes of a cell.

The Psychological Basis of Universal Mechanics

So much for the epistemology of mechanical physics; its merely psychological starting-point is given by the science of acoustics: here we actually know that a body emitting sound is "the same" as is "also" a body moving in a special manner.[2] We cannot discuss here the most important words

[1] It was the great fault of many modern phenomenological physicists to confuse theoretical mechanics as a rational and aprioristic science with the knowledge of the actual motions of perceptual bodies. In fact, rational mechanics is above experience, and is only called into existence by it. Rational mechanics cannot be "false," it would hold, even if all *actual* movement in the universe did not obey the law of Galilei—as modern electrodynamics asserts, at least for very great velocities. Actual movement then would not be pure "mechanical" movement, but would be pure movement corrected by an electromagnetic field. Rational mechanics is nothing but enlarged mathematics, or rather a step beyond real mathematics in general categorical ontology.

[2] The corresponding perception of two "senses" is also the chief reason for distinguishing practical "reality" from "illusion."

"the same" and "also,"[1] which lie at the very root of philosophy, in spite of their everyday character; it is enough for us here that acoustics forms the most simple bridge from quality to motion in constellation; from sound to heat is but a step.

We repeat that the kinds of motion "corresponding" to heat (in general words—molecules, atoms, and electrons) are in their epistemological character as "real" as are the moving particles of air corresponding to sounds. Or better: all of them are either "non-real" or "real," as you choose; certainly they are of the same *degree* as to "reality," the word reality being taken in the sense of "possibility of perception." Hypotheses come in here, of course, as to the specificity of what is not yet actually perceived; but that there must be a "something," with regard to discontinuity, which is of the degree of the molecule or the atom or the electron, is not an hypothesis but an assumption immediately suggested by certain facts.[2]

The best reason, finally, which forces us to make the subject of science proper not "sound" and "heat," but the movement of a something, as soon as there is any evidence that there is "also" movement where there is sound and heat, is epistemologically given, as we know, in the possibility

---

[1] Compare Hegel, *Phänomenologie des Geistes*.

[2] If molecules or atoms were ever "discovered"—perhaps by the aid of an "ultramicroscope"—what would be immediately perceived would be sensations, though—on account of the length of the waves of light—not sensations representing the molecules or atoms directly. But would therefore the molecules or atoms be "red" or "green," or at least "dark" or "light"? By no means, but discontinuities *with regard to* sensations would compel us to say that here we have a field for applying certain *concepts* which are waiting for application in our mind. As *concepts* atoms would be *points* from which fields of force are radiating. All this is not metaphysics, but analysis of "enlarged Givenness."

of applying nothing but geometry. Psychologically we here find ourselves face to face with the simple fact that "pushing and pulling," *i.e.* mechanical causality in the crudest form, is the only kind of causality we are able to perform ourselves. In this sense alone do we "understand" mechanical causality.

I have said more about the philosophy of mechanics than might seem to be required in a biological discussion, because at the present time mechanical physics has been discredited in the utmost degree. It was necessary to rehabilitate it to a certain extent, in order that it might not be regarded as altogether valueless to analyse the relation in which autonomous biology stands to the mechanical type of inorganic science.

β. THE DIFFERENT FORMS OF UNIVERSAL MECHANICS

We now return to our biological problem. What about entelechy and inorganic nature as a system of uniform elements in motion, now that we understand the relation of entelechy to the inorganic universe as a system of qualitative energies or even qualitative energetical elemental centres?

It is important to notice at the very beginning of our study of the rôle of entelechy in a world that is considered mechanically, that it matters little how the mechanical view of nature is conceived in detail. Whether the dualism of ether and mass, or in other terms, of primary and secondary matter, be solved or unsolved, whether the ultimate elements of mass be regarded as particles or as dynamical points, or, in the kinetic fashion, as specified permanent states in a continuum—all these questions, though of the greatest importance for the ontology of the Inorganic, have no bearing at all upon the problem before us, at least in its most fundamental form. And it would not affect us if movements in nature were one day proved to be essentially electrodynamical, or if rational mechanics were shown to be actually at work in nature. In the first case, as is well understood, natural mass would not be the "mass" of analytical mechanics, whilst in the second case analytical and empirical mass would be identical.

Mere Movement and the Causation of Movement

The problem of the relation between entelechy and mechanics has to deal not with movement as such, but with a certain possible kind of causation of movement that is irreconcilable with the causations of movement occurring in the inorganic field. It will soon become apparent what that means.

Hertz remarks, in his famous posthumous treatise on mechanics, that his most general principle of movement, which is a combination in some way of Galilei's principle of inertia and the Gaussian principle of the least action—that this most general principle, though only stated for inorganic systems, would also hold for systems in which life-processes are concerned, as the *effect* of every vital process always could be imagined as being the *effect* of a system of the inorganic class. From this statement and, indeed, from the whole of Hertz's analysis, it is clear without further discussion that his principle only deals with the character of motion, as far as it *has been caused* in some way and is now existing, but not with the causation of motion. Be that causation what it may, it will always *result* in a force of special intensity and special direction, acting upon the special element of mass, and precisely the same sort of *result*, of course, might follow from the action of some inorganic combination.

Under such a view there is room for all sorts of causes of motion, whether they consist in the effect of systems of "hidden masses," or in the effect of *anything* else: motion, and motion alone, is studied by this kind of mechanics.

That the special mechanical system of Hertz is kinetic at bottom, that it knows only motion as the cause of motion, and therefore knows only one kind of energy, viz., kinetic energy, does not come into account here; his principle of movement as such would hold for any other theory of dynamics equally well.

The Forms of Mechanical Causation

But the problem of inorganic causation of motion—almost put aside by Hertz and "solved" in a rather abrupt manner [1]—now demands an answer. The two chief classes of possible mechanics—kinetics and dynamics—at least require to be considered.[2]

Kinetic mechanics knows only motion as the cause of

---

[1] By the assumption of stiff or rigid "connexions." This assumption fails even to fulfil the requirements of the theory of elasticity.

[2] Kinetic mechanics may appear in two different forms, the one founded upon the hypothesis of the continuity of matter, the other upon discontinuity. Dynamical mechanics, of course, regards matter as discontinuous with regard to its atoms, which are "centres of force," but its "lines of force" fill space continuously—whether they be regarded as mere abstractions or as "states" of a continuous ether. Kinetic mechanics based upon continuity cannot speak of "motion" in the ordinary sense of the word. "Motion" becomes equal to "continuity and contiguity of change of elements of space."

THE INDIRECT JUSTIFICATION OF ENTELECHY 217

motion; all other forces are only apparent to it. The principle of the conservation of the "quantity of motion" (mv) of a given system is its only principle, including of course the conservation of kinetic energy, the only energy kinetic mechanics knows. But whenever nature is regarded as a mechanical system of the dynamical type, it is conceived as a typical arrangement of mass-elements possessing central forces, and in this system all becoming depends on the original state of actual motion and the amount of these forces. There are *two* kinds of energy—the actual form $\frac{m}{2}v^2$ and the potential form—and all becoming is represented as an increase and decrease of the amount of these two forms correspondingly, their sum total remaining unaltered in each of the three dimensions of space. The potential form of energy is as subsidiary here as any subsidiary energy in the field of qualitative energetics. But, in any case, the sum total of energy existing cannot be imagined changeable; and this principle is valid with regard to each co-ordinate separately.

The principle of the conservation of the quantity of motion (mv), of course, does not hold in a theory of mechanics that is dynamical: it is contradicted by potential energy.

What rôle then could entelechy play in a world of either mechanical type?

Pure Kinetics Negligible

As far as I am aware, there is not any kinetic system of mechanics that could claim to be pure. In order to explain the totality of physical phenomena *some* kinds of "forces" are always being introduced, at least where it is a question of molecular dimensions. Thus pure kinetics is in fact always given up in the long run.

Therefore, I think we can allow ourselves to neglect kinetic mechanics [1] altogether, and may simply ask: What is the relation of entelechy to dynamical mechanics?

γ. ENTELECHY AND DYNAMICAL MECHANICS [2]

As entelechy is non-energetical, it certainly does not change the amount of energy of a limited system in any case whatever;[3] but it might do everything that can be

[1] If in fact only motion were the cause of motion in the Inorganic, the rôle of entelechy in becoming in space—since it has been *proved* not to be of the inorganic type—would be confined to the real creating or annihilating of motion. But since kinetics is far from being the only legitimate form of mechanics, we are not *forced* to go thus far. The modern views about the electrodynamical foundation of *real* (not of analytical!) mechanics are intentionally neglected here.

[2] In the standard work by the late L. Busse, "*Geist und Körper, Seele und Leib*" (Leipzig, 1903), a very thorough critical discussion of all current theories about the relation of "mind" and mechanics will be found. We only mention here what we ourselves think to be valuable. It seems strange, considering the eternal nature of the problem, but, as far as I know, our *first* hypothesis, to be brought forward hereafter, seems never to have been advocated in its present form; it will be seen to be an application of our views—which were also new—about entelechy as augmenting the amount of diversity of distribution.

[3] Busse, Schwarz, and probably others have admitted an increase of the amount of mechanical energy, when discussing the relation between "mind" and matter. I should not like to go so far, unless facts really forced me to do so; though it must be conceded, that nothing unthinkable would be postulated; for the "mind" (or the entelechy) would be a something that is *external* to the system in question. Compare the last note but one. The view has also been advocated occasionally that "mind" acts on "matter" by disturbing so-called labile equilibria. Such equilibria are, however, extremely improbable. Apart from this there would be no *logical* argument against the "lability" theory, as the amount of energy that is required in order to disturb a labile equilibrium is infinitely small (dx), and thus might be regarded as belonging to another sphere of Being. Compare the important concept of "Behaftung" in K. Geissler's valuable work, *Das Unendliche* (Leipzig, 1902); see in particular page 406.

imagined to be done without relation to the quantity of the energetical state of a system as such. Now it seems to me that there may be non-energetical modifications in this state of two different kinds, one of which we already know from qualitative energetics.

Entelechy in its Relation to the two Forms of Mechanical Energy

I am thinking in the first place of entelechy as *suspending* the becoming that otherwise would happen. The process of compensation of potentials, in the most general meaning of the word, such as differences of coupled intensities, could as we know be suspended by entelechy. Does anything similar happen in pure mechanics with its two and only two kinds of energy? Kinetic energy and potential mechanical energy, of course, would be the only fields accessible to the action of entelechy. Now it would certainly not be a legitimate hypothesis to assume that entelechy is able to transform any potential energy into the kinetic form by removing some kind of obstacle that has hitherto impeded this transformation, for this process of so-called "Auslösung"—to use the untranslatable German word—requires a certain finite amount of energy in any case, and entelechy is not energy. But the problem acquires a very different aspect as soon as we assume that kinetic energy, *i.e.* "happening," is always the given material entelechy has to work with, but that entelechy is able to transform actual happening into a state of mere potentiality by suspension, and that it can only set free such "potentials" as it has itself created by its suspension of happening. A combination of processes of the following kind, it seems to me, is well able to explain what I suppose to be the work of entelechy. An element of mass m moves with velocity v, until it comes within range of a repulsive force; its velocity then decreases constantly until it becomes zero. That point will be reached when the amount of its original kinetic energy $\frac{m}{2}v^2$ has been equalled by the potential energy derived from the repulsive agent. Finally, the element m receives an impulse in a direction opposite to the original one, and this impulse—decreasing from moment to moment, as velocity increases—will last until the element has reached its original velocity, and also its original kinetic energy $\frac{m}{2}v^2$, taken in the opposite sense.

Now imagine that the process of constantly decreasing motion just described, is *suspended* by entelechy at some stage or other—say at the moment in which the velocity is v_1—in such a form that the amount of $\frac{m}{2}v_1^2$ is transformed into an equivalent amount of "potential" energy, localised at the place of m and kept there until it is set free, that is, transformed into the actual kinetic energy $\frac{m}{2}v_1^2$ again. Could not such a thing happen without any relation to questions of energetics? Certainly it could, for the process of suspending would not touch the amount of energy in any way, though it would interfere with inertia; and the process of relaxing suspension would be in no sense equivalent to an "Auslösung" or removing of obstacles. The mechanical process we have imagined is represented very clearly by an inelastic body moving with the velocity v and entering during its motion into an elastic ball. It will move into this ball for a certain time with decreasing velocity, come to rest for a moment, and then move in the opposite direction with increasing velocity again: let this process be stopped at the moment when the inelastic body has traversed say one-third of the path into the elastic mass. There is no contradiction to energetics in such an event, *provided, of course, that after the suspension has ceased the mechanical and energetic events continue their course from the point where it was broken.*[1]

So I think that even in mechanics proper we have the possibility of formulating in a strict logical sense what is done by entelechy.[2]

Entelechy, *by its very nature*, may suspend movement, transforming kinetic energy into potential energy, and it may set free suspended movement as circumstances require.

Of course, as we saw with regard to general energetics, entelechy can only be regarded as able to set free those potentials which it has *made* "potentials" by its own suspending action, but not potentials that owe their existence to any inorganic cause. This important feature would lead us to a discussion of the continuity of suspension

---

[1] Our hypothesis, of course, implies that a movement like that of a pendulum, which changes its direction periodically, passing through states of mere potential energy at the point of change, may be suspended in this point of change, in which there is *no* movement. This case, of course, is more simple than ours, and would not charge entelechy with an actual stopping of kinetic energy. But our more general hypothesis seems to me to be legitimate as well.

[2] A similar view, with regard to "psycho-physical" interaction, has been urged by Wentscher and others; but as a rule "suspending" and "Auslösung" have not been distinguished clearly enough.

222 SCIENCE AND PHILOSOPHY OF THE ORGANISM

by entelechy, as seen in inheritance, but we regard our previous remarks on this point of the theory as sufficient (see page 181).

Entelechy as Transporting Mechanical Energy

Before discussing our result any further let us turn to the second possible way in which entelechy may influence mechanical systems. The discovery of this possible rôle of the Non-mechanical in mechanics goes back to Descartes. In our own days Eduard von Hartmann in particular has investigated more carefully what is supposed to happen here. Descartes, strictly speaking, was not trying to study the influence of entelechy as a natural factor on mechanical mass and motion, but to fix the interaction of "mind" and body. You are aware that we ourselves regard such a problem as not legitimately formulated. But Descartes' analysis holds well on a different epistemological basis in the form that any non-mechanical agent, though not able to change in any way the amount of energy in any dynamical system,[1] has the faculty of reversing any mass-element it likes, and of thereby changing the *direction* of forces and motions. It might be objected that a certain amount of energy would be necessary for any "turning" of a mass-element, there being required a certain force, or rather pair of forces, from the side on account of inertia. Where is the necessary energy to come from, since entelechy itself is regarded as

[1] Descartes, strictly speaking, according to his theory of the continuity of matter, knew only kinetic energy; the so-called "quantity of motion" (mv), therefore, was the mechanical quantity he would not allow to be altered by mind. For this reason our first hypothesis about the relation between entelechy and mechanics would have been impossible for him. Even his own statement about this relation—or rather about the relation between "mind" and matter—does not acquire any very clear meaning on the kinetic theory.

non-energetical ? Hartmann tries to avoid this difficulty by assuming that entelechy—or, as he calls it, the "Unconscious"—may transport energy from one axis of space into the other. The energy it needs for the process of turning as such is taken from the one axis and placed at the other : the sum of all the energies remains unaltered, there only are energetical changes with regard to the three chief co-ordinates x, y, and z, and thus the action of the vital principle would pass the boundaries of mechanics, *i.e.* of inertia, but not of energetics in general. But I can hardly agree that this complication is necessary. Entelechy *is* a natural agent *per se*; why not assume that its action in changing the direction of force and energy is an action "*per se*" that is implied in its intensive manifoldness ? The true laws of mechanics are broken in *any* case, and entelechy must by no means be imagined as a mechanical apparatus : it is just the negation of that. We must free ourselves from all the conventional images as completely as possible. You may say if you like that entelechy, when turning a mass particle, acts upon it at right angles to its path—this kind of action requiring no energy—but even thus there would only be a pseudo-obedience to the laws of real mechanics, since entelechy must be regarded here as non-energetical, and as interfering with inertia at the same time.

The Suspending and the Transporting Action of Entelechy Discussed Together

If now we consider the theoretical probability of the two possible ways in which entelechy or anything non-mechanical whatever *may* influence mechanical systems, it seems to me that our first hypothetic statement dealing with the possibility of a suspension of becoming in mechanical systems offers several advantages which are not afforded by the doctrine of a changing of the direction of forces. According to the latter theory entelechy would seem to be limited by practically nothing except the amount of existing energy, whilst, according to the former, it would be limited not only by energy as such but also by pre-existing differences with regard to velocities and potentials. And we do in fact see that entelechy *is* limited and restricted in its actions to a rather high degree. But I confess that the theory of "turning" and thus changing the direction of forces and energies must also be regarded as a possible solution of our problem. In any case it would assume less than any hypothesis about the real creation of energy by entelechy.

Entelechy in Contrast to General Mechanics

Is there any "contradiction" to mechanics in our two statements? Certainly, as far as the *exclusiveness* of mechanics is concerned. Wherever there is life in the universe something happens that is not present in the given mechanical constellations as such: something is introduced, not changing the quantitative side but changing the *actuality* and *direction* of mechanical events. But I should prefer to speak of a "contrast" instead of a "contradiction."

It might seem as if there were more contrast between entelechy and mechanics than there is between entelechy and energetics, as far at least as the energetics of ordinary textbooks is concerned. For both of our formulations of the possible relation between entelechy and mechanics assert that a something which is non-energetical interferes, though not with the amount of mechanical energy as a whole yet with inertia, and therefore with the amounts of the two types of mechanical energy respectively. But let us not forget in this place that there also was a great contrast between vital phenomena and the *complete* " science of inorganic or spatial becoming " that is to be written in the future. Entelechy, as endowed with the faculty of enlarging the amount of diversity in the distribution of given elements, was in opposition to that future science.

Of course, what we have said about entelechy and mechanics would imply most clearly that entelechy can augment any " diversity of distribution." Thus this point does not need any further explanation in this chapter. The work of the " demons " of Maxwell is here regarded as actually accomplished.

δ. CERTAIN BRITISH AUTHORS ON LIFE AND MECHANICS

That life must be most intimately related to the direction of the motion of masses is no uncommon view with physicists and chemists, especially in this country. Lord Kelvin speaks of the organism as endowed with the power of " directing and moving particles," and Tait regards it as simply " unscientific " even to *attempt* a mechanical explanation of life. Both these statements [1] are rather general.

---

[1] Lord Kelvin, *Popular Lectures*, ii. p. 464 ff. ; *Fortnightly Rev.*, 1892, vol. li. p. 313. Tait, *Contemp. Rev.*, 1878, 31 Jan., p. 298. Lord Kelvin also refers to the impossibility of understanding the fact of inheritance on the theory of an accidental concourse of atoms. Our second proof of vitalism (see vol. i. p. 226) implies the same statement.

But, as many of you will know, Professor Japp [1] some years ago advocated a vitalistic theory that was most markedly based upon the concept of *direction*. That certain lower organisms are able to consume or to produce only *one* of a pair of corresponding asymmetrical chemical compounds proves, according to him, that specific direction as an elementality plays a fundamental part in organic life; besides those organisms only the conscious mind of the chemical experimenter is able to do the same. I should not like to regard the biochemical facts alluded to by Professor Japp as really proving vitalism by themselves—they only prove a certain kind of specific statical teleology, it seems to me—but certainly the rôle of specific direction in life is most clearly shown by them, and for that reason they are mentioned here.

[1] "Stereochemistry and Vitalism," *Report* 68*th Meeting Brit. Assoc. Bristol*, 1898, p. 813.

6. How Entelechy is Affected

We have discussed at full length how entelechy may possibly act with regard to an energetical or a mechanical inorganic system, or in other words, what it may change in any way in such a system. But we have not even mentioned so far the corresponding question: how may changes in any inorganic system affect entelechy? But this problem, of course, needs at least to be mentioned as well as the other. In the theory of so-called psychophysical interaction both problems, as a rule, are treated on equal terms: the "Psychical" is regarded not only as affecting the "Physical," but also as being affected by it.

a. THE PRINCIPLE OF ACTION AND REACTION AS RELATED TO ENTELECHY

In the first place we are, I think, obliged to inquire whether in the work of entelechy there may occur anything comparable with the Newtonian principle of action and reaction, this principle, of course—as in "electrodynamical mechanics"—being understood in the widest possible ontological sense. Of course, since entelechy is neither an energy nor any factor of the mechanical type, the principle of reaction cannot apply to it in any physico-chemical or mechanical sense. But, even then, entelechy is an "agent" or a "factor" in nature, entelechy is a something acting univocally with regard to the inorganic, as we know, and therefore there must be something in this relation that is comparable with the principle of reaction in a general logical sense though beyond inorganic causality. For all becoming—not true causality alone—must always be conceived under the form of a mutual interaction. Whenever a factor A affects B, not only is B affected but so is also A. With regard to pure causality this principle holds irrespective of all our special definitions of a "cause," almost all of them being formulated with reference to practical purposes.[1] I believe now that we can easily find out how to relate the concept of a "reaction" to entelechy. Entelechy when performing any act in a system becomes changed with regard to its intensive actuality by this act itself; the "having done" changes its "doing," for doing is no longer necessary after having done. Thus entelechy is affected by the accomplishment of its own performance, in acting as well as in morphogenesis. We here meet the first case in which any kind of affection of entelechy occurs.

β. THE TYPES OF AFFECTION OF ENTELECHY

We now turn to a short survey of the possible ways in which entelechy may be affected by a mere change in inorganic nature as such.

[1] Comp. vol. i. p. 99 ff., and vol. ii. p. 158 ff.

Morphogenetic Entelechy

The organism, we know, is a system the single constituents of which are inorganic in themselves; only the whole constituted by them in their typical order or arrangement owes its specificity to entelechy. Therefore the single constituents of an organism also stand in energetical or mechanical possible relations to many external constituents of the inorganic universe. These possible relations may disturb the whole as governed by entelechy: by some such disturbance entelechy, in the first place, may be possibly affected, may be called into activity, so to say.

We here meet the problem of the stimuli of restitution and adaptation again.

In order that adaptation may happen, the fundamental state of the organism must be disturbed in its normality: this fact affects or calls forth entelechy.

In cases of restitution we were not able to state anything in detail about the precise stimulus that sets this process going: but, since in all restitutions the morphogenetic performance, though occurring on the basis of indefinite possibilities, was always in the most typical and specific relation to what had been disturbed, we were able to say that the stimulus of restitutions is most probably something connected with the *specificity* of the disturbance of the normal whole. This "something" must be regarded as affecting entelechy.

In short, morphogenetic entelechy in cases of adaptation or restitution is affected whenever the state of normality, based upon a specific suspension of possible inorganic becoming on the part of entelechy, is changed by the effect of external becoming. Entelechy then at least tries to modify its suspension in such a way as to reduce that external becoming to normality.

But such a view fails in the face of *normal* development. Here, we know, fertilisation or some substitute for it is necessary in order that entelechy may come into action. What does that mean? It seems to me that we shall meet the point if we assume that fertilisation or its substitute affords here some necessary means, some necessary specific potential differences, as it were, without which entelechy is condemned to inactivity, just as it is in the absence of oxygen. Artificial parthenogenesis, as analysed by Loeb, lends strong support to such an hypothesis. But this would mean that even in the case of normal development entelechy is called into activity in the proper sense *by missing its normal result where it might exist potentially*, and thus normal development would be regarded as a mere example of all restitution. Fertilisation or its substitute would thus play a rather secondary part. It would not call forth entelechy by itself, but would only allow entelechy to act after it *had* been called into activity already by the mere existence of a living fragment of an organism.

Of course, this is no answer to the problem why the organism *does* actively form " fragments " in the service of " reproduction "; but this problem leads beyond the theory of " personal " entelechy as the subject of embryology, and will shortly be mentioned again on a later occasion.

Any restitution, like normal morphogenesis, is accomplished by a great number of consecutive single performances, or, in other words, single stages. What about the manifestation of each stage by entelechy? We may say here briefly, I believe, that the spatial existence of, say, the stage A affects entelechy with respect to its performance of the next act leading to stage B. Thus morphogenesis—and not morphogenesis alone—becomes a series of events that occur between matter and entelechy, and *vice versa*.[1]

The Affection of the Psychoid

As to the affection of the psychoid or the entelechy of real acting by external inorganic events, we must not forget that the concept of "normality" comes in here only so far as a certain actual liking and willing takes the place of normality; to will a certain thing at a certain time is "normal" for the psychoid at that time.

If we restrict our analysis to such acting as ends in a distinctly visible result, say an object of art or of handicraft, we may say: the psychoid, its specific willing being given, is affected by the very *specificity* of combination of what there is, compared with what there ought to be according to its willing. In this way a printer will always take up his work at the point where he left it the day before. A similar view would hold with respect to acting in general.

Psychologically all passivity, or rather receptivity of entelechy with regard to external changes, is expressed by

[1] We avoid by this formulation the difficult concept of an intra-entelechian "causality," which plays its part, for instance, in Lotze's writings—in a very different form and terminology, of course. It must be granted that introspective psychology might seem to lend support to such a concept—we shall speak ourselves of an "intra-psychical series" on a later occasion—but it is better avoided by the philosophy of nature.

232 SCIENCE AND PHILOSOPHY OF THE ORGANISM

the words sensation and sensibility. We can hardly avoid describing, at least analogically, what *must* happen in the affection of entelechy in general by words similar to these, just as we have spoken of a primary knowing and willing of entelechy. But, of course, our postulate that an affection of all entelechy by external changes *must* exist and that this affection relates to specificities of order or combination is more important than mere terminology.

As in discussing the affection of morphogenetic entelechy we came back to the stimuli of restitution, so here we could analyse again what we called "individualised stimuli" when we were discussing action. Both times the analysis of the type of affection of the vital "something" itself constitutes a proof of vitalism and forces us to call this "something" entelechy.

γ. THE CONTRAST BETWEEN AFFECTION IN THE ORGANIC AND THE INORGANIC

To sum up: Entelechy is *affected* and thus called into activity by *changes of any normality* governed by it which are due to external causes, and these changes *do not affect entelechy as a mere sum of changed singularities but as changes of normality as a whole.*

This point is very important, for, on the other hand, our careful analysis of the relation of entelechy to energetics and mechanics has taught us that the activity of entelechy relates immediately to *single* inorganic events, though in the service of normality.

The fundamental contrast between the affection of entelechy from without and any kind of affection in the

THE INDIRECT JUSTIFICATION OF ENTELECHY 233

Inorganic is well illustrated by the mere fact that in the case of entelechy the affecting inorganic combinations act as totalities. It was for this reason that we said that the "analysis of the type of affection" by itself forms here a proof of the "autonomy" of what happens, whilst in our discussion of the active rôle of entelechy, with regard to energetics and mechanics, we had to start from the autonomy of life as proved, and had to study what might follow from such autonomy with regard to *single* effects in inorganic nature.

All changes of normality that affect entelechy are "causes," of course, in so far as they are changes of given realities in space, though their effect is not an immediate spatial effect but one that has passed through entelechy. *Qua* causes, they are as specific as is their final spatial effect induced by entelechy. Thus we meet the strange fact here that, as regards biology, first cause and final effect are in the most intimate relation to one another with regard to *specificity*, though not in an immediate relation. This sort of relation between cause and effect occurs nowhere in the inorganic except in *pure* mechanics, and there in quite another form. A general ontological theory of relation—I do *not* say of "causality"—might take advantage of this most important logical fact.

General Conclusions

Entelechy related to Space and therefore belonging to Nature, but Entelechy not in Space

THE contrast between the Non-living and the Living has appeared in all the discussions of this long part.[1]

But the contrast always was a contrast with regard to nature, or rather *in* nature as the "Given" in space. We have at no time lost sight of nature by what we have said.

This contrast is indeed of a most fundamental character: there is quite a new type of natural becoming revealed to us, whenever entelechy is at work, actively increasing in a regulatory way the amount of diversity of distribution on account of its intensive manifoldness after it has been affected by individualised stimuli. Inorganic becoming relates to extensities and is measured by energy; we may say that energy measures the amount of causality which is spatial in

---

[1] The same contrast would appear if we were to relate entelechy to a certain modern type of analysing inorganic systems, *i.e.* the so-called "principle of phases," which also rests upon aprioristic considerations. I have discussed entelechy under this aspect in my *Naturbegriffe*, p. 182; but it seems to me that the result to be possibly obtained would not repay a long analysis in these lectures. Entelechy is a "parameter" of its own kind helping with the inorganic parameters to determine "equilibrium" and "degrees of freedom." This is the whole result to be obtained.

itself. Entelechy is a diversity or a manifoldness in itself but not in the sense of spatial extensities, therefore it has nothing to do with the amount of spatial causality as such, though it relates to events in space, and therefore it is not measured by energy. In fact, entelechy is affected by and acts upon spatial causality as if it came out of an ultra-spatial dimension; *it does not act in space, it acts into space*; it is not in space, it only has points of manifestation in space. This analogy with some theoretical views that are advocated by so-called spiritualists to explain the facts which are admitted by them to exist is a very good *description* indeed of what happens in any natural system upon which entelechy is acting. At present it must be enough to lay stress upon the great difference [1] between the two great classes of becoming in nature, both of them, as we know, subject to univocality : the one spatial, extensive, quantitative; the other non-spatial, intensive, and arranging only; but both of them realising themselves in spatial events, *i.e.* in nature.

The Problem of " Entelechy and Causality " only partly solved

But, after all, how does entelechy stand to causality? Is it a special type of causality itself?

I am sorry to say that the answer to this ultimate problem must once more be put off until considerations of another kind have been weighed.

[1] It is upon this difference as formulated in the text that the very essence of vitalism, of "non-materialism" rests. It matters little how materialism is formulated in detail; energetics is but a new form of materialism, and is far from being its *Überwindung*, as Ostwald claims.

Justification of our Cautiousness

We have charged entelechy with the minimum amount of non-physicochemical performing that is possible in regard to its dealing passively and actively with inorganic causality. From the point of view of energy we only admit entelechy as a factor which suspends occurrences that would be possible according to the inorganic order. Perhaps we have charged entelechy with too little, though what we have done stands in harmony with our actual knowledge, which has shown us *limits* of regulability at many points. Let us not forget that there may exist many realities, which we do not know yet and possibly shall not know for some hundred years, on account of their minuteness perhaps—the word "realities" to be understood here in the sense of "possible objects of experience," as long as metaphysics is excluded. Let us not forget how late the phenomena of radio-activity have become known to us. In other words: there may be still more fundamental actions done by entelechy than those which we at present know of and therefore admit. May not entelechy have an individualising action upon electrons directly? And what about the first origin of life? But here we are already touching some problems which belong to the next chapter.

Perhaps it will really become necessary some day to admit that entelechy not only suspends potentials, but that it creates potentials—perhaps by coupling or chaining uncoupled differences of intensity—and thereby creates energy; something similar would be expressible in purely dynamical terms. We have no reason to deal more fully here with such an assumption, which, of course, would have

THE INDIRECT JUSTIFICATION OF ENTELECHY

to consider the problem of the finiteness or infiniteness of the universe; for it was our endeavour in this chapter to draw only such theoretical conclusions as are nearly related to known facts.

The "Moment of Regulation"

Let us then close this chapter with a certain consideration which most intimately relates to biological facts in general.

In all phenomena of morphogenetic regulation and adaptation and of acting we are by no means forced to assume that entelechy by its counteracting inorganic becoming works all along the single phases of the process in question. In adaptation especially it would seem to be quite sufficient for fulfilling the needs of the organism, if entelechy were to break the inorganic chain of events at one special point, the rest being inorganic becoming again. In restitution and acting something very similar may happen. The term "moment of regulation" would be well descriptive of this one special point of happening where entelechy sets in. But we do not know anything special about this problem.[1]

[1] Compare our remarks on catalysis, p. 186 f.

C. ENTELECHY AND SUBSTANCE

a. THE CATEGORY OF SUBSTANCE AND ITS APPLICATION IN GENERAL

THE late Eduard von Hartmann says somewhere in his *Kategorienlehre* that all philosophy has been a struggle about the concept of "substance"; and I doubt if any one who knows the history of philosophy would say that he is wrong.

Substance and inherence, in fact, are the most common of all categories; even the child knows very much earlier how to use them than how to apply causality; but in spite of that the problem of what is properly to be regarded as "substance" remains the unsolved problem in all the various fields of philosophical research.

The categories of substance and inherence, as all of you know, find their simplest application whenever "things" are regarded as possessing properties, as being the "bearers" of their properties. But science proceeds on its way and soon regards the "being a thing" as a property itself. What sort of a property? What then is the criterion of *not* being a property?

We see here that from the very beginning a very remarkable principle of ontology is coming into action, at first almost hidden to consciousness, but in an advanced stage of philosophy consciously applied: the principle that there must be a something in enlarged givenness which is absolutely *unchangeable*, and that only this unchangeable something deserves to be called a "substance" definitively.

INORGANIC SUBSTANCE

Of course, in our biological lectures we cannot pursue the subject of general ontology and epistemology: so we only mention that *inorganic* sciences have ended in our days by regarding as the true substance either discrete dynamical points generally called "atoms"—though not in the more restricted meaning of chemistry—or space itself. Space in this sense is not merely a "form of intuition" but is identical with what is generally called "ether" as far as the latter is taken as a continuum. In fact, if you think about all the so-called properties of the "ether" of physicists, you find that all of them are non-properties, or at least nothing but the mere expression of possibilities,[1] that they are mere negations and that space alone is left as the substantial continuum, as the bearer of phenomenological reality, at the end of the discussion.

The doctrine which regards space as *the* inorganic substance applies more strictly than any other the principle of stability, or conservation, or unchangeableness: space cannot even change its "place," whilst all sorts of atoms are changeable according to their position in formal space. But on the other hand this identification of space and substance seems to go too far beyond the common application of the category of substance, which in its most

[1] With reference to the electromagnetic field.

primitive form was to signify a "thing." So it comes that advocates of the space-substance theory generally introduce still another kind of inorganic "substance," which they call merely distinctly marked elements of their space. But these also have the character of unchangeableness except in respect to motion, and are almost identical with the atoms of the other theory.

In fact, there seems to be some force compelling the human mind to admit some substance *in* space and not merely space as the substance. The principle of the constancy of the sum of all inorganic or material substance would then be guaranteed for the simple reason that its coming out of space or its coming into space is quite an unimaginable and unthinkable event. Here, indeed, are the very sources of the aprioristic principle of the conservation of material substance.

There exists a very close relationship between the principle of the conservation of substance and the principle of the conservation of energy: both of them in some respect resting upon the character of (formal) space as an all-embracing something which neither may be left nor be entered. It is probably this relationship that has seduced some modern authors into asserting the identity of substance and energy, a doctrine which seems to us to be absolutely impossible. For this assertion forgets that what is measured by "ergs" is only the amount of causality as far as the latter has quantity and is therefore measurable, whilst substance relates to what is not touched by causality at all. The two principles of conservation relate to two absolutely different branches of ontology. Energy "is" not, but is realised in change; substance *is*.

It is true that ordinary energetics has not a very good opportunity to discover the proper equivalent of substance in nature, but the fault is its own and does not lie with the category of substance. As soon as the problems of the "being material" are not neglected, the category of substance would become applicable even in the realm of qualitative energetics; of course it becomes much clearer in mechanical physics. In fact, might we not say that the irresistible tendency to apply the category of substance has been one of the fundamental *sources* of the mechanical view of inorganic nature altogether?

INORGANIC SUBSTANCE OF ANY TYPE RELATES TO EXTENSITY

But enough at this place about the meaning of "substance" in the inorganic world; enough also about the difficulties remaining still unsolved here. In what follows we shall only use one fundamental result, common to all the different theories of substance relating to the Inorganic. Inorganic substance either is *extensity* itself, that is, space as the bearer of phenomenological reality, or it is a something consisting of absolutely single elements which are one beside the other *in extensity*. All extensities in the Inorganic are built up out of such substantial elements. That the substantial elements of inorganic nature relate to extensities and to extensities alone also holds good, if the substantial elements themselves are understood dynamically, that is, if they are regarded as certain elemental "spheres" in space which are each the seat of forces going out from a centre. Even in this case, though the centre of the force is a point and is not extensive in itself, the substantial element in space as such is an extensity. We have no desire to advocate the dynamical atomistic theory by what we have said, at least not without restrictions. We only wish to emphasise the fact that inorganic substance in *any* possible form relates to extensities, and that if it relates to varieties and manifoldnesses it does so with regard to *extensive* ones and to nothing else.

We now turn back to our proper field of research—biological philosophy in its relations to the category of substance.

β. ORGANIC "ASSIMILATION"

In the first place we shall have to deal with some characteristics of life which are by no means philosophical by themselves. These introductory remarks will serve at the same time to fill a certain gap in our survey of life phenomena. You probably have noticed that there *was* still a gap in that survey, though, I hope, our following discussion will show that this gap was only apparent and implied only a pseudo-problem.

RESPIRATION

Respiration and assimilation are generally regarded as the most fundamental functions of organic life, as the very foundations indeed of all physiology.

Respiration in its scientific meaning is the oxidation of any chemical compound of the body, that is, its combination with oxygen, in order, as text-books tell us, to provide a source of energy for functional performances. The compounds to be oxidised may be split into simpler ones before oxidation or they may not. The last result of the process of oxidation is the production of carbonic acid, uric acid, urea, and some other compounds, which are poisonous to the organism if care is not taken for their removal.

As we have said already, oxidation is generally regarded as a source of energy exclusively; or, better, as a source of so-called free energy, that is, energy that may do work on account of differences of coupled potentials. But this rôle of oxidation would never explain its absolute necessity. If such a doctrine were the whole truth, the stopping of oxidation would only stop the functioning of the organism; but the organism is not only damaged, it *dies* if oxidation is not allowed, and death is well known here *not* to be due merely to a poisoning by the final products of oxidation such as carbonic acid, for the removing of which the most elaborate arrangements exist in the organism. Therefore there must be yet another part played by oxidation. We should not be wrong, I suppose, to formulate this rôle in the following way :—The organism by its merely synthetic or analytic metabolism seems to produce some substances which are poisonous to it, *i.e.* which disturb the order of its metabolism in an irreparable manner if they are not converted into an innoxious form: *this conversion into an innoxious form is done by oxidation.*[1]

For a long time the foundations of organic oxidation were an absolute enigma to biology, and all sorts of theories were invented to solve it. All these theories, as, for instance, the one which utilises the effect of oxygen in its

[1] I advocated this theory as early as 1901, at a time when only Noll held a similar view with regard to organic oxidation. But at present the theory of the anti-poisonous action of oxidation seems to be gaining ground, the new discoveries of Winterstein being most favourable to it. Comp. vol. i. p. 199.

so-called active state (O_3), have become antiquated owing to the discoveries of the last few years. It was the mistake of all former theories of oxidation to look upon respiration as a process in which the organism plays an almost passive rôle. Either some compounds of the organism were regarded as attracting the oxygen of the medium by their own affinity, or oxygen itself was regarded as attracting parts of the organism. Modern biology has shown that oxidation is an *active* function on the part of the organism for the benefit of the whole. Wherever it is necessary either to destroy noxious compounds or to gain energetical potentials, the organism forms catalysers or calls into activity so-called zymogens, which set up oxidation that would otherwise not have taken place.[1] The fuel consumed for the *supply of energy* consists generally of those constituents that are derived from the food—though hardly without some intermediate change first taking place—but it also may be more important constituents of the tissues themselves, as we have learnt in our analysis of the metabolism of fasting. Oxidation as a mere *process of anti-poisoning* attacks all the so-called by-products of metabolism in general.

Thus the most general result gained by modern biological research is the knowledge that oxidation is like all the other processes of metabolism; that it is as regulable and as limited in its regulability as they; that it only seems to be more important on account of its universal presence in all forms of life.

[1] Our description is a little schematic: former theories of respiration have made a difference between so-called "primary" or fundamental oxidation, which is necessary for life in general, and "secondary" oxidation, subsidiary to special functions. It is highly probable that this difference will disappear in the light of modern research, but the matter has not yet been fully decided.

We therefore leave the theory of oxidation and approach the general subject of metabolism; of this general subject oxidation has proved to be but a part.

"ASSIMILATION" AND "DISSIMILATION"

Metabolism, *i.e.* the change of chemical specificities during the differentiation, growth, and functioning of the organism, is generally considered under the two headings of "assimilation" and "dissimilation." Few terms in science are more ambiguous and problematic in meaning, and few terms are used so freely and recklessly. Of course nobody would mind if they were only used to signify that some of the processes in the organism which lead to chemical results proceed from the simpler to more complicated chemical compounds, while the rest proceed in the opposite direction. In that case one could only object that the words synthetic and analytic, as commonly used by chemists, would suffice for the needs of physiology also. But, as a rule, something else and something more is meant whenever the words "assimilation" and "dissimilation" are used — and this "something more" is extremely problematic.

We here must enter the realm of so-called physiological chemistry, with which I must confess I am not at all familiar; but in spite of that I hope that the following discussion, dealing with some very general and almost purely logical questions exclusively, may serve to elucidate a little what might be called the central point of physiology.

Whenever the words "assimilation" and "dissimilation"

are to signify anything specifically determined, that is something other than what chemists call "synthesis" and "analysis," and whenever at the same time they claim to be used in any strict meaning at all, they *can* only mean that there is a something of a specific chemical nature, yet intimately bound up with life itself, which has the power of making other less complicated chemical materials *like itself* or of producing *from itself* less complicated materials by an analytical process.

Let it be clearly understood : the word "assimilation" does not mean that there is a fundamental material *A* of given quantity, to which *external* means and forces add a further quantity, but it expresses that the material *A* increases by its *own* action at the cost of the components of the medium in the broadest sense.

Taking the word assimilation in this usual sense, the question of course would arise as to the kind of forces "assimilating," that is, equalising foreign materials to the material *A* and seated in *A* at the same time. But it seems to me that another question should be settled first, which is perhaps of a still deeper importance, though it does not sound so theoretical.

The " Living Substance " in the Chemical Sense

I am thinking of the very simple but very fundamental question : Does assimilation in the sense we have indicated really take place ? Does the chemically distinctive substance *A*, the so-called "living substance," exist at all ? Are there any criteria of its existence ? There are in fact many theoretical authors who have answered these two

THE INDIRECT JUSTIFICATION OF ENTELECHY 247

questions affirmatively; and they have almost always been of the materialistic school. But is it not remarkable that the positive investigators of physiological chemistry never say one single word about the problematic material A and the problematic process of real "assimilation"?

What then does physiological chemistry really teach as the result of its experiments?

There are many specific chemical compounds present in the organism, belonging to different classes of the chemical system, and partly known in their constitution, partly unknown. But those that are not yet known will probably be known some day in the near future, and certainly there is no theoretical impossibility about discovering the constitution of albumen and how to "make" it. All the substances present in the organism have a definite range of possibilities regarding their physiological origin and their physiological destruction. They may originate in a certain number of different ways, and may be destroyed in a certain number of ways. Organisms behave differently in this respect. Fungi, for instance, are able to build up all the chief classes of their constituents—fats, carbohydrates, and albumen, out of one organic compound of rather variable constitution, while all animals require constituents of all three classes in their food, or, at least, are not able to live without receiving albumen. The modes of constructing and destroying the constituents of the organism almost always differ to a great extent from those used in the laboratory: to mention but one difference, what is done by heat in the laboratory is generally done by ferments in the organism. And, finally, upon this use of ferments by the organism depends the most remarkable feature of organic metabolism. Metabolism occurs in a regulatory manner which is to the benefit of the whole: at one moment one chemical construction goes on here and at another moment another chemical destruction occurs there according as the need exists in those places; all the regulations, of course, being confined within certain limits presented by the fact that a certain sum of specific compounds forms the absolutely necessary food of the organism.

In these chief results of metabolistic physiology not a word has been said about our special living substance A and its "assimilation." In fact, the specific constituents of the organism may be said to be "assimilated" in so far as they are liable to an increase of their amount; but this pseudo-assimilation is always due to the action of some *other* constituent of the organism, never to themselves. Thus the word "assimilation" seems justifiable only so far as the organism as a whole is considered. In that sense, however, it would mean nothing of importance.

Negative Results only

What then is gained by our discussion of the most general results of physiological chemistry for the central problem of this chapter, the problem of the relation of entelechy to substantiality? The facts suggest no reason for assuming that a "living substance," assimilating and dissimilating in the strict sense, is the real base and foundation of life. On the contrary, physiological chemistry knows nothing about a living substance and nothing about "assimilation" and "dissimilation." The facts revealed by this science, though not amounting to a real proof of the operation of an autonomic factor in life, such as our entelechy, are certainly very easily reconcilable with its existence.

A chemical "living substance" does not exist.

γ. ENTELECHY INCOMPATIBLE WITH A "LIVING" CHEMICAL SUBSTANCE

We shall now regard our problem from its other side. We *know* that the facts show no indication of a "living substance" in the chemical sense, we further *know* that an autonomic regulatory factor is at work in organic processes. What then, let us ask, follows from the concept of this factor or agent itself with regard to the existence of a living substance of a specific chemical constitution, as the foundation of vitality? Does an analysis of the concept of entelechy lead to the admission of a "living" chemical substance in spite of the negative facts of physiological chemistry, or do the results of such an analysis stand in harmony with our actual present knowledge of metabolism? In the first case science would have to go and search for the "living substance" until it found it and could show it in a test-tube; in the second case its main work might be said to be completed in this field.

I now hope to be able to show you from the meaning of the concept of entelechy—that being a well established elemental agent in nature—that entelechy can be neither the consequence of any sort of specific chemical compound —when it might be represented by such a compound as "living substance"—nor the outcome or consequence of any constellation of different specific chemical compounds of any sort, which might otherwise perhaps be regarded as the *materia viva*.

No Chemical Substance Possible as the Basis of Entelechy

Entelechy, we know, is an intensive manifoldness, *i.e.* it is an agent acting manifoldly without being in itself manifold in space or extensity. Entelechy therefore is only an agent that arranges, but not an agent that possesses quantity.

What then would be the significance of saying that a specific chemical substance is the bearer of entelechy? To say so would be to attribute the property of extensity to a something that has nothing to do with extensity at all, to a something which in a certain respect may be said to be the negation of extensity.

It gives a good idea of the strange consequences to which the doctrine of a "living substance" as the bearer of autonomic entelechy would lead, to recall the fact that, of course, a living substance in the sense of a specific chemical compound would be measurable by weight like any other chemical compound. We should have to speak of, say, six pounds of lion-substance, or a pound and a half of eagle-substance, or three ounces of earthworm-substance; and all these chemical compounds would some day be sold in the market perhaps. We here see most clearly that it is quite impossible to assign the characteristic of extensity to an agent which is simply a determinant of *order in* extensities; for our lion-substance, of course, would not signify so much of the actual substance of a given lion, but would mean so many pounds of that *homogeneous* chemical material which is supposed to represent the "being-a-lion."

Of course nothing is said by our remarks against the hypothesis that there may exist real chemical compounds, which are characteristic of organic specificity in the sense of being necessary means of morphogenesis, and which perhaps play their rôle in the process of inheritance as far as its material side is concerned. In fact, the new discoveries in hybridisation, as we know, seem to advocate such a view to a certain extent. These substances, however, are by no means identical with entelechy but are used by entelechy.

There is still another very grave objection against the material character of entelechy: if it were material it would be subject to energetical changes, for it would be energetical itself; but that we have seen is an impossibility. And, moreover, to assume that the disintegration of a certain amount of chemical material, homogeneous in itself, could explain real differentiation during ontogeny, would clearly contradict the principle of univocal determination.[1]

No Constellation of Chemical Substances Possible as the Basis of Entelechy

But now you might reply to our discussion: "Good, a specific chemical compound cannot be the basis of entelechy in the sense that entelechy always appears whenever this compound is formed, by the very fact of its formation. But could not entelechy be a consequence of a specific relative constellation of different chemical compounds of specific states of aggregation? Could there not appear a

[1] Comp. vol. i. p. 134 ff.

new and elemental factor owing to the constellation of some other factors already known? Do we not see such an event happen whenever electricity is generated by rubbing a glass rod?"

Let us try to answer this objection at first in a narrower sense. If the typical constellation of the inorganic agents A, B, C, and D is to originate a new sort of activity, which does not come to them from without, but is regarded as their true and real consequence, how would it be conceivable at all unless you imagine that one of the four constituents, A, B, C, and D, possessed the new agent in question already in a state of potentiality, comparable to the state of a so-called zymogen in fermentation, which is waiting to be transformed into a ferment? But, if it gives this turn to the problem, the constellation-theory represents no great advance on the purely chemical theory of entelechy already refuted. One of the four elements of the hypothetic constellation creating entelechy would have to perform almost the same rôle that is performed by the specific compound of the chemical doctrine.

But to pass to more general considerations: is it at all possible that new elemental kinds of natural changes can be created by the mere constellation of agents already known? Can such a constellation possibly be followed by more than a mere resultant action of the sum of the elemental actions of its constituents?

It has been said occasionally by modern writers that a system, by the mere increase of its amount of material, may begin to exhibit marked differences in its behaviour. Take for instance a homogeneous sphere in rotation. It will simply be flattened at its poles, if it is small, but a large

THE INDIRECT JUSTIFICATION OF ENTELECHY

sphere of the same material and moving with the same angular velocity will throw off its equatorial substance in the form of a ring, and a satellite may be formed out of it; for the absolute amount of peripheral velocity increases enormously with the increase of the total amount of substance. So there *may* result very different definitive forms from systems which differed only in size at the outset.

But, of course, it is clear from the very beginning that the origin of new *elemental* factors is not touched at all in this example.

But how about the relation of rubbing a glass rod to electricity, how about the rise of the electric current from chemical potentials, as we see in the familiar galvanic cell?

It is true that at the first glance there may seem to be a real creation of something fundamentally new by a mere constellation: phenomenalism in its purest form, in fact, would advocate such a view. But the history of physics shows that it is impossible for human reason to rest content with such a conception. Science always has been in search of some pre-existence of what seemed to be new, and, in fact, science has always managed to find this pre-existence in some way. Either it has attributed the new thing that arose to what existed already, endowing the latter with it in the form of a potentiality, expressed under the name of a so-called "constant," or it has gone further and has tried to conceive the possibility under the form of a substantiality. Mathematical phenomenalism takes the first line, the modern theory of electricity follows the second; the mere E of the first, marking the "being potentially electric" as an irreducibility, becomes the electron of the second, in the sense of the elemental quantity of the new phenomenality in question. In some respect our mind is satisfied by both methods, though more by the second. For our present purpose it is enough to know that there exists in our mind a demand for some such satisfaction: newly arising elemental agents must be conceived as already pre-existing in some way.

It will have become quite clear, I hope, from our discussion, that any theory which tries to make entelechy arise as a new elemental consequence of some constellation must result in taking one of the constituents in the real sense of a "living-substance." But the living-substance theory has been already refuted.

Entelechy and Physiological Chemistry

Entelechy cannot be regarded as arising from material conditions of any sort. What follows from this result for the facts of physiological chemistry, which formed one of the earlier parts of this chapter? It follows, so it seems to me, that what physiological chemistry studies is only *results that are chemically characterised* — not results of processes that are *chemical processes*. It is very important to understand well what this means. Of course, chemical potentials have formed the general basis of all physiological chemical results, but these results, as we know, are not due to the mere play of these potentials as such, but to the intervention of entelechy: therefore something purely chemical is found in the results only, but not in the processes. Without entelechy there would be other chemical results.

Entelechy controls not only oxidation but "assimilation"

and "dissimilation" also; without it a chaos of chemical processes would occur, and would soon disturb organisation and functioning. Previous analytical work has taught us that entelechy acts by means of setting free pre-existing potentials the compensation of which it has suspended before; this applies also to its work in the fundamental phenomena of all physiology. It probably is the production and actuation of ferments that is immediately controlled here, oxidation or any kind of chemical synthesis or analysis thus being purely chemical processes that *follow* the fundamental vital act.

Ancient Problems

In a certain respect the problem dealt with in our present considerations is identical with the famous Aristotelian question whether the concept of a house be subordinated — in more than a formal manner — to the concepts of wood or stone as its higher classes. Aristotle answers the question negatively, as we should do also. But it is exactly the same thing, only in a still more general form, to deny that entelechy itself is connected with or dependent on chemical substances.

And still another famous problem has been solved by us implicitly: the "enigma" how it might be possible for matter to "think," a question which plays a great part in one of the well-known addresses of Emil du Bois-Reymond. The answer is simple, for the problem is a pseudo-problem: "matter" not only does *not* "think," but "matter" is not even the foundation of life in *any* sense. Entelechy is something different from matter and altogether opposed to the causality of matter.

δ. SUBSTANCE AS A CATEGORY IN ITS RELATION TO ENTELECHY

By proving that entelechy is not identical with or a consequence of any chemical compound, or the constellation of such compounds, we by no means have solved the chief problem of our present chapter, which deals with the relation between entelechy and substance as a *category*. May not entelechy, though absolutely unlike everything that can be called substance in the inorganic world—whether it be conceived purely chemically or in the sense of a theory of matter—may not entelechy be called a "substance" in the most general philosophical sense of the word, that is, in the sense of a something irreducible, which remains the always unchangeable bearer of its changeable qualities?

Then there would be two substances with regard to nature, and our theory would become very similar to some theories of the past, though with the remarkable difference that our idealistic view would not allow us to regard one of these two substances as "psychical," as all other similar theories have done—Lotze's being one of the latest. There would be one spatially extended substance—"matter" and one non-spatial intensive substance—"entelechy" both substances forming part of that branch of enlarged given reality called conceptual scientific nature.

Let us first note a few very characteristic features of what may be called the behaviour of entelechies; the analysis may perhaps afford us materials to decide our fundamental problem.

The Concept of Divisibility not Applicable to Entelechy

At the risk of shocking you with an apparent absurdity I might say that entelechy has the power of preserving its specific intensive manifoldness in spite of being divided into two or more parts. The fact which we have called the genesis of complex-equipotential systems seems to favour this view at the first glance, and so do all the experiments relating to the development of isolated blastomeres of a germ into whole organisms of smaller proportions. Moreover, we directly founded our second proof of vitalism upon the evidence that, though a typical machine-like constellation of agents, different in its arrangement along the three axes of space, cannot be divided and remain whole at the same time, yet there exists in the living organism a something which *does* show these two incompatible characters.

The question now arises whether in a deeper sense we are entitled to speak of entelechy as remaining whole in spite of its "division" into parts.

It is very difficult to free the philosophical analysis of entelechy from all that is familiar to us from our acquaintance with extensive phenomena; and yet we *must* free it from all that belongs to extensity. It was the great achievement of Kant to show that space is the inevitable form of our intuition of the Extensive. Now, as to entelechy, there is no intuition, and therefore space and all sorts of relations about space have practically nothing to do with entelechy. Entelechy itself is *con*ceived only; it is *per*ceived only in its extensive results. Entelechy is not spatial, but only acts into space—I do not say "in" space—and the word "into," of course, is itself not at all of a "spatial" character here. In this respect, as will come out fully later on, there is quite a gulf between entelechy and such natural agents as forces and energies, though the latter are also concepts, not percepts. Now it is clear that "dividing" is always understood as something spatial, and therefore it follows from all we have said that this word in its strict meaning is not at all applicable to entelechy. When we speak of "dividing" we always think of a something which we can cut into pieces. But entelechy cannot be cut in this manner, for the simple reason that it has no spatial dimensions at all: the "having dimensions" would contradict altogether the meaning of the term.

Therefore we had better not speak of entelechy as an agent which "remains whole in spite of its division into parts," but simply say that entelechy may manifest itself wholly even after the division of a certain organic body, on which, had it remained one whole, entelechy would have manifested itself as *one* whole also. Entelechy always *manifests* itself individually: but our analysis proves that so-called individuality of the real organic *body* is not without further discussion to be identified with the deeper meaning of entelechian individuality.

The Concept of Localisation or Seat not Applicable to Entelechy

An agent which is of a non-spatial nature cannot be said to have a definite seat or a definite localisation in space. Entelechy therefore cannot possess a "seat." It cannot at all be imagined like a point consisting of a some-

THE INDIRECT JUSTIFICATION OF ENTELECHY

thing and moving through space, now in this and now in that direction. Descartes, as is well known, regarded the soul as having its seat in a specific organ of the brain, the so-called pineal gland. We may follow him so far as to say that there may be specific points of the organism with respect to which entelechy is active while at other points it is inactive. But these would only be points of mutual relation, not points of rest.

"Entelechy" so far a Mere System of Negations

I fully see how difficult it is to say anything positive about entelechy without contradicting other statements regarding it. I say once more that there is nothing at all to be "imagined" in a picture-like manner about entelechy: the non-spatial can never be realised by our imagination in spatial images. It may be hard on us, but so it is. And at the same time we always must bear in mind that in dealing with entelechy we are not dealing with anything psychical, or absolute, or metaphysical: we are analysing an agent at work in nature. We know concerning this factor that it cannot be spatial in any sense, that it has no seat in space nor any dimensions, but merely acts "into" space; in one word, that it "is" not in spatial nature but only acts with regard to spatial nature.

In fact, the characteristics of entelechy form only a complicated system of negations so far, and little more. Nor can it be otherwise unless we are prepared to change our whole view of reality, and of natural reality in particular, as in fact we very soon shall.

And thus at present the question whether entelechy is a

"substance" must remain as open as the previous question about the relation of entelechy to causality. Entelechy was a kind of "quasi" causality, and now may be said to be an enduring "quasi" substance. But still we feel that our reason craves more than this.

ε. INSOLUBLE PROBLEMS

At the end of this chapter you probably will expect the discussion of a few questions which interest you more than any others, and the answering of which perhaps you have hoped would be the final result of all our analysis. But such remarks as I am able to offer about the origin and end of individual life, and the origin of life in general, can claim merely a subjective value. Materialists profess to know a good deal about all these eternal problems, but I confess that I know nothing at all about any of them.

The Origin and the End of Individual Life

In the face of these fundamental questions let us remember, firstly, that our present task is neither a truly psychological nor a metaphysical one. We therefore have nothing to do with the problems of immortality as relating to the Ego; we are only studying phenomena in respect to the Ego. In fact, even if a "principle of the conservation of entelechy" could be established, and if we were able to speak about what might be called a phenomenological metempsychosis, it would all relate to phenomena in the first place, and it is well worth noticing that without further discussion spiritualistic phenomena, if proved some day,

THE INDIRECT JUSTIFICATION OF ENTELECHY

would also be mere phenomena to the Ego and nothing else. At the end of these lectures we shall devote some time to certain considerations that might probably lead us beyond this theoretical Egoism.

With the starting of a new actual individual, entelechy begins a new manifestation, and with death it ends one; that is all we can say. What that manifestation, *qua individual*, was before that beginning, and what it is after death is absolutely unknown to us. We are not even able to say whether it was and will be anything "individual" at all in these two periods or not—the words "was" and "will be" to be understood in a non-metaphysical sense, that is to say, in the sense of a "possible immediate experience." For the ideal or Platonic existence of entelechy as an individualising agent does not, of course, guarantee any sort of permanence of the individuals which, on account of an entelechian manifestation, form part of the given universe at a given time.

Spiritualists claim to have some knowledge about our problem, saying that after death the manifestations of entelechy preserve their individuality though using a new (so-called "astral") kind of material. But I say once more that I can form no opinion in this matter, though I should like very much to be able to do so. Science, in fact, ought to deal with these questions even at the risk of finding a mere chaos of defective criticism and actual fraud: but one single fact, positively established, would well repay the hard work of generations.

What science knows about death is simply this: a certain amount of matter that was formerly controlled by entelechy becomes freed from this control, and then obeys the laws of physico-chemical causality exclusively. Does entelechy actively withdraw from matter or not, and, if actively, then why? Why has "regulation" become impossible?—But it is of no use formulating any more of these unapproachable questions.

The Origin of Life in General

The question about the so-called primary origin of life is as incapable of being discussed as is the problem of death, in spite of the great number of popular works written about it. We certainly cannot grant that life has originated by a fortuitous concourse of inorganic constituents—that is clear without any further discussion from our analysis of entelechy in its relation to matter in general.[1] Constellations do not create entelechy, but entelechy governs constellation. But nothing can be said concerning the absolutely primordial relations between entelechy and elemental materiality.

Whilst speaking about entelechy in its relation to intensities of energy, we mentioned that our theory postulates the continuity of life which is well illustrated by the fact of inheritance. From this we may conclude that there are no gaps in entelechian manifestations: there is a continuity of a constellation of specific kinds of matter always maintained by entelechy, always overcome, so to say, by its suspension of inorganic becoming.

If we accept the theory of descent we may say that

[1] It therefore is only an argument of minor, *i.e.* merely empirical importance against "generatio equivoca" by contingency, that organic compounds, even of *low* complexity, do not exist on earth except if produced by organisms.

THE INDIRECT JUSTIFICATION OF ENTELECHY

the type of manifestations of entelechy has changed in the course of their continuous line. But we never come to any kind of beginning.

In any case it must appear very strange that life is only known to us in immediate relation with very complex chemical compounds of a few classes. Why does not entelechy act upon the elements of matter directly? Or is the present state of relation between entelechy and matter a consequence of the long time that life has continuously existed? Has entelechy, so to say, altered its behaviour with regard to matter? Or are we simply in ignorance of other types of its manifestations?

And so the series of questions and problems might be continued—but there are no answers.

It seems to me that this is the right place to point out that the whole problem of the origin of life on earth is of far less theoretical importance than the problem of the *laws* of life, though the common opinion almost always argues otherwise. For this reason we have devoted ourselves so closely to the study of the vital law and all its consequences. The solution of all problems of secondary importance will follow the knowledge of the law some day; but without this knowledge no *real* solution of those problems would ever be possible.

Conclusions of Part I

We have reached the end of the first part of our philosophy of the organism; let us then rest for a moment and look back upon the path we have traversed.

Our scientific discussion had shown us that the phenomena of life are not explainable by the concepts and laws we know from inorganic science, but that something new and elemental must be introduced by the science of biology. The first part of our philosophy of the organism was devoted to the justification of our newly introduced factor, in a special sense of the term "justification." It has been our endeavour to show how our new elemental agent and its law may be put into relation with the general ontological and logical principles concerned in the science of inorganic nature. But we have only formulated this relation between the Organic and the Inorganic by using those ontological aprioristic principles which are empirically realised in the *latter*, and that has led us to mere *negations* with regard to entelechy.

But, of course, still another kind of justification of our entelechy is required. We not only have to show that there is no contradiction between our new conception and those elements of the system of apriorities which are concerned in inorganic sciences, but we have to

THE INDIRECT JUSTIFICATION OF ENTELECHY 265

demonstrate the legitimacy of our factor itself as a part of the aprioristic system of natural factors or entities. We have to show that epistemology entitles us *positively* to introduce into science such a something as entelechy is. In other words, we have to establish vitalism from what may be called the organisation of the Ego.

That will be done, and the following pages will prepare the way for it.

All the proofs of vitalism given in our merely scientific section were indirect proofs, or proofs *per exclusionem*; all the possibilities but one were wrong, and therefore that one possibility was true.

Our next endeavour will be to prove vitalism directly. And upon this direct proof the positive epistemology of entelechy will afterwards be founded.

PART II

THE DIRECT JUSTIFICATION OF ENTELECHY

A. THE DIRECT PROOF OF THE AUTONOMY OF LIFE BASED UPON INTROSPECTIVE ANALYSIS OF COMPLETE GIVENNESS

1. ANALYTICAL PART

THE way which is generally followed in biology, as in almost every branch of science and philosophy, leads from the simple to the complex, both words being taken in the sense of formal logic. But another method of analysis is possible also, and this method is now to lead us to an important result. We shall once more *begin* our analytical study of biological phenomena, but we shall begin it not with the most simple but with the most *intimate* facts, that is to say, with those facts which are related more closely than any others to the Ego.

My own body as a scientific object is to be the starting-point of this new type of biology; my own body in the strictest possible sense.

But my own body is not to be regarded here as a constitutive part of objectified "nature," at least not for the very beginning of the analysis. The whole series of what is "given" to my consciousness whilst I am acting is to form the subject of our analysis, and only at the end of it will one part of that whole be considered as "nature." Thus our method will not be biological, nor even strictly "scientific," so to speak; it will analyse *Givenness* in its completeness, not only so-called "natural" Givenness. The consecutive series of the phenomena which present themselves to my consciousness whilst I am acting will be formulated. In the second place only shall we try to separate what properly may belong to "nature" and what does not belong to it. We thus shall find out, I hope, how nature and natural factors may be most elementally conceived in their relation to life-processes.

I am sitting in my chair and want to write; a lamp recently bought and not yet quite known to me in its construction stands on the table; the lamp begins to smoke—it is here that our analysis is to begin.

This analysis will not relate to "given" phenomena in their mere passivity, *i.e.* not to mere "sensations," but to those objects of consciousness exclusively in which some sort of activity or "apperception" on the part of the Ego is concerned. True "perceptions," of course, belong to this domain of mental activity.

a. A CASE FROM COMMON LIFE

The Case

My having an optical perception of the smoking lamp, in short, my *optical lamp* is followed by the desire to stop the smoking; in order to do that my attention is directed towards the construction of the lamp, which I compare with that of other lamps already known to me. This consideration ends in the will to move a certain screw of the lamp. I see and feel my hand touching and moving the screw; the smoking of the optical lamp ends.

These are the most general lines of the process; it is worth while to mark them in a more detailed fashion. My seeing the smoking lamp, to be quite accurate, is first followed by the remembrance of what a lamp's smoking is; then comes the associative remembrance that the consequences of its smoking are very unpleasant; the will arises to stop smoking; this recalls past cases of such a stopping, and the recollection of them recalls previous ways of doing so; that calls my attention to the construction of the lamp; this is found to be different from known constructions but similar to them; a certain point of similarity relating to the means of moving the wick is noticed; the specific will arises to perform the movement; my hand is felt and seen moving the screw in question; the smoking lamp is seen not to smoke any more.

The whole of a special excerpt from given reality in which "I myself" am playing a part has been described here as a continuous series. All of its constituents are phenomena presented to my conscious Ego. All of them follow each other in order of time with regard to their originating, though the amount of their velocity in following each other may vary to a great extent. Only a few of the constituents are "spatial." By saying that all of the constituents follow each other in order of time it is not stated that only one of them is presented to the Ego in each element of time; on the contrary, my seeing the smoking lamp continues during the whole of the series, and some remembrances of past cases of smoking lamps and of lamps of different construction may also continue during the whole. But what may be called the *active* rôle [1] of the Ego only relates to *one* of the constituents of the continuous [2] series in one element of time. I only am conscious that it is "I" who experience the phenomena with regard to one, and only one, of their constituents; the permanency of other parts of the series, though existing, is of no more consequence to me than the seeing of the room in which I am sitting during the whole of the process to be analysed.

What Common Life Learns from the Case

Taken in a quite immediate and unprejudiced manner, there cannot be the smallest doubt that the Ego, as far as it is "willing," is an active factor in the whole that happens in our example. The willing Ego is influenced and is influencing. It is a real link in the whole chain of events, and this whole chain—in other terms, the whole of the consecutive series of constituents which forms the process in question—must be regarded as univocally determined so far as it is an object of reflection at all. It is for this very

---

[1] If only one phenomenon were *passively* presented to consciousness altogether at a certain time differential, the acts of identification and of comparison would be impossible. We cannot enter here into the important psychological and epistemological question that arises in this connexion. Compare the remarkable discussion of these problems (and of association also) by M. Palágyi in *Philosophische Wochenschrift*, 1907, vols. vii. and viii.

[2] The word "continuous" therefore must be understood here in a rather wide sense. Space is continuous, but so may also be called the series of cardinal numbers.

reason that *every* single element of it must be said to influence the next, and to have been influenced by the preceding one. We now shall get a result of greater importance, if, at this point of the analysis, we take advantage of the different character of the constituents of our process with regard to *spatiality*. Only the first and the last phenomenon of our process were spatial ones, what there was between them was only in time but was not objectified in space. Thence it follows that spatial phenomena may be univocally connected by phenomena which are not spatial; the latter forming a group by themselves.

What we have described and considered here is practically the view taken in common life, with the only exception that common life regards spatial phenomena as absolute realities, and not only as realities to the Ego.

Science now will tell us that our analysis has been very incomplete, that we have regarded our body not as an organism, but as something that is extremely simple.

β. THE SAME CASE IN A SCIENTIFIC FORM

Let us then try to complete scientifically our study of the phenomena which are immediately given to me during my acting; let us consider my body as an organism playing its specific part in this particular series of phenomena as a consequence of its organisation; but at the same time let us never forget that we are analysing at present a certain series of phenomena presented to my consciousness, to my Ego, and nothing else.

An Hypothesis

The organism then, *my* organism, may be looked upon as playing its full rôle. I now must beg you to allow me a certain hypothetical liberty at the very beginning. In order that a full and complete analysis of those of the phenomena concerned in our process which relate to my body may become possible, let us make a supposition, which, in fact, is not true, but which easily may be imagined to be true without exceeding the limits of our present researches. We shall assume that we are able to touch every single element of our whole body, including the brain and the nerves. It is true, we cannot in reality touch our own brain at any point, but it seems to me that there is no objection in principle to assume the possibility, as in any case brains in all their parts are what we call tangible things.

The Case Once More

After these preparations let us begin to analyse the phenomena of the smoking lamp once more. Let us imagine that we possess a complete knowledge of all physiology, but that at the same time we do not forget for a single moment that we have to do with phenomena in respect to my Ego and with nothing else.

The optical phenomenon of the smoking lamp—the "optical lamp"—is again the starting-point. Physiology tells us that this lamp first affects the retinas of our eyes; from the retinas an influence goes out to the optic nerves, and from these to parts of the brain. But let us stop here a moment; how could the "optical lamp"—to put it briefly

—be the antecedent of processes of which it is notoriously the effect? In other words, how could the optical lamp influence the retinas and the nerves, since we know that our seeing the lamp as an optical image *follows* the irritation of these parts of our organisation? It would be an absurdity. We therefore must *not* begin our analysis with the "optical" lamp, but must begin it with something else. Certainly a "lamp" may be assumed to exist as the first link of the phenomena in question, but, briefly speaking, it is a "tactile" lamp, tangible say by my left hand; this *tactile* lamp, as a constituent of immediate Givenness, influences my retina, also taken in the tactile sense, which may be admitted at least in principle. Stimulation of my "tactile" —or at least tangible—optic nerve follows, and then follows stimulation of my tactile brain, and only at the end of all these processes is the "optical" lamp given to me.[1] It is a *smoking* lamp; and now this smoking calls forth the whole series of conscious phenomena mentioned before: identification with former cases of smoking, remembrance of their unpleasant effects, desire to stop smoking, remembrance of past cases of such stopping, of the means to effect

---

[1] Our whole instance might be reversed, of course: the "optical" lamp might be the beginning of the process studied and the "tactile" lamp the end. In this case all the processes of the nerves and brain would have to be considered as "optical" also. But the whole example would become rather clumsy in this case. A good instance of this class would be a wasp that flies upon my hand and is then removed by "myself." The reader is advised to analyse this example by himself. The phases of the "continuous series" would be these: (1) "Optical," *i.e.* "seen" wasp; (2) optical skin affected, *i.e.* changed; (3) optical sensory nerve affected; (4) optical part of brain affected; (5) "tactile wasp" experienced. All the subsequent phases (identification, association, will, moving the hand) are the same as in our instance discussed in the text. Of course the new instance would force us to assume hypothetically that we can *see* our nerves and brain—at least by means of a mirror.

THE DIRECT JUSTIFICATION OF ENTELECHY 273

it, attention to the construction of the lamp, comparison with known types of construction, noticing of a certain screw as an important thing, specific will to move this screw, feeling and seeing my hand moved: the optical lamp ceases to smoke.

γ. THE DIFFERENT TYPES OF ELEMENTS IN GIVENNESS

Spatial and Non-spatial Elements

It now seems to me important to inquire which of all these phenomena may be regarded as *spatial*, that is to say, as being extensities in *any* sense, whether in the tactile or in the optical sphere.

There certainly is a *continuous* series of phenomena given to consciousness, leading from the givenness of the tactile lamp through the stimulation of retina, nerves, and brain as tactile phenomena, through my seeing the "optical" lamp, and through very many other phenomena down to the moving of my hand as a phenomenon that is optical and tactile at the same time. Moreover it is very important to notice that the single constituents of this continuous series *follow* one another with the predication of univocal necessity. The "optical lamp" *follows* the tactile phenomenon in the brain, which for its part has *followed* the tactile phenomenon in the optic nerve, and the "optical lamp" is *followed* by the phenomenon of identification. But it is by *no* means clear from the very beginning that this continuous series must consist of phenomena of tactile and optical, that is, of *spatial* character exclusively. On the contrary, introspective analysis shows most distinctly that the opposite is true. The first process that relates to the brain, following the stimulation of the optic nerve, we allow to be spatial, *i.e.* noticeable as being tangible in some way. This phase in consciousness is then followed by "seeing" the lamp, which was only "tangible" before, that is by a conscious act which is spatial also, but belongs to quite another class of so-called qualities. Now the first processes of remembrance and identification appear; the smoking lamp is regarded as "similar" to smoking lamps of the past. There certainly is nothing of a "spatial" character in this process of comparison as such, even if the images of lamps formerly experienced, which are among the pre-requisites of identification, are regarded as spatial. Here follow the remembrance of how unpleasant the effects of smoking may be and the wishing to stop smoking. All these processes completely lack the characteristic of spatiality or extent. The moving of my hand is the first spatial process again, at least for the unscientific observer, though the scientific physiologist will tell us that this process follows a certain change which is spatially related to some part of the ("tactile") brain, and that between these two there occurs a spatial phenomenon relating to some motor nerves, *i.e.* centrifugal nervous conduction. Careful psychological introspection might still add that a certain optical imaginary idea of my moved hand is intermediary between proper willing as such and that change in the brain on which nervous conduction and actual moving finally depend.

Would it then be advisable to separate all those phenomena of our conscious series which are spatial in any sense from those which are non-spatial? It seems to me that another kind of distinction would lead to more important results: this distinction starts from the fact that *three different portions* of phenomena may easily be distinguished in that part of our continuous series of conscious events which begins with the stimulation of my retina and ends with the moving of my hand.

The Elements of Givenness in their Relation to the Brain

The *last spatial* phenomenon of the *first* of these portions of the continuous line of conscious events is a certain phenomenon relating to the brain as a "tangible" thing following the irritation of the optic nerve. The *first spatial* phenomenon of the *last* portion of the series of conscious events is again a phenomenon relating to the brain. But the *middle* portion of that series had nothing to do with the brain whatever, though also this middle portion of the conscious series is composed of different links following one another univocally.

Thus the being or not being related to the brain, or rather to my body, gives a very clear reason for dividing the conscious series, so far as it begins with the stimulation of my retina and ends with the moving of my hand, into three different portions; and at the same time we notice that the phenomena belonging to the first and third of them are all spatial, whilst the second portion, beginning with "seeing the lamp," consists of spatial and non-spatial elements.

Now it seems to be very important at this point of our analysis to inquire whether we could not say a little more about the *last* phenomenon of the *first*, purely spatial, portion of our conscious series and about its relation to the *first* phenomenon of the *last*, purely spatial, portion of it, both of them relating to the brain as a spatial something.

Spatial and Non-spatial Elements among those which do not Relate to the Brain

But first we must analyse a little further what is meant by saying that the second portion of our continuous series of conscious events consists of spatial and of non-spatial elements. Indeed, the middle portion of our conscious series, which does not relate to the brain at all, does *not absolutely* lack the characteristic of spatiality. Its first and its last elements certainly do not lack this characteristic, the first of them being the "optical lamp," and the last, as we have said, probably a certain optical idea of my moving the hand; and some of the so-called associative phenomena concerned in "identification" and "finding-similar" are spatial too. But nevertheless, there remains a fundamental difference between the last phenomenon of the first portion of our series and the first phenomenon of its second portion, in spite of their both being spatial. The first phenomenon of the middle portion of the series does not relate to the brain in any way, but *is the lamp* as an optical phenomenon; and a similar relation holds between the last element of the middle portion, the optical idea of moving my hand, if compared with the first phenomenon of the last portion of our series which relates to the brain again. Thus we understand that the middle portion of the conscious series, so far as it relates to spatiality, does so in quite another sense than do the first and the third portions,

THE DIRECT JUSTIFICATION OF ENTELECHY 277

which relate to spatiality exclusively. Spatiality comes into account here only in the sense of a relation to so-called external " things " or imaginary " ideas " of things, but not to the " brain " or any part of " my body."

The last element of the first portion of our conscious series is univocally followed by the middle portion of it, and first by its first element, the " seeing the lamp " ; not, however, by this first element alone, but thereafter by all the rest of the middle portion. Here we are faced by a very important problem.

δ. THE CONNEXION BETWEEN THE CEREBRAL PORTIONS OF ELEMENTS

The Last Cerebral Element of the First Portion. Relations to the Scientific Analysis of Acting

The principle of univocal determination [1] demands that the *last* phenomenon of the first portion of our series, relating to my brain, *be such* as to allow the whole of the non-cerebral phenomena of the middle portion to *be such as they are*. But what is the consequence of this? We here come into close relation with some analytical results gained already in another part of our lectures, though from quite a different point of view. Whilst dealing with the analysis of action as a phenomenon in Nature, we gave the name " historical basis of reacting " to one of the chief features upon which acting rests: acting not only depends on the individuality of the stimulus which is present but also on the specificity of all former

[1] I do *not* say the principle of "causality."

stimuli and all effects of them. We said that in psychology the words "association," "memory," "experience," "abstraction" and so on are generally used to signify what can only be called "the historical basis of reacting" by the true naturalist. But at present we *are* dealing with "psychology" of the most exclusive nature, for all that *is* is regarded as psychological in our present consideration. The second portion of our conscious series now shows us fully developed what from another point of view had been included in the one phrase of the "historical basis." And so we understand that the ultimate event that relates to the brain in the first portion of our conscious series must be such as to allow the "historical basis" to come into manifestation. Now, on the other hand, this "historical basis" has been created by series of phenomena similar to the one we are studying; that is to say, *cerebral* phenomena were also included in these series: and thence it follows that the ultimate process of the first portion of the conscious series we are studying, whenever it acts at all in such a way as to awake the historical basis, must be *different*, say, on the fourth time of its going on from what it was the first, second, and third times. But, as all the *former* steps of the first portion of our conscious series are *not* different the fourth time from what they were the first, second, and third times,[1] they cannot bear in themselves the sufficient reason for the becoming different with consecutive repetitions of the *ultimate* phenomenon of that first portion. Therefore the reason of this becoming different *must* lie *in the brain* itself as a phenomenon. A certain ultimate process of the first portion of any conscious series

[1] Except perhaps in as far as "functional adaptation" comes into play.

of our type—a cerebral process—is thus proved to become different each different time of its happening, because the brain itself has been changed by the *former* happening of this process; and the brain has changed in such a manner as to allow the second portion of the conscious series to go on as it does. Therefore—the lamp is not only "seen" but is also *identified* as a lamp, and reminds me of all my former experience.

In other words, as in our former chapter, we have here stated again what is to be regarded as actually cerebral in the phenomenon of the "historical basis" and what is not. The brain is certainly important; it manifests, so to say, the elements of the historical basis; but it does not use them. Its manifesting property may some day probably be shown to depend on so-called physico-chemical peculiarities. In this sense, *but in no other*, may mechanical foundations of "memory" be spoken of.

On "Identification"

The question may arise here whether the second portion of our conscious series—beginning with "seeing the lamp" in our instance—may not be broken into parts by single elements which are "cerebral." Might not so-called association, happening at different points of the second portion of our series and most decidedly at the beginning, where the "seen smoking lamp" is "identified" as being a smoking lamp, might not this association be the immediate consequent to a cerebral antecedent, *i.e.* speaking idealistically, to a conscious elemental event referred to "my brain," as the last element of the first portion of the whole conscious series was? A detailed discussion of this problem would belong to so-called physiological psychology. I only mention here that there are strong reasons, it seems to me, which allow us to deny *a limine* such a possibility. As to the "identifying the lamp," it must be kept in mind that we here have not *two* psychical events, firstly, the seeing, and secondly the identifying, but only *one* ; the lamp seen the second time *is quite immediately* a different thing psychically from the lamp seen the first time. There is no need therefore to refer to the brain in the *midst* of the second portion of our series. It was for this reason that we said the *brain* must have been altered by a "first" stimulus with respect to its reacting to the same stimulus the second and third time. I fully agree here with the excellent analysis of "reconnaissance" given by Bergson.[1]

The "Intra-psychical Series"

But let us return to the three portions of our conscious series. The first of them, as we now have learned, ends in such a cerebral act as will allow the second portion to go on in its specificity ; and this second portion, of course, ends by allowing the appearance of the last portion. The second portion alone is not of a cerebral character at all, but at both its ends it is connected with cerebral phenomena. There are very important consequences resulting from this fundamental relation.

First let us try to find a proper terminology for the

[1] *Matière et Mémoire*, Paris, Alcan. Rehmke, on the other hand, though a partisan of the "interaction" theory, regards what we shall call the "intra-psychical series" as permanently broken by cerebral acts; compare his *Psychologie*, and his excellent little book, *Die Seele des Menschen*.

second portion of our conscious series as contrasted with its first and third portion.

It is well understood, I hope, that in the whole of the present discussion we have only been dealing with phenomena of consciousness: we have studied how one state of my consciousness is influenced by a former one and influences a later state; in this respect *all* of our objects have been "psychical" ones. But, in spite of that, the psychical phenomena we have studied differ from one another in so far as their first and their third portion consist in conscious phenomena which have the peculiarity of being objectified by the Ego as relating to what is called "my body" and "my brain" in particular, whilst the second portion of the series of our phenomena is not objectified in such a manner, but is either objectified to so-called "other things," the lamp for instance, or not objectified at all. Without forgetting, therefore, that the phenomena we study are without exception psychical, let us give the name of "*intra-psychical series*" to that second portion of the whole of our conscious series of subjective events which does *not* stand in relation to *my* so-called body in any respect.

ε. THE DIRECT PROOF OF VITALISM

And now let us abandon our strictly subjective view and let us look upon the Given as science does. We, of course, have no intention of taking a leap into realism; the "Given" will not cease to be a phenomenon to me, but we now shall call "Nature" or "the Objective" that part of the sum of phenomena presented to me which I am forced to relate to so-called bodies in space; and out of this "Nature" we in the first place study "my body" as the most immediate object in biology.

My Body as my "Object"

If we now try to relate the results of our discussion to "my body" in this sense of "my object," we find the most remarkable fact that certain processes which we are forced to regard as going on in my body may show a *gap* in the midst of them, *so that there exists a point where their consecutive univocal line is interrupted in such a manner that it is impossible to understand its second half from its first half*, as far as bodily processes—*i.e.* conscious phenomena objectified as relating to "my body"—are concerned. There is "reality" between the two halves as far as states presented to consciousness are reality, but there is no reality between them as regards "my body."

From our subjective point of view we gave the name "intra-psychical series" to that line of conscious events which fills the gap in the whole of the phenomena; from the point of view of natural science we are not allowed to do so, we are not allowed to mix up psychical elements with phenomena which have been objectified into so-called physical ones. But now there must be created some sort of *scientifically* legitimate correlate to the intra-psychical series of the *subjective* point of view as advocated before. Here then we meet our old friend the "*psychoid*" again, a sort of entelechy as a *natural* factor.

We thus have shown on the mere basis of subjective or introspective analysis that *vitalism is not only possible but necessary* as far as "my body" is regarded as an object of biology. From the point of view of strict idealistic epistemology, which studies "Givenness" without any metaphysical assumptions at all, the phenomenological series of conscious states related to my body is *broken* by a series of states which cannot be related to that body in any sense. Psychology can fill this gap in the bodily world by the "intra-psychical series"; *science* has to restrict itself to saying merely [1] that there *is* a natural factor concerned in the events going on in my body, a factor which is an "intensive manifoldness" and may be called "psychoid."

Thus phenomenological idealism leads *by itself* straight on into vitalism, at least for one single object of biology—my body.

Other Living Bodies

It now remains for us to pass beyond the limits between "my body" as a natural object and other living realities, in order to establish our directly proved vitalism in the most general form; and this transition is by no means difficult. The first step leads from my body as a phenomenon objectified into a constituent of Nature to the bodies in Nature which are very similar to mine: to the bodies of other men. We have actually proved that the behaviour of my body in Nature cannot be understood by a mere

[1] Modern authors very often do not appreciate clearly this state of things. Everything we know about is "psychical," they say, and in this way a real "monism" or "psycho-monism" is the end. That is certainly true, but is at the same time of no use to natural *science*. Natural science deals with objectified spatial phenomena, and its only aim is to discover the principles and laws that are valid for these. Therefore with regard to spatial phenomena exclusively the problem of "mechanism or vitalism" arises. That the *complete* series of phenomena which are immediately presented to consciousness is not a "mechanistic" series—even if the word "immediate" is understood in an enlarged meaning—is self-evident; the terms "mechanism" and "vitalism" lose their meaning in *this* field.

combination of single events relating to extensities, and thence it follows by analogy that the behaviour of the bodies of other men will also not be explainable in such a way, that to account for it a sort of intensive manifoldness, an entelechy or psychoid, must also be introduced. So we reach quite the same conclusion, by our new and direct method, as we have reached already indirectly, by analysing action as a natural phenomenon. The next step leads from men to higher animals which show at least some similarities in behaviour, and we even may be led to the lowest organisms in this way as far as their behaviour in acting is concerned. But, of course, such a method of demonstration would fail as soon as phenomena of the instinctive or metabolical or morphogenetic kind are studied, and it is here that the indirect proof, as applied by us in so many of the previous lectures, is the only one admissible.

"Understanding" Vitalism

The present rather subtle discussions have not been undertaken with the object merely of proving vitalism as a fact of theoretical biology; I hope at least that this has been done sufficiently by our previous analytical researches. Our object is philosophical in this section and not merely scientific: we did not want here to prove vitalism but to *prepare its epistemological justification*, which is much more. If in fact we have got a direct sort of proof of the autonomy of life-phenomena, or at least of some of them, by a mere analysis of phenomenological Givenness, by an analysis of the complete series of conscious events as such, by an analysis of self-consciousness, in other words, we can fairly claim that now we *understand* vitalistic becoming on the basis of our most intimate psychological experience. The Ego feels itself to be the vitalistic agent. So the common view asserts, and so our analysis has shown.

This "self-feeling" and "understanding" will form the starting-point of what is to follow.

In fact, the common opinion about life-phenomena, which of course is neither analytical nor theoretical in any sense, claims that "I" can move my body by my "will," and that every living being has a so-called "soul" by which it can do the same. This view, suggested by ordinary unscientific experience, can now be said to have been transferred from a non-analytical and non-theoretical to an analytical and theoretical sphere, and to have been proved and psychologically justified in this sphere. In fact, "I" am a link in the univocally determined series of phenomena, so far as I "will"; my volition is both influenced and influencing.

I am conscious of this faculty of my willing in quite an immediate manner, not through experiences but only on the occasion of experience. And this experience, which, so to say, awakes my knowledge of willing, is always of a very peculiar sort. Whenever any state of the phenomenological reality is either liked or disliked, my volition comes into action as far as seems suitable in this particular case. And I am conscious of yet more concerning my power of willing: I know that by my will there can result external events which end in typical complications of elemental realities, and that these complications are not referable in any way to other complications pre-existing in space.

My power of volition is thus the only immanent and

a priori means of my consciousness by which I am able to understand how the happening of specific complicated results without pre-existing external specifying causes is possible. It has often been remarked already that certain other most general terms relating to what is given have a similar origin. For instance, I only understand "causality" as the necessary relation between a certain earlier and a certain later state of events in space, because I am able, so to speak, to feel causality, or, in particular, "force." Again, I "understand" reality in the form of "substance and inherence" only because I feel the permanence of my Ego in spite of its varying states. In exactly the same sense I feel that I am a willing agent as far as the origin of the Complicated out of the Non-complicated is concerned.

At this point our analysis will be resumed in the next chapter. But at first we must leave pure analysis, and must enter into very important discussions of a polemical nature.

2. Polemical Part

The theory of so-called psycho-physical parallelism negates what we believe we have proved. It asserts that as in any and every natural phenomenon so in man's actions also there is an *unbroken* series of bodily, of physico-chemical causality; that there is no non-bodily part of events filling the gap between two bodily parts; that mechanical causality runs throughout the brain as a bodily, *i.e.* material system.

a. THE IMPOSSIBILITY OF THE VARIOUS CURRENT FORMS OF PSYCHO-PHYSICAL PARALLELISM

Parallelism has assumed two chief forms, one of them decidedly realistic and metaphysical, the other pseudo-idealistic.

Metaphysical Parallelism already Refuted

The first form goes back to Spinoza. One unknowable reality manifests itself in two unbroken independent but parallel series of events, the psychical and the physical series. Both of them are complete in themselves, there is no interaction between them. It affects the completeness of the psychical side, though not the unbrokenness and completeness of the physical series, if a certain concession to metaphysical materialism is made by regarding the psychical as a mere "epiphenomenon" of the physical.

This form of parallelism, of course, being metaphysical throughout, cannot be refuted by an immanent introspective psychological analysis like ours, but can only be refuted by general considerations, or by showing on the basis of so-called objective happening that the completeness of the physical series does not exist. By the latter means we have already refuted parallelism in our analysis of action.

As to general anti-parallelistic arguments, let me add in the first place to what was said before [1] Lotze's argument that it is impossible to regard the "soul" as a parallel resultant of single mechanical events, since a "resultant" in the clear, *i.e.* mechanical meaning of the term always relates to the effect of forces acting upon *one and the same* material element. Besides this the *strict* parallelistic theory, maintaining the completeness of *both* its "sides" or "aspects" of the Real, may be refuted by showing that it leads to absurdities of a very remarkable kind. Only the psychical acts upon the psychical, only the physical upon the physical, so the theory advocates. But this implies that any and every inorganic event or state has its "psychical" counterpart, which, of course, is simply absurd. Rickert [2] has well observed against parallelism that, according to this theory, the effect of alcohol on the human mind would be not the effect of C_2H_6O but of the "psychical" that "corresponds" to C_2H_6O. C_2H_6O as such would only act upon the human body. It seems to me that there is no reason whatever to assume that every inorganic event or state "represents"

---

[1] See page 115, note 1.   [2] *Festschrift für Sigwart*, 1900.

something psychical. Inorganic events, to a certain extent at least, always are sums; but psychical events are not. This alone, it seems to me, overthrows strict parallelism and may even be regarded as refuting *every* kind of parallelism. It is not in any way intelligible how the movements or changes of the parts of a mechanical or energetical system, that is, of a system which is notoriously a mere aggregation of its parts, could be "accompanied" by a something, or could be the "Erscheinung" of a something that is quite certainly not an aggregate. There is nothing like "wholeness" in any mechanical system except in a purely formal geometrical sense. On the contrary, it is the chief characteristic of an energetical or mechanical system that every event occurring in it is independent of the whole, and only dependent on its own immediate conditions and cause. If part of a machine of any kind whatever is broken or disturbed, single events may go on well and typically in the unbroken and undisturbed part. For this reason a mechanical or energetical system—a "machine"—though it may well be the *result* of the manifestation of an intensively manifold whole, can never be its parallel or "Erscheinung."

Pseudo-idealistic Parallelism Refuted

The second form of parallelism pretends to be idealistic, but is, in fact, realistic and metaphysical also. All so-called reality is regarded as being phenomenological, as "being" only with regard to a subject. But this subject is not identified with "my Ego" exclusively, but an indefinite number of possible subjects is assumed to exist. The parallelistic statement then is as follows: What are perceptions of things or conceptions of any kind whatever for myself, that is to say for subject A, are movements or changes of energy and potentials in the mechanical or physico-chemical system called the brain for subjects B, C, D, and so on.

Strict idealistic criticism must object to this doctrine, that nothing about the real and absolute existence of the subjects B, C, D and so on is known or even knowable. Thus the theory fails as an " idealistic " one.

Besides that there is one very remarkable difficulty in this doctrine, which may best be formulated shortly in the following way. A sees a lamp, B sees the corresponding movements in the brain of A which are supposed to be parallel to A's seeing; but B's act of seeing must have a corresponding parallel itself in the brain of B; this movement in the brain of B may be seen by A again; then this new act of A's seeing must have a cerebral correspondence which only " is " as far as it is seen, say by B; and so on, *ad infinitum*. In short, pseudo-idealistic parallelism, granting that reality is throughout phenomenological, but at the same time maintaining the " existence " of different subjects, is driven into absurdities. A new " psychical " parallel is always found to be wanted on going to the bottom of the matter, and this want of a new parallel never ends.

In this respect the plain metaphysical parallelism is clearer, operating as it does with the Physical and the Psychical as two types of manifestations of the Real.

Parallelism Impossible on a Truly Idealistic Basis

Let us now return to the sphere of strict idealism, chosen as our basis of analysis, and let us see whether there be any possibility whatever of the parallelistic doctrine on such a foundation.

We simply ask: is it imaginable or thinkable in any fashion that to my "seeing a lamp" or to my "thinking $(a+b)^2$" there corresponds parallelly a movement or a change of energetical intensities in my brain? To "correspond parallelly" means to "be simultaneous with"; to "be," on the other hand, means "being perceived by, or at least being perceivable to myself," if strict idealism is maintained. We know already that in principle at least my brain as a whole may rank among the things perceivable.

Then we have the following chain of events as postulated by the parallelistic doctrine, each link being checked by idealism. I see the lamp; at the very same moment, I either see or touch a specific fact in the brain as my object. But this "perceived fact" is most obviously not my "perceiving the fact";[1] for the latter a new perceivable fact or change in the brain is required, the perceiving of which requires another fact or change, and so on—just as in our analysis of parallelism founded on a pseudo-idealistic basis. There is a series of postulates with regard to "parallels" which never ends.

We can express the whole problem still a little differently. I see the lamp after the occurrence of all the changes in the retina, the optic nerve, and the brain that I have

[1] The "perceived fact" may be green, but my "perceiving the fact" is certainly not green.

perceived, let us say tactually, before. But *I know* that, before I could perceive in any form the cerebral parallelism that is supposed to accompany my seeing the lamp, there must *first* have been a perceivable change in the retina and nerves, or the tactile skin and nerves. These must be changed *before* I *can* perceive the cerebral change that corresponds to my seeing the lamp. Thus the so-called parallel effects would always be *late* with regard to that to which they are said to be " parallel "—in other words, there would be no parallelism at all.

Thus on the basis of strict idealism the parallelistic theory is a simple impossibility.[1] *Idealism therefore strictly implies that the series of bodily causality with regard to my body when I am acting is broken.* In other words : *Idealism implies vitalism in a certain field of reality.* We repeat : it is for this reason and for no other that we "understand" vitalism.[2]

We have shown by an analysis which was free from any metaphysical prepossessions whatever that the willing " Ego " plays its elemental part in my acting, and we have now proved by another analysis, similar to the first but polemical, that any kind of " parallelism " is impossible on the basis of idealism, pure or impure. Our arguments, of course, hold good on an idealistic basis

[1] There are many authors that have not realised this truth. Verworn, for instance, in his *Allgemeine Physiologie* begins by establishing pure idealism, then concludes wrongly that all science is psychology (comp. page 283, note 1)—as he does not see that the Given consists of two parts, only one of which is objectified in space—and at the end, strange to say, rejects vitalism and advocates the physico-chemical explanation of life most emphatically.

[2] Compare the various writings of H. Bergson (*Essai sur les données immédiates de la Conscience*, 5th ed., Paris, 1906 ; *Matière et Mémoire*, 1896). There are many points of contact between his and my way of regarding reality and life in particular.

THE DIRECT JUSTIFICATION OF ENTELECHY 293

exclusively; that is to say, they only hold good if "being" is regarded as equivalent to "being perceived or concerned by a conscious subject." As soon as any metaphysical concessions with regard to absolute or independent being are made—and we ourselves shall make them anon—our arguments fall to the ground. But in that case our analysis of action takes their place.

β. A NEW FORM OF PARALLELISM

If finally we turn back to the part which "my body" and its "psychoid" play in objectified nature, that is to say the part which they play as the objects of natural science, we are met at the first glance by a rather strange difficulty, or rather ambiguity.

My body and the part played by it were first considered as phenomena to the Ego only, just like volition, judging, etc.; afterwards my body was understood as belonging to objectified nature, though also within the bounds of idealism. What was the intra-psychical series in the first case became the psychoid in the second. Of course, the intra-psychical series was an immediate experience of consciousness, whilst the psychoid is only a concept, or better still a conceived factor in nature, created to fill a gap in the chain of events, which otherwise might exist in objectified nature, as has now been proved both indirectly and directly. The direct proof of its "existence," in the sense of phenomenal objectification, has been based in part upon the impossibility of the parallelistic doctrine—and now apparently our discussion ends in a sort of parallelism again! For there can be no doubt that the immediate conscious experience of the intra-psychical series is "parallel" to the part played by the psychoid. But, in fact, this "parallelism" is quite different from what is called so in common practice. We regard it as impossible to accept parallelism in its common form, namely, in the sense that the intra-psychical series might be paralleled by a series of events composed of single conscious acts of the type of so-called sensations, or, speaking objectively, by events of the mechanical or energetical class. But our new sort of parallelism does not assert anything of the kind. If for once we allow ourselves an excursion into metaphysics, *i.e.* an assertion about the hypothetic character of absoluteness—as in fact we shall do to the full extent at the end of this book—we may say that the intra-psychical series, or briefly "the Psychical," "the Conscious," is parallel to, or rather an epiphenomenon of a certain metaphysical happening (unexplainable in detail, but most certainly not resembling anything mechanical, not even by analogy) which interferes with the metaphysical correlate of so-called mechanical reality.

Conclusions

Among all the living bodies in Nature there is certainly one whose vitalistic autonomy can be proved directly, viz. "my body"; its "psychoid" being the immediate correlate of the intra-psychical series, as soon as the introspective point of view is changed for the point of view of natural science.

In these words the chief results of the present chapter are summarised.

The argument brought forward here against the doctrine

THE DIRECT JUSTIFICATION OF ENTELECHY

of parallelism and establishing the discontinuity of material causality by idealistic introspection, though it occurred to me independently before I had any knowledge of the existing literature, cannot claim to be quite new. You will find it in a somewhat different form in Busse's work entitled, *Geist und Körper, Seele und Leib*, where the whole problem of parallelism is discussed critically at great length, with reference to the opinions of the majority of psychologists and philosophers; and you will also find it in the writings of Leclair[1] and Bergson,[2] not mentioned by Busse.

But what is new, I believe, is my connexion of the direct refutation of parallelism on the idealistic basis with vitalism as a general doctrine. *By* refuting parallelism, and *by* establishing the Ego as acting by its will, vitalism *is* established, at least for *one* natural body—my own.

Let us carefully note that to refute the parallelistic doctrine is by no means to establish the independence of the Ego's willing or of the psychoid's manifestations of mechanical or energetical constellations in the brain. On the contrary, we know that a very close mutual dependence exists here, and we have tried to discover what it is. But dependence and parallelism are two absolutely different things.

And now we are prepared to pass from psychology to epistemology.

[1] *Der Realismus der modernen Naturwissenschaft*, Prag, 1879.
[2] See page 292, note 2.

B. THE CATEGORY "INDIVIDUALITY"

a. CATEGORIES IN GENERAL

Definitions

I "UNDERSTAND" vitalism, for "I" am a vitalistic factor myself.

In the same way I understand causality in Nature, and pushing and pulling in particular; for I can accomplish pushing and pulling in Nature with parts of my own body.

And I understand what an unchangeable substance is, with its changeable attributes, since I feel myself such an unchangeable enduring substance in spite of the changeable phenomena present to my consciousness.

So far vitalism would seem to be psychologically justified, and it would only require some further analysis to realise what my understanding of vitalism really implies.

Is any other kind of direct and positive justification of vitalism possible?

Mere psychological self-analysis can only afford a rather uncertain and doubtful conviction, it seems to me, with regard to what happens in "Nature" irrespective of my own acting. It is true, what I immediately feel whilst acting gives me a clue to understand certain phenomena observed in Nature, but that would always remain an understanding

THE DIRECT JUSTIFICATION OF ENTELECHY 297

by mere analogy, and there might be very many types of phenomena in Nature which would be unintelligible by this means.

You all know what an ontological category is. A category is a constituent of the irreducible conceptual scheme according to which reality becomes the object of human consciousness. Whilst Aristotle and the medieval logicians regarded categories as the unchangeable characteristics of absolute objectivity, Leibnitz, Locke, Hume, and Kant put the conceiving mind in the place of that objectivity, and thus brought the whole question into the subjective sphere.

Of course we can only say a few words here about the different problems—by no means solved to universal satisfaction at the present day—which relate to the epistemological nature of categories.

A category is a certain concept or proposition which is applied in any attempt to understand the Given. It seems to me that there is hardly any doubt with regard to the mere presence of such categories in the human mind. Even Hume and his modern disciples would not deny it, though they see nothing more in the categorical system than the mere effect of a "habit" or an "economy" of the mind, which may be strengthened by "inheritance." We ourselves do not believe that individual habit or economy would have been able to endow the categories with the character of *absolute* validity which they undoubtedly possess—at least with regard to the subject; and to admit any kind of "inheritance" with regard to them would seem to us both metaphysical and self-contradictory, for the concept of inheritance is itself a result of categorical conceiving.

Fundamental Difficulties

At this point we are led to some rather difficult considerations. The categories allow of statements regarding so-called objectivity which cannot be denied, which must be admitted as soon as their meaning is understood: in *this* logical sense they are *a priori*, *i.e.* prior to ordinary experience. Even the concept of objectivity itself, with its relation to subjectivity, is due to them. But the categories are not prior to ordinary experience in the temporal sense: they are awaked *during* the process of conscious experience, but are logically *a priori*, since they are "awaked" only and are not induced or inferred. They are independent of the *amount* of ordinary experience.

So far there is hardly any difficulty of a serious character.

The question now arises: Are the categories properties which are inherent in the conscious Ego in such a way that the Ego is forced to conceive Givenness with their aid exclusively? Is the Ego in possession of certain innate properties? This view, recently styled rather inappropriately the theory of "psychologism,"[1] was held by many of Kant's successors; it is much in vogue nowadays, and Kant himself must be said to have made certain concessions to it, at least in the first edition of the *Kritik*, though his chief intentions went in another direction.

Without any doubt I feel forced to apply the categorical system when I conceive the Given and in particular Nature;

---

[1] This name would be good with reference to ordinary psychology as an inductive science. But it is a little ambiguous, as the name "psychology" also *might* be used in a very wide sense, embracing the knowledge of everything that is related to mental life in any sense, including epistemology, ethics, and aesthetics.

I feel convinced that there would be no experience about Nature at all without my possessing this system. And yet so-called "psychologism," as the ultimate foundation of the categories, it seems to me, is wrong.[1]

It is wrong, but *not* (as Kant himself supposed in the second edition of the *Kritik of Pure Reason*, and as many of his modern followers say) because on a mere psychological basis of apriorism the character of objective and universal validity would be wanting to our aprioristic statements. Objective and universal validity in an *absolute* form *is* in fact quite unattainable by the human mind, to which "universal" validity will always remain a question of its subjective conviction controlled by what the majority agree to.[2] The categories therefore, though they "objectify," do not guarantee "objectivity" in an absolute sense; these two derivates of the word "objective" have been very often confused. But any "psychological" basis of apriorism, that is to say, any foundation of the categories that rested upon *ordinary* "psychology" in any sense *is* in fact not sufficient; nay, more, it is *illogical throughout, because all ordinary psychology itself rests upon the categories.* To say that a something called "my Ego" is *forced* to apply its

[1] Here and later on, when referring to absoluteness, the reader will find my epistemological point of view changed to a certain extent, as compared with the epistemological chapters of my *Naturbegriffe und Natururteile* (1904).

[2] I fully agree with those of Kant's critics who maintain that Kant *himself* regarded his "transcendental deduction" as sufficient to refute "psychologism." But it is another question whether Kant was right to think so. It seems to me that the ultra-psychological foundation of the categories can *only* be demonstrated by the argument in the text and not by means of Kant's transcendental deduction, and that absolute objectivity can only be introduced by a certain other argument that will interest us in the last part of this book. Absolute objectivity is quite certainly unattainable by means of Kant's "deduction"; the *Bewusstsein überhaupt* is nothing but "my" fiction.

categorical properties implies *necessity*, which *itself* is a *constituent* of the system created by these " properties," and to conceive the Ego as the *bearer of properties*—to say nothing of the term " innate " properties, very much out of place here—would be to apply to the Ego the category of substance-inherence, which also forms *part* of the categorical system. Thus, in order to explain what categories are, psychologism uses certain of the categories themselves! The Ego as a " substance " is the *result* of my categorical reasoning, and " being forced " has an intelligible meaning only on the basis of the categorical system itself! Therefore *my* establishing the categories, at any rate, cannot be founded upon psychology.[1]

But what are we to do in the face of this enormous difficulty?

An Irreducible Kind of " Experience " the Foundation of Categories

All that the categorical system allows me to say about the Given is logically prior to ordinary experience and therefore not ordinary experience itself. But what about my discovery, or rather my becoming conscious of the categorical system itself? The discovery of this system is quite certainly not " experience " in the ordinary meaning of the word, not " experience " in the sense of inference, but is it not experience in a certain *most general* sense? Is it not the becoming consciously convinced of a certain something?

[1] What about " other " subjects? Compare the next section (β) with regard to this strange problem, which cannot be discussed here at greater length.

Kant founded his *Tafel der Kategorien* upon the different possible forms of judgments; judgments being regarded, so to say, as objectified reasoning. Was it not a certain kind of "experience" to become convinced that these forms of judgments were possible? And would it not be a certain kind of "experience" to discover by introspective analysis immediately what kinds of elemental concepts and relations pertaining to Givenness are quite inevitable to my mind?

Thus, I think, we may be permitted to say in a very neutral form that the categorical system is revealed to me by immediate analytical "*experience*" of an absolutely *irreducible* kind. This sort of "experience" simply states, "The categories are valid as they are," and at the same time expresses the conviction that all science, *including psychology*, rests upon the categories, and that even such concepts as "Ego," "Subject and Object," "Reality," form part of the categorical system. We shall soon have a good opportunity of verifying what we have learned, in a special case.

A Few Remarks on Categories and Ordinary Experience

The categories are established in the conscious stream of immediate Givenness—in the irreducible form of "experience" just described—but once acquired they are capable of directing the conscious subject, systematising in this way all further truly empirical ordinary experience; for we only understand the Given as far as it is formulated categorically. Thus categories become *axiomatic*. Indeed, all concepts and propositions in science, so far as they are based upon the categorical system, ought to be called axioms; the word "postulate" being reserved for certain suppositions with regard to contingent constellation in Givenness, as will be shown by analysis later on.

Categories may also be said to create scientific themes, whether these themes may be solved easily or with difficulty or never. The theory of matter is a good instance of a categorical theme that is, so to speak, half-solved. It will be important for our future discussion to keep well in mind that the existence of categorical themes and their solution are two absolutely different things. But the very nature of the categories implies the confidence that this solution is not impossible.

The Problem of the System of Categories

Now the further question arises : Is there any relation discoverable among the single constituents of the categorical system ? In other words: *is* this system a real "system," is it one whole ? Kant himself did not make any attempt to show that only these kinds of categories *can* exist and no others. His "deduction" only proves the *general* fact of their being founded upon the various forms of judgment and their being pre-requisites of ordinary experience. Hegel's system of the categories, on the other hand, founded upon his dialectical method, does not guarantee completeness and does not clearly separate primordial and derived categorical concepts.[1] But, no doubt, it will be the chief task of the philosophy of the future to establish a rational system of the categories in the place of the mere aggregative systematics of the present day.

[1] The same is true of the categorical systems of Hartmann and Cohen, and of many others of minor importance.

THE DIRECT JUSTIFICATION OF ENTELECHY

We now shall study the theory of the categorical system with special regard to our bio-philosophical purpose. Our task does not require a complete analysis of this system—however desirable it might be—but will be accomplished by the discussion of two main classes, the categories of relation and of "modality" in the terminology of Kant.[1]

β. THE CATEGORY OF NECESSITY

Let us begin with a few words about one category of the latter class, which seems to us to stand at the head of all: *necessity* or *univocal determination*, which has been shortly discussed from a narrower point of view on a former occasion.

All that "is," "is" of necessity, whether immediately or mediately derived from other necessities. This axiom, expressed in the concept of "function" in its widest, say in its metamathematical meaning and connected in some way with the logical principle of identity, embraces all others. Therefore it is much wider than the axioms of substance-inherence, causality, and so on, in short, than any axiomatic statement with regard to any special kind of relation.

Vitalism, in what form soever it appears, must be subject to it, as we know already, and need not repeat here.

The Fundamental Paradox

But necessity only relates to Givenness. We here reach a very important point, already mentioned in a more general

[1] We do not mean to say that we agree with Kant's system of the categories; in the first place, we are far from allowing that his four main groups are *co*-ordinated with one another. But to open up here the problem of the categories as such would complicate our special theme in an unnecessary manner.

form, when we were dealing with the character of the categories. My "thinking necessity" cannot be regarded as "necessary," and therefore, as we have said, the categorical system cannot be founded upon ordinary psychology—it cannot be "founded" at all, it simply "is." A very strange antinomy meets us here: my "thinking" as a conscious act is not subject to necessity but creates necessity, but your thinking and, strange to say, my own "having thought" are elements of phenomenological Givenness to myself and may even be a very real element in Nature, in the form of a book, for instance. My "having thought" and your thinking are therefore necessarily and univocally determined with respect to my "thinking." Is therefore *my* "thinking," are any of my "actings," *qua* actual and present actings, *free*? On a previous occasion we maintained that the psychoid cannot be regarded as "free" in its manifestations, because it is an element of Nature; we were dealing then with the psychoids of *others*. At present I am dealing with *myself*, not even with my psychoid but with my "thinking."

"Freedom" a Mere Negation

Of course, this is not the place to discuss at full length the philosophical problem of problems, and therefore I only say that, in my opinion, we *may* speak of the "freedom" of *my* thinking or of any of my mental acts in a *negative* sense, in the sense of non-necessity. But our reason is unable to conceive anything positive under this expression. For we are so obliged to conceive under the form of necessity that, as we have said, even my "having thought," as soon as it belongs to the past, must perforce be looked upon as necessitated. We regard it perforce as if the natural equivalent of my Ego, my psychoid, had contained the sufficient reason for it, though, it is true, we only know about this reason *after* its manifestation. And this holds for *all* manifestations of psychoids in " others " : it is always *post factum* that we know about the reason of any of their manifestations ; we simply throw back the accomplished fact upon a " faculty " of the psychoid and then say it is " necessitated " by a something that was by no means known to us before. There can be no doubt that our reason *is* limited in this way.[1]

Freedom thus escapes analysis altogether,[2] for " analysis " would mean subjection to necessity.

γ. THE CATEGORIES OF RELATION

Our proper and final conception of vitalism will be based upon a study of the categories of relation, and thus

[1] I refer to Bergson's profound reflections on "*liberté.*" I doubt whether he has solved the problem. "Intuition" is not a legitimate solution. As he says himself, we are all born Platonists ! Even the "élan vital" *must* be conceived categorically if *clearly* conceived.

[2] In no other field may the antinomy of the concept of necessity be better understood than in the field of morality. I know that my past actions have been univocally determined, and yet I feel free whilst acting and may judge about my past actions that they "ought not to have been " ; in short, I feel responsible. And I make other people responsible for their actions in spite of my knowing that their actions were necessitated. It is true, with regard to others, "pardoning" on account of inevitability is generally regarded as a sign of a high moral level, and thus the antinomy may seem to be solved here. But is pardoning *myself* an act of morality ?

Almost all moral philosophers have searched for a solution of this antinomy on metaphysical grounds. No other solutions indeed seem possible. Personally we must confess that the solution offered by Schopenhauer appears to us better than any other. To a certain extent—but only with regard to the starting-point—this " solution " is identical with the Kantian one.

we enter upon the chief part of our whole bio-philosophical system.

We have learnt in a former chapter of these lectures that entelechy, though not a substance in the proper meaning of the word as used in the inorganic sciences, resembles "substance" in so far as it endures in spite of changes; and we have also learnt that entelechy, though it is not causality in the proper meaning of the word, resembles causality in so far as it determines changes in nature with univocal necessity. We may say that entelechy is causality and substance, but that it is also something more, that entelechy implies causality and substance, just as causality implies substance because it cannot be thought of without a bearer that endures in spite of all change.

What then "is" entelechy categorically? There seems no place left for it, at least in the categorical system of Kant, where so-called "interaction," "Wechselwirkung" in German, takes the third and last place among the categories of relation.

Introspective Psychology and the Categories of Substance and Causality

In the first place, let us study a little more intimately the way in which the categories of causality and substance come to consciousness and acquire their bearing on science.

Categories, we know, render "experience" possible with regard to all that is given except themselves, they being "experienced" immediately and irreducibly during our becoming conscious of Givenness. Categories, in other words, create nature so far as the latter is a cosmos instead of a chaos; the cosmos is systematised in science. Categories are brought to consciousness by only a limited amount of acquaintance with Givenness, but, as soon as they *are* brought to consciousness, they direct consciousness in all future experience of Givenness: the systematisation of nature by means of categories thus becomes a "problem."

It is by psychological introspective experience that categories are, though not created, yet *most immediately* awaked. The category of substance is brought to consciousness in this immediate way by experiencing the permanence of the Ego during the change of the consecutive conscious states; the category of causality becomes conscious, whenever I feel that I move bodies in nature by the movement of parts of my body, which is a body in nature itself.

By mere *analogy* at first the categories of substance and of causality are applied to the relations of bodies in nature *among one another*, without relation to my body; psychological self-experience thus being the connecting link between the categories and objective nature. One body pushes the other, so it is said, because it is in possession of a moving "force," just as "I" am in possession of such a "force." It is only by degrees that categories become applied to external nature *directly*; in other words, that they are strictly conceived as "categories." Theoretical mechanics in fact has to a great extent freed itself from the physiological so-called "anthropomorphic" connexion between the categories and external Givenness.

The category of substance thus became the foundation of all theories of matter, the category of causality became the foundation of dynamics in *any* of its forms, whether classical or electro-dynamical. And the category of causality, as we have said, must be formulated here in such a way as to imply substantiality in a certain sense—though it is more than substantiality.[1]

Inorganic events can thus claim to be "understood" by means of the categories of substance and causality, the word "understand" being used here in a sense higher than the merely psychological.

The Problem of a New Category of Relation

Are there no categorical means of understanding vitalism in the same way as mechanics or energetics were understood? *Would our analytical discussions about vitalism and entelechy have been possible at all if there were no such categorical means?* The question itself, in fact, seems to offer us a key to its solution.

It seems to me that we encounter here a very grave defect in the categorical system of Kant. To put it shortly: among the categories of relation the place of his "Gemeinschaft" or "Wechselwirkung," which only is a sort of commentary on causality, has to be taken by a quite different kind of category, and this new category must be such as to allow of the scientific analysis of life. It is true, in the *Kritik der Urtheilskraft*, Kant most fully discussed the concept of "teleology," but he did not regard it as a category, but only as of a certain "regulative," not of any "constitutive" importance. That this is wrong will be demonstrated by showing what is right. Kant was too much a Cartesian with respect to our problems. Eduard von Hartmann, as far as I know, is the only philosopher

[1] Once more we repeat that "energy" is not substance, but only a standard of measurement of causality (see p. 162). The substance that exhibits causality would be the ultimate units of matter.

THE DIRECT JUSTIFICATION OF ENTELECHY 309

who most decidedly established "finality" as the third real category of relation. But we shall develop our views without reference to the discussion and terminology of this author.[1]

Unlike causality, "teleology," considered purely as a kind of description, never relates to single phenomena in nature as such, but always applies to the spatial or temporal combination of phenomena in its specificity. We ask "for what purpose?" whenever we see anything happen that bears on the realisation of a certain *typically combined* whole, "typical" either on account of any kind of symmetry or on account of its existence in indefinite exemplars. We ask this question—in particular the simple uneducated man asks it—because we know that there *does* exist at least *one* elemental *combining* factor, manifesting itself with regard to nature—our own *will*. But what does this mean except that our experience with regard to this one factor has awaked a certain category which now seeks for further application, just as did the categories of substance and causality, which at first belonged to introspective psychology exclusively? It is very interesting to note in this connexion that among primitive peoples and in the child the new category, here in question, plays a far greater rôle than causality: all facts in nature which relate to any kind of constellation being conceived as due to

---

[1] When this chapter was already definitively written I learnt from the *Logik der reinen Erkenntnis* of Cohen that this author regards the concepts "purpose" and "individual" as true categories. But he does not draw the conclusions, it seems to me, that ought to be drawn from such a statement, and his theory of the Organic, therefore, does not go beyond a sort of Kantianism: mechanical causality remains the ultimate effective and constitutive principle of nature, the two organic categories he introduces do not serve to formulate natural agents of a new and special class.

elemental principles of willing, or rather as facts forming parts of some constellation that is foreseen. In this way nature becomes "animated." Later on causality overshadows the new category—at least in so-called science. But can it ever overshadow it in practical life? Does the materialist really regard his parents and friends and children as mechanical systems?

But if there *is* the way open for a new category carrying in itself its proper intellectual theme, why not formulate as strictly as possible the real *science* of this category?

I hope we have tried already to begin this work.

δ. THE CATEGORY "INDIVIDUALITY"

Previous Preparatory Work

In our last lecture, whilst analysing my own acting immediately, we formulated scientifically facts which every human being knows: we showed how the new category is awaked to consciousness by introspective psychology. And in our so-called indirect proofs of vitalism we discovered certain types of constellations of natural phenomena which needed the application of a new category of relation, besides substance and causality, if they were to be understood at all.

What did we actually do in our discussion of the differentiation of the harmonious-equipotential system? We formulated the problem like a mathematical equation, and by discussing the precise nature of the problem we found the solution. A certain "unknown," our "E," was introduced as if it was found already, and then we showed by analysis what this unknown might stand for and what it might not. It was found to be irreducible, autonomous, and not an aggregate of extensities. These were all negations, and could only be negations in the realm of the categories of substance and causality, as the necessary relations between changes in spatial nature.

Negations now become affirmations after psychological introspective self-analysis has awaked a new category. Entelechy now becomes a *positive* concept, created as the manifestation of the *new* category that was wanted. We now " understand " entelechy. The ultimate results of our indirect proofs of vitalism—though they are by no means superseded by the "new category"—acquire their proper intelligible meaning only at the moment when the foundation of entelechy upon a special category of its own is appreciated.

In truth, we *have* worked already on the theme established by the new category without knowing it quite consciously. We studied the question whether a certain new category came into action in this special field of nature or not. But that implied the semi-conscious conception of the new category. Otherwise it would have been impossible for the whole problem about the mechanical or non-mechanical character of life to have been formulated at all! I venture to say that the mechanists also march under the banner of the new category which they deny. They know a certain manifestation of it from themselves, and then ask: " Is the category also at work elsewhere? " They would not like to find it elsewhere, but that they regard it as a possibility is shown by the very fact that they discuss it, which otherwise would be meaningless.

"*Individuality*"

I propose to give the name of *individuality* or *constructivity*[1] to the new category we are studying here. This name would seem perhaps to require some justification and explanation. It was chosen in order to render the aspect of the category as little psychological and anthropomorphic as possible. In fact, by saying that "individuality" leads to individual construction and is elemental in itself the rôle of this category seems better expressed than in any other way. Some special category we *must* have in order to acquire any systematised experience about specific and typical constructions at all; there would not be *any* such experience without it.[2] The construction itself may be spatial or temporal or both; that is to say, the whole of the construction may be a typical order of elements in space or in time or in both; no matter, its logical aspect remains *construction of individual wholeness* in spite of its being composed of parts.

---

[1] At the end of the "Beweis" of his "Dritte Analogie der Erfahrung" Kant uses the word "Composition" instead of his "Gemeinschaft" or "Wechselwirkung." Does it not look as if he had here perceived the *true* third category of relation?

[2] This is not the place for a real "deduction" of the category of individuality. I only say here that it might easily be discovered as an analogy to a certain class of judgments, or rather of the logical elementalities concerned in judgments, just as Kant discovered his "table of categories." But judgments would have to be studied *completely* for this purpose. Strange to say, this has never been done either by Kant or by Kantians: the *final* judgment ("in order that," "damit," "afinque") has always been overlooked. And yet it is irreducible! The disjunctive judgment, which belongs to another main group altogether, has wrongly taken its place.

"Finality" a subclass of Individuality

The categorical concept of causality, at first awaked in the form of the faculty of pushing and pulling, needs a great deal of refining, so to say, in order to become useful for natural science; in the end pushing and pulling appear only as *sub*classes of causality. So it must be with the category of individuality: it needs sifting scientifically, anthropomorphisms must be eliminated, and at the end of this process the special kind of "constructivity" known to myself by introspection will only appear as a *sub*class, as in causality. This subclass of constructive individuality, apparent in *my* acting, alone deserves the names of *finality* in the proper sense, or purposefulness or teleology: here alone is the "*finis*" consciously anticipated in a clear and distinct manner, and here alone does it account for the special type of each *single* phase of what the "individual" factor performs. In a certain sense we even might apply the name of finality to each *single* performance of such a totality of occurrences as acting is.[1] You will remember in this connexion that with regard to morphogenetic entelechy it was only by descriptive analogy that we applied the words "willing," "judging," and "knowing."

[1] Bergson (*L'évolution créatrice*) denies "*finalisme radical*," the term being understood, as far as I can see, in the sense of a general plan of the universe in every detail. At the end of this book we shall do the same. But Bergson also objects to "*finalité*" as a principle of life; he puts his "*élan vital*" in its place—granting that it resembles "finalism" more than mechanism. I think that our "individuality" meets the point—but I consider it as a category and believe that Bergson also found nothing but a new category by his "intuition." Individuality, in fact, rests upon a sort of "intuition" as far as *all* categories rest upon it. Bergson only analyses phylogeny; in ontogeny *le tout est donné*—and *yet* there is "vitalism." Compare my article on Bergson in *Zeitschr. f. d. Ausbau d. Entw.-lehre*, ii. 1908.

ε. CERTAIN DIFFICULTIES IN THE CATEGORICAL CONCEPT OF INDIVIDUALITY

Well-known difficulties crop up in the ontological concept of causality. Of course, it cannot be our task here to mention them all, and so it may be enough to remind you of such problems as the *actio in distans*, the "seat" of a force, the time between cause and effect, the boundaries between two bodies in pushing, and so on. The infinitesimal calculus was invented in order to overcome these difficulties, which to a great extent are difficulties of space-analysis; for causality always relates to changes in space exclusively; both cause and effect are spatial changes.

We therefore must not be astonished, it seems to me, if now, whilst entering upon the scientific refining of the category of individuality, we meet with quite a number of difficulties at once, though almost all of them are quite different from those which appear in the analysis of causality.

An Analogy to a Mere Functional Conception of Causality

If we were satisfied with a mere functional conception of nature—as certain modern authors pretend to be—that is, with a conception of nature which simply states on what elemental natural factors any being or happening univocally depends, without distinguishing different kinds and degrees of necessary dependence, the difficulties we should meet would not be very numerous. We then might simply reason as follows :—

The whole process by which individuality manifests itself may be called the process of individualisation. We study the question: What are the factors determining the precise events at a given moment t of the process?

Let $\phi(E)$ be the psychoidal or entelechian factor itself, E denoting the "end," and the function $\phi(\ldots)$ denoting that not "the end" itself but something depending thereon is at work. Let s be the state, *i.e.* the amount of the whole constructive individualisation already accomplished, and let a be some specific alteration of this state coming from without. Then the events B at the moment t would be expressed by the formula: [1]

$$B = f\,[\phi(E), s, a]$$

If it can be shown that $\phi(E)$ cannot be resolved into other elements it follows that some factor based upon the category of individuality is at work.

But all this would not amount to very much; it would be far too summary, so to say.

No "Causa Finalis"

Let us begin our further analysis by referring once more to our formula.

We have written $\phi(E)$ and not E; this implies a very important statement indeed.

We know already that our entelechy is no kind of causality, though it resembles causality. A cause is only a change in space which univocally determines another change in space; entelechy therefore is not a cause. But what then of the famous "*causa finalis*"? Simply this, that the term is completely absurd without further explanation. In the first place, as we know, there is no *proper* "*causa*";

[1] This formula will be found discussed at full length in my *Localisation morphogenetischer Vorgänge* (1899) and in my *Organische Regulationen* (1901), p. 172.

and in the second, how could *the end*, which is not yet reached but is *to be* reached, be an acting factor at all ? The " end " determines entelechy to be what it is : for instance, it determines a psychoid in its specificity by so-called imagination ; but " the end " does not act : the " having the end in one's imagination " acts !

Entelechy and Causality

But is it really true that neither entelechy nor any factor similar to it is causality ?

It simply is true by reason of definitions, and the definitions correspond to irreducibilities : causality relates to singularities only, but entelechy has to do with the construction of complexes which are unities. And besides this : a *causa* is spatial like its effect, but entelechy is not spatial, though its effects are. We thus may say that with reference to spatial *effects* the category of individuality *implies* causality in a certain sense, just as causality implies substance. But there is no identity at all ; and, on the other hand, entelechy is by no means " causality seen from behind," as is occasionally asserted by those philosophers who have not realised that individuality or teleology is as true a category as causality, able to establish really elemental and irreducible natural agents.

We shall get a still more explicit idea of the relation between individuality and causality, if we remember that all factors created on the basis of individuality—such as entelechy, for instance—are *intensive* manifoldnesses. That is to say, they are composite, though not in space, and their single—but merely conceptual—constituents, *qua* single, act into space. In so far as the *single* manifestations of the *single* constituents of the intensive manifoldness entelechy are concerned, there is something like a "cause," though an extra-spatial cause. Now the principle "no effect without a cause" remains true: there indeed is *something* single responsible for this single spatial effect in all spatial manifestations of entelechy, but it is the manifestation of an element of a composite intensive unity. And the converse is also true: every single change *in* space may be a "cause" and have its "effect": but this effect will not *always* be in turn a spatial change. It may also be a sort of affection of a single constituent of entelechy, which then will lead to some kind of manifestation of it. Thus the chain of causes and effects is unbroken—but part of it is unspatial. We have proposed to apply the name of finality to those singlenesses in a manifestation of individuality that take the *place* of causes in the manner described, though they are not "causes" pure and simple.

In *this* way individuality "implies" causality.

Entelechy Supra-personal

As entelechy is unspatial, the question "where" entelechy is, is meaningless. Entelechy is the individualising agent, but it would be just the reverse of truth to assume that there are in space as many entelech*ies* as there are individuals, or so many kinds of entelech*ies* as there are different forms or types of individual entelechian manifestations.[1] This would be wrong, for the simple reason—besides many others—that in many cases there might be formed two or

[1] If, in spite of this, the word entelech*ies* occurs in the text on many occasions, this is only for the sake of terminological simplicity. For instance, the phrase "forces and entelechies" means, strictly speaking, "forces and acts of manifestation of entelechy."

more individuals out of one by an artificial separation of parts. In this sense entelechy, though individualising, is *supra-individual* itself—as E. von Hartmann pointed out most clearly—or may rather be said to be " supra-personal."[1]

ζ. CATEGORIES AND FACTORS IN " NATURE "

Before turning to our most important task, namely, to show how the category of individuality may serve to establish a clear and distinct class of agents or factors in *nature*, the concept of " nature " with special relation to the categories requires a general analysis.

" *Ideal Nature.*" The " *Ontological Prototype* "

All the elemental constituents that science operates with are modelled and formed according to the categorical system, each of them corresponding to a special ontological category of relation. Specificities with regard to quantity, quality, space, and time serve to give the definite character to each constituent, and the general notions of actuality and possibility complete the picture. Thus the constituents of nature, which are known as " mass," " force," " potential energy of distance," " constant," etc., are created.

All these instances are such as occur in the sciences of the Inorganic; only the two categories of substance and of causality are at work here, as far as ontological relation is concerned.

The system of all these constituents and their relations

---

[1] Bergson also has seen this point. He adds that, considered as "*finalité*" the organic finality would be "*externe,*" as even in ontogeny the whole is formed by the self-limitation of totipotent parts. I believe that these difficulties disappear from our new *categorical* point of view. Comp. p. 313, note 1.

THE DIRECT JUSTIFICATION OF ENTELECHY

in general *is* "ideal inorganic nature" in the scientific meaning of the word. Ideal inorganic nature as a whole corresponds to the totality of possible relations which may be established from the point of view of pure ontology or "transcendental logic" in the sense of Kant, always in combination with the simple categories of quantity, quality, space, time, actuality, and possibility.

On the basis of all the categories just named a certain number of irreducible *principles* of relation, a certain number of "*ontological prototypes*," as they might properly be called, are established, and the task of science is to co-ordinate natural Givenness with these ontological prototypes.[1] Natural Givenness can only claim to be "understood" so far as this co-ordination has been successful.

Now all inorganic nature, as the total system of all the constituents at work in it, is *in space*; and all potentialities, such as potentials, potential energies, constants, have their proper spatial locality. "Causality" then means that one spatial change is univocally followed by another.

Organic Nature

The category of individuality quite certainly allows of creating elemental constituents *with regard to* spatial nature,

[1] Kant maintained, as is generally known, that his "transcendental logic" rests upon the faculty of "synthetic judgments *a priori*." It may appear questionable whether in fact this concept meets the point, and whether it would not be more advisable to speak of the faculty of establishing a certain system of irreducible *concepts* as the fundamental faculty of reasoning, all proper "judging" *a priori* being analytical. But I agree that this would only be another explanation of the same fundamental *fact* of consciousness. Poincaré, in his *Science et Hypothèse*, advocates the view that a good deal of so-called synthetic apriorism is analytical, since it simply rests upon definitions. This assumption, it seems to me, though not wrong, is certainly incomplete. The question arises: "Why are there just these definitions and no others?"

but *not* "in" spatial nature. This is the most important characteristic of this category. Therefore all constituents of external nature created on the basis of individuality, such as entelechies and psychoids, are completely and absolutely *unimaginable*. All that is imaginable must have spatial characteristics, and it is quite impossible to form an imaginable idea of something that is manifold but not in space.

All constituents of nature the ontological prototype of which is based upon individuality can only be conceived but never imagined, though their effects are realised in imaginable nature. All entelechies and psychoids are νοούμενα in this sense, but they are not νοούμενα in the transcendent sense of Kant, for they are constituents of the world of φαινόμενα, as far as the "world" they relate to is given to the Ego. Thus entelechies, though transcending the realm of the Imaginable, do *not by reason of their logical character as such* form constituents of metaphysics in the sense of something absolute and independent of a subject.[1] Even morality, if there were need to assume yet another new kind of category to be at work here, would not depart from phenomenality in the widest sense.

Thus, whilst we conceive "nature" as *the totality of what may be related to spatiality in any way*, and include in nature vitalistic principles, acting, and morality, all of which indeed relate to spatiality, the whole analysis of so-called objective Givenness acquires a far more

[1] Once more I repeat, that entelechy is not identical with "consciousness" or "the Psychical." Even if we were to proceed from our methodological critical idealism ("solipsism") to metaphysics, entelechy and psyche would not be identical, though they might then be nothing but two forms under which one and the same reality is expressed. Comp. also p. 294.

coherent aspect than it does under the views of orthodox Kantians.

With Kant, as with a Cartesian in this respect, nature is only *in* space; the "moral world" is a world by itself, and life receives a very ambiguous position altogether. The whole of Givenness is broken into two or even three parts, and this is the more regrettable, because one part of it, morality, is transferred to the sphere of νοούμενα, or intelligible things in the transcendent sense, the absolute intellectual inaccessibility of which had been affirmed just before; and because a second part, life, is at least said to be inaccessible to "science." Thus the three parts of Givenness appear quite irreconcilable.

In opposition to this Kantian doctrine it seems to me that the concept of *nature* must be enlarged, so that "nature," always in the sense of objectified Givenness, consists of one completely spatial and one only partly spatial portion.[1] The logical process, in fact, on the basis of which the concept of a "force" as an irreducible

[1] Only in this way, it seems to me, do the chapter of Kant's *Kritik*, "Möglichkeit der Causalität durch Freiheit, in Verbindung mit dem allgemeinen Gesetze der Naturnotwendigkeit" and the "Erläuterung" following this chapter, acquire a really clear meaning, even from the point of view of the "analytical" part of the *Kritik* itself. Kant's "Freiheit" only has an understandable sense if conceived as a non-mechanical and non-spatial form of determinated and *natural* happening—just like our entelechy. Nothing metaphysical comes into account here as long as acting is studied as an element in Givenness. As to "my" acting and "my" thinking see page 304. That the so-called "antinomies" of Kant's "Dialektik" are not really such, has often been noticed. All of them are capable of being solved *within* the range of Givenness and do not touch at all the problem of the "Absolute." Mind within the range of Givenness is more perfect than Kant allowed it to be. Also the problem of the finiteness or infiniteness of the universe is very understandable and soluble within Givenness, and does not perforce relate to something else. It was a mistake of Kant to connect his "thing-in-itself" with all sorts of problems about pure Givenness.

constituent of ideal nature, and the concept of an "entelechy" as an irreducible constituent of ideal nature are formed, the first with the aid of causality, the second with the aid of individuality, is exactly the same so far as spatiality is excluded the second time. Let us not forget that even a force or a potential energy or a constant, though they are *in* space, are not immediately imaginable but only conceivable; they are "realities" in the sphere of the conceptual world, but only express *possibilities* with regard to the real in the sense of *immediately* imaginable Givenness. The sphere of reality has to be enlarged in order to embrace them. It is just the same with entelechy, except that entelechy has no spatial localisation.

If we may be permitted to say a few words about our concept of morality in this place, we find the Kantian conception of "nature" untenable once more. How could morality have any meaning whatever to a human being, if it were to relate to something not only quite inaccessible to science, but even, as Kant claims, *absolutely* unknowable and undiscussable, and not to a something that forms a part of Givenness in the widest sense? It seems to me that morality *is* Givenness itself—if it were not, it would be undiscussable. Morality, *i.e.* the application of a categorical concept of a special and elemental kind to the actions of other men and oneself, relates to "nature" in our enlarged meaning of the word. Therefore, moral acting is natural acting, at least part of it, and it is very misleading to oppose morality to nature: morality is part of nature itself.

Conclusions

Thus we may finally say that entelechies and psychoids *are* as truly as are potentials and constants—they all *are* not immediately, but only in an enlarged meaning of the word. They all *are* as products of the intellectual elaboration of Givenness: all of them, and morality too, are parts of *one* system, which some day may be revealed to humanity in its completeness, and may then receive its metaphysical interpretation.[1] *Nature* is *one*, whether it be merely "natura naturata" or also "natura naturans," to speak in the terminology of the scholastics. And Life is "understood" by the concept of entelechy just as well as is inorganic nature by the concepts of energy, force, mass, etc. There is no need of further "explanation."

In a certain sense we may say that all conceptual constituents of nature are created in order to understand logically the singularities of Givenness as being subsumed to generalities: in this sense also there is no difference between the natural agents which only "relate to" and those which "are in" space.

---

[1] It seems to me that many modern philosophers, exaggerating certain mistakes of Kant, tend to subdivide philosophy, that is "knowing," into a number of branches, entirely lacking in connexion. Psychology and logic, logic and ethics, nature and the "intelligible world," science and history, are regarded as being respectively quite apart. It seems to me that nothing can be farther from the truth than this. Experience is *one*, and Givenness is *one*, and philosophy as the understanding of Givenness by "experience" must be *one* also, whether the different branches of "experience" follow their separate methodological path for a while or not. But this is not the place for a system of philosophy. The reader will note, I hope, from various remarks, that we regard as very nearly related psychology and epistemology and logic, science and history, nature and morality.

η. RATIONAL SCIENCE

Though a theory of epistemology is not the theme of these lectures, yet the connexion of constituents of nature, based upon categories, with immediate Givenness, requires a few words of explanation.

Rational Science and " Ideal Nature "

All science that goes beyond mere description and empirical classification deserves the predicate "rational," for it is "science" only so far as it is based upon the characteristics of reason. These characteristics of reason are the faculty of forming categorical statements that may be concepts or propositions, and the faculty of concluding from premises. The raw material of science, of course, is immediate perceptible Givenness in space and in time. This raw material is transformed by "science" into the concept of *ideal nature* in so far as categorical statements, say ontological prototypes, are connected with mere spatio-temporal inductive generalisations. Whether this connexion is possible at all and within what limits—that is a problem of a special kind, which we shall briefly discuss later on.

Rational Science and " Causal " Science

It is very far from the truth to regard rational and *causal* science as one and the same. But rational and causal science are in fact very often confused, and it seems to me that this logical error is due to the ambiguous word *explaining*.

In its legitimate use this word denotes the relation of the general to the singular. A single event in Givenness, say the fall of a certain stone with a certain acceleration, is explained by a generality resting upon a categorical principle—in this case by the law of gravitation. The generality as such is a "causal" one in this instance, and may be formulated by the use of the term "force," or "potential," or whatever you prefer.

But people also speak of "explaining" when they apply the category of causality—which has nothing to do with explaining singularities by categorically formulated generalities—to immediate givenness with regard to its *temporal sequence*. In this case the falling of the stone is explained if you know that it was pushed from a table by a child. In a logical sense there would not be a whit of explanation in this case, unless you were in possession of Newton's, or at least Galilei's law.

In short, the law resting upon a categorical principle *explains* falling in general, in the real sense of the word "explaining"; knowledge of the child's act *explains* a particular case of falling in quite a secondary meaning of the word. Causal "explaining" is always simply historical. It ought rather to be called "causal reference."

Ideal Nature and Natural Factors

It seems to me that the confusion of rational explanation and causal reference—so common nowadays—is almost always due to the following reasons:—Wherever laws of nature resting upon the principle of causality are the generalities which "explain," they do so not merely in their property of general statements in the sphere of mere ideal concepts, not merely as *constituents* of "ideal nature," but more particularly in so far as they have served to create typical *agents* or *factors* in immediately given nature. Thus the law of Newton is not only an expression of the generality of attraction, formulated with respect to quantity, but *by* the law of Newton we are entitled to endow the bodies here before us with potential energies and forces as parts of the *given* world in its contingent specificity. Though remaining in the domain of concepts we here proceed from a Platonic to an Aristotelian point of view. Thus, in our instance of the child pushing a stone from the table so that it falls, the *constituents* of the *general law* of Newton are concerned in any *factor* concerned in the causal series of events inaugurated by the child. The child not only pushes "a stone," but a stone endowed with a definite amount of potential energy with regard to the earth: it is for *this* reason that the stone will fall when in its course it leaves the surface of the table. But explaining and causal reference remain two very different kinds of necessary connexion all the same—one of them logical, the other ontological.

Now all we have said holds with regard to entelechy also. The concept of entelechy as an effective extra-spatial intensively manifold constituent of nature, based upon the category of individuality, *explains*, say, the restitution of the Ascidian *Clavellina* in *general*. The restitution, however, of the *particular* specimen before us is *referred* "causally" or historically, not by the mere act of my cutting the animal into two parts, and not even by my creating a special restitutive stimulus—unknown in detail—by the operation. The historical reference lies in the fact that my cutting the animal and thus creating a restitutive stimulus *affects a given organism that actually is the point of manifestation of a natural factor*, viz. of a certain form of entelechy, just as the child in our instance pushed not only "a stone," but a stone endowed with a specific potential energy.

By these considerations, it seems to me, not only the logical and ontological similarities between entelechy and the other natural agents have been put into the clearest evidence, but also the general relations between *laws* of "ideal nature" or "Platonic ideas" and *factors* in natural Givenness—as far as it is conceived and not merely immediate Givenness—have acquired a certain sort of final elucidation. A deeper analysis, of course, would belong to a theory of knowledge.

The Problem of Entelechian Systematics

Now, as to entelechy just as with respect to space there is still a third kind of "explaining." In this sense the typical features of a certain specific type of entelechian manifestation, say of a dog or a bee, may be said to be "explained" by entelechy as a whole. This new sort of explaining is nearly related to explaining in the real rational sense, though it is not identical with it. We approach the realm of this sort of explaining if we now turn to devote a few words to the problem of entelechian systematics, shortly mentioned already on another occasion.

It certainly is a problem whether or not the category of individuality would allow us to predict how many *types* of manifestations of entelechy—culminating in man—might be possible, and for what reasons these manifestations are what they actually are in fact, just as the category of space [1] allows

[1] It would be useless for our purposes to make a sharp distinction between the categories of "imagination" and the categories of ontology.

us to predict the number of regular bodies and their characteristics. Here we meet the problem of systematics once more.

No attempt has been made, so far, to answer the first of these questions, except a few rather fanciful constructions by the school of Schelling. In fact, it is difficult to see what the ground of division for a system of entelechian manifestations could be. It probably could only be gained from introspective psychology,[1] from an analysis of different types of volition; but that would not go beyond mere analogy at present.

As to the second question, the problem "why" these very singularities are connected in one unity, it is here that the third special kind of "explaining" above mentioned comes into play. The old French morphologists, Cuvier for instance, saw this problem; only E. Rádl[2] has seen it in our own day. It is the problem of necessary but non-causal connexion, which also plays its rôle in geometry, and in everything connected with geometry. "Explaining" would occur here on the basis of the "Satz vom Grunde des Seins" in Schopenhauer's terminology. But there exists not even an attempt at a solution of this fundamental problem.

A few aprioristic special statements with regard to different forms of entelechian manifestation, though *not* with regard to systematics, are indeed possible. It might,

[1] To a certain extent Bergson tries to derive the different types of organic beings—plants, echinoderms and molluscs, arthropods, vertebrates—from the character of his supra-conscious *élan vital*. This common source would also explain the harmonies among those types, especially that between plants and animals in general.

[2] See in particular his *Geschichte der biologischen Theorien*, vol. i., Leipzig, 1905; vol. ii. in preparation.

for instance, be predicted from the very nature of an organism, that it would restore itself, after disturbances of its organisation, *either* by regeneration *or* by re-differentiation, that is to say on the basis of *either* an harmonious- *or* a complex-equipotential system. But this aprioristic distinction is not gained from an analysis of entelechy as such, but from an analysis of the nature of the perfect organism.

θ. A FEW REMARKS ON THE PROBLEM OF TIME

We know that autonomous vital phenomena are founded upon natural factors and laws which we are able to conceive by the aid of a special category of relation, individuality. We know also in what relations these factors stand with regard to inorganic factors and laws and how they act with regard to space—they are non-spatial but manifest themselves in space. But one point of great importance has only been incidentally mentioned—the relation of entelechy to time.

Somewhat mysteriously I said in a former chapter[1] "being and becoming are united in entelechy," "time enters into the timeless," namely, into ideas in the Platonic sense. That is to say, entelechy, though an elemental ontological entity, cannot manifest itself completely in any case without taking a definite amount of time; and this, at the first glance at least, seems to be contradictory to the concept of a Platonic idea, which expresses the timeless, the non-historical *par excellence*.

Let us first consider the process of morphogenesis

[1] See page 149. Compare also my *Organische Regulationen* (1901), p. 204.

once more. Morphogenesis is a succession of typical stages; when one stage is perfect the next stage begins. The validity of these statements is not affected by the fact that, as the experiments of Klebs have shown, in so-called "open" forms, such as plants, the different stages may be lengthened or shortened or even completely suppressed under certain external conditions. In any case an embryo of a plant would not form a flower until it had formed its first leaves, the so-called cotyledons. Now we have said on a former occasion that the fact of there being consecutive stages in all morphogenesis may well be understood on the assumption that entelechy by its *having* performed stage A, *i.e.* by the spatial existence of A, is summoned to perform the next stage B. In this way morphogenesis would consist in a permanent interaction between entelechy and matter. But even then, the activity of entelechy always wants time in order to manifest itself completely. This is true even if the single steps in the process of an entelechian manifestation are regarded as *strictly instantaneous, i.e.* requiring the time zero.

As to acting, it is enough to remark that a conscious aim, say the creation of a work of art, is invariably reached by stages, one completed stage provoking the completion of the next stage. The psychoid therefore cannot manifest itself except in time.

And what about introspective self-experience? Is not the most immediate fact presented to the conscious Ego the fact of its own duration? Bergson, in fact, has made the concept of *la durée*—not *le temps*—the centre of all epistemology *and biology*.

The important question here arises, whether we shall

make the "Temporal" in any form a constituent of what we have called "ideal nature" or not. Ideal nature only "is" in the sense of an eternal, *i.e.* timeless, validity; it is *the* non-historical. The Temporal—so it seems—*cannot* have a place in this ideal world. Time is said to be properly a subjective phenomenon in the strictest sense; time seems to be, if you will allow me to say so, still "more" unreal than space is. But, on the other hand, there is nothing more "real" to immediate self-experience than duration; memory, the prerequisite of all experience, nay, of all knowing, ordinary and scientific, demands duration. Without the duration of my Ego, I might perhaps be conscious of single "Givennesses" in space, but they would be lacking in connexion; there would not be *one* Givenness, there would be a permanent forgetting: no change, no movement, no past and future—only the present. And there would also be no morphogenesis and no acting: there would only be stages, but, since stage A would be forgotten when stage B arrived, there would be no connexion between the stages.

But my Ego *does* endure, and I *do* conceive change and movement and morphogenesis and action—my own and other people's.

What then is to be preferred: my postulating an absolutely timeless ideal world and looking upon all realisation in time as a merely subjective thing—as a sort of imperfection of my conceiving that ideal world—or my immediate knowledge of duration, my knowledge of time as the most "real" of all realities?

There is no doubt that memory and duration are almost identical. And it is equally true that what, strictly speaking, is called *time*—in particular, scientific time—is nothing but a certain constituent of enlarged Givenness, conceptually invented and "measured" on the analogy of space, and by no means identical with immediately given duration. In this respect Bergson's analysis is fundamental. I may add to it a certain remark of Lotze's that time, in the objectified or scientific sense, saves us from assuming that instantaneous Givenness comes from and passes into nothing.

Would then duration be something absolute in the strict sense, and would entelechy, at least *my* entelechy, since it implies duration, be something absolute also? Then duration would really be a constituent of "ideal nature." On a later occasion we shall see that memory is indeed one of the few paths that tend to lead us towards something like absoluteness—though in another form than we are now speaking of. At present let us conclude these fragmental considerations by merely saying that to introduce duration into ideal nature would *not* be to introduce scientific time — time as defined by Kant—in the same sense as duration. The "Temporal" implied by entelechy would be objectified *duration*; and this is "timeless" in the scientific meaning of the word.

But let us regard the problem of "entelechy and time" from still another point of view. It certainly is one of the most *universally* known facts in biology that the adult organism is formed out of the egg by a *consecutive* series of processes, by a consecutive line of stages. And because this fact is known so universally and is observed almost every day, people—even scientific people—hardly realise

THE DIRECT JUSTIFICATION OF ENTELECHY 333

sufficiently how very strange this fact is. *Why* is not the adult formed in the egg by an instantaneous act of entelechy? You *cannot* reply to this question: "Because, of course, entelechy can only do one strictly single act at a given moment"; for in the differentiation of an harmonious-equipotential system entelechy does produce, though not the complete, yet a *certain* composite totality instantaneously,[1] and we all know that we ourselves are able to produce *certain* specific individual totalities of a composite character in strictly one element of time—*e.g.*, when we strike a chord on the pianoforte. We may even say that on account of this being so, the concept of entelechy was introduced. But again: *why* are there consecutive stages in ontogeny? *Why* does time enter into each manifestation on the part of entelechy?

We can only confess that we do not know. Theoretically, it would appear more reasonable if there were no such thing as "ontogeny." But, on the other hand, we all know that a painter, though he conceives or rather imagines the picture strictly as a whole instantaneously, and though he is able to produce *certain* composite totalities also instantaneously, is yet far from creating the complete whole in one moment. And this may serve us as an analogy; it may teach us something more about the dependence of entelechian acts—not of entelechy itself—on non-entelechian factors; for it is because he is dependent on his organisation and on many other things that a painter cannot paint a whole picture instantaneously. Indeed, only on the basis of some such dependence are we able to understand the existence of

[1] That totality which is produced on the basis of the *explicit* prospective potency of a certain organ. See vol. i. page 83.

ontogeny as a consecutive series of stages. The problem of "entelechy and time" may therefore be said to be partly solved by noticing the dependence of entelechian manifestations on inorganic means. But, I confess, this is only a partial solution.

Conclusions of Part II

SUMMARY

We now have tried to solve as far as we could the problem of " individuality " and the natural factors established by its aid, or, to speak in the usual terminology, the problem of teleology. Teleology is by no means " causality seen from behind," as many of our dogmatic philosophers maintain. Teleology or individuality is as elemental as causality.

The category of individuality entitles us to introduce into " ideal nature " a special kind of elemental constituents, and into given nature a special kind of elemental factors, which are unspatial but imply duration. Entelechy and the psychoid are types of them. We are entitled to introduce them since the ontological category of individuality is possessed by consciousness; for this reason life is really *explained* by entelechy.

Immediate psychological self-analysis shows us this category at work. With regard to objectified nature indirect proofs are required. Some such proofs have been found; they relate to typical and specific combinations in organic nature, which are typical and specific with regard to space, or time, or both.

Entelechy in a certain sense implies causality and substance; it may *counteract* true or inorganic or material causality, but it *acts*. Its chief performance is the augmentation of the degree of diversity of distribution among given elements; this action may also be formulated with regard to mechanics.

Entelechy *uses* matter and material causality for its "purposes." A material system in space left to itself will behave differently from what it would do if controlled by entelechy. In other words, spatial conditions form only a part of the sum of all conditions on which organic becoming depends. It is for this reason that all vital becoming strikes us as something that is new and primordial, though in fact the part played by entelechy does not imply creation but implies regulatory admission of pre-established possibilities only. This final statement implies that entelechy is *alien* not only to matter but *also to its own material purposes*. This, in fact, is a point of great importance: the concept of a "self-purpose" is contradictory in itself, even formally; a "purpose," as we know from a former discussion, is always a certain state of the surroundings that "ought to be" with regard to a subject external to it.

Therefore, at the end of all, the often mentioned difference between organisms and things made by art, with regard to the relation between the "material" and its "user," disappears: *material* and *user* are *two* entities not only with regard to objects of art and handicraft, but *also* with regard to organisms. For entelechy when at work in the organism —leading its morphogenesis or governing its motor organs— is also not "in" the material organism but only *manifests* itself in this material. The only difference then that remains between organisms and things made by art is the following: in products of art matter is formed *through* an entelechian manifestation pre-existing already, in morphogenesis and in the process of acting itself matter is affected *immediately* by entelechy. But in both cases non-spatial individualising entelechy is at work in the last resort, and entelechy is *external* to its "material."

The Method Applied

We now are at the end of our theory of the individual living organism, both scientific and philosophical.

In the first place, let me remind you again on this occasion of the path that we have followed during our long analysis and synthesis. It seems to me that the chief and most characteristic feature of our method—I might even say the feature which alone enabled us to pursue our theoretical construction so far as we have done—is the specific character of the concepts from which we started. These concepts were not "collective" concepts, as used in ordinary biology, not concepts such as "the cell," "the nucleus," "the gastrula," "secretion," "nervous conduction"; these only had their place in our introductory remarks. But the concepts we really worked with were of a very different character: "the prospective potency," "the equipotential system," "regulation," "the historical basis of reacting," "the individualised stimulus" are a few instances of the concepts that we employed. All of them are categorical concepts, concepts built up by a specific arrangement of pure categories; and to them we owe the possibility of reaching finally the realm of the pure categories themselves.

Definition of the Organism

And now let us briefly summarise in a special form all we have learnt about the organic living individual. Let us close our discussion with an *analytical definition of the individual living organism.*

As an object of science, or, in other terms, as a constituent of ideal nature, or from the point of view of enlarged phenomenalism, the living individual organism is a typical constellation of different elements which are each chemically and physically characterised; its typical constellation is preserved in spite of so-called metabolism, *i.e.* a permanent change of the material it consists of. The organism exists in innumerable exemplars; it exhibits the phenomenon of development and possesses as its most important properties the faculties of regulation, reproduction, and active movement. The character of all the properties or faculties the living individual organism is endowed with is such that the organism cannot be conceived as a constellation of inorganic parts which is inorganic *qua* constellation. There is something in the organism's behaviour— in the widest sense of the word—which is opposed to an inorganic resolution of the same and which shows that the living organism is more than a sum or an aggregate of its parts, that it is insufficient to call the organism "a typically combined body" without further explanation. This something we call entelechy. Entelechy—being not an extensive but an intensive manifoldness—is neither a kind of energy nor dependent on any chemical material; more than that, it is neither causality nor substance in the true sense of these words. But entelechy is a factor

THE DIRECT JUSTIFICATION OF ENTELECHY 339

of nature, though it only relates to nature in space and is not itself anywhere in space. Entelechy's rôle in spatial nature may be formulated both mechanically and energetically. Introspective analysis shows that human reason possesses a special kind of category—individuality—by the aid of which it is able to understand to its own satisfaction what entelechy is; the category of individuality thus completing the concept of ideal nature in a positive way.

This is a detailed analytical definition of the individual living organism.

PART III

THE PROBLEM OF UNIVERSAL TELEOLOGY

INDIVIDUALITY or teleology as a real ontological category of relation being established, the problem presents itself for discussion, whether its range of application with regard to Givenness in space or "nature" may not be wider than the mere biology of the individual organism.

To restrict the application of individuality in a dogmatic manner to this limited field would be equivalent to saying that natural agents of the entelechian class can only manifest themselves with respect to certain chemical compounds, of the albumen group in particular, and this, of course, would seem to be very strange and inconceivable.

In order to find out to which domains of nature individuality as a category may relate, at least hypothetically, we shall do best, I believe, to review once more the reasons which actually led us to set up the entelechian natural factors where we did.

a. RETROSPECT

We began with certain classes of natural processes which were of the type of *specific combinations* of qualitative and quantitative chemico-physical singularities in space and in time and which were repeated in an indefinite number of exemplars. These classes were first pronounced "teleological" in the descriptive sense of the word. The question then arose, secondly, whether the combination of these states and processes was such as to allow us to regard it as the outcome of another primarily given physico-chemical combination of a fixed character — as we understand the combination of processes in an artificial machine from the combination of its parts — or whether the specific combination of our objects was guaranteed in itself, *i.e.* immanent. In short: " Is the teleology of our classes of the 'statical' or of the 'dynamical' type?" With regard to morphogenesis, inheritance, and acting, the dynamical kind of teleology was found. Thirdly and finally, a special category, "individuality," was discovered, upon which our whole discussion had rested, unconsciously at the beginning, consciously at the end.

Consequences of the " Machine-Theory "

It is worth while to lay stress upon the fact that the category of individuality would have also come on the scene if the "machine-theory" of life had proved to be right, say for the case of morphogenesis. Even in that case we should have been forced to ask for an intrinsic reason of "individual constructing," if not for this actual machine A — the egg — yet for the other hypothetic machine B which is supposed here to have been the basis of its originating. And if this machine B again had proved to be the effect of another machine C, we should have asked for its reason of constructing, and so on *ad infinitum*. Thus even on the machine theory of morphogenesis the search for a really immanent-teleological or entelechian factor would have become a scientific *task*— an unending task perhaps. For, whenever we find typical constellations of the statical-teleological class, we are forced to conclude that there must *have been* in some former time some autonomous intrinsic activity. The category of individuality *forces* us to conclude in this manner.

This consideration, of course, is superseded, as soon as we have proved the entelechian factor to be *immediately* at work in every single originating organic individual; but it will not be without importance for our future discussions to have alluded to it here.

Different Types of Entelechian Effects

A further distinction will also prove to be valuable for what is to follow. We have called the entelechian factor of morphogenesis typical with regard to order, whilst the psychoid, except when it resulted in products of art, was typical with regard to sequence exclusively. Morphogenetic entelechy always manifests itself in visible constellative products—the organisms. The psychoid may manifest itself in such constellations, as in objects of art and handicraft, but does not do so in everyday acting. But that does not prove anything against the character of the typical specific combination being realised in everyday action. The single phases of a conversation are unities in spite of their not being condensed, so to speak, in visibility.

There is, indeed, one difference between visible constellations which are the effect of entelechy and those which result from acting. The first are points of manifestation of vitalistic factors themselves—at least as long as life endures,

THE PROBLEM OF UNIVERSAL TELEOLOGY 343

as long as there is no corpse; the latter are inorganic constellations or machines, and in this sense correspond to a corpse only. "Die Tätigkeit ist in ihr Produkt übergegangen," as Hegel says—activity has gone over into its product. But this difference does not come into account in our present considerations. We know from our previous discussion that it is not a fundamental difference.

General Plan of what Follows

After these preparations let us set to work. Let us try to find out in which departments of the whole of nature real individualising processes may occur or may have occurred—at least hypothetically; in which fields the concept of individual unity is justifiable.

We know that we should be able to find what we are searching for whenever there were such combinations or sequences of states or events as are "teleological," at least in our well-defined descriptive meaning of this word.[1] In this case, and in this case only,[2] there at least *may* be more than aggregates or sums, whilst otherwise nature, except in

---

[1] By these words we most decidedly exclude from "teleology" everything that does not relate to combinations or sequences as such. We therefore cannot agree with those who have regarded certain forms of the most fundamental mechanical principles under a "teleological" aspect. In the "principle of least action" there is nothing teleological; the principle is only another expression of the principle of causality with regard to Euclidean space. See my *Naturbegriffe*, pp. 47 and 97; also Petzoldt, *Maxima, Minima und Oeconomie*, 1891. Something similar is true with regard to the principles that bear the names of Lenz and Le Chatelier, in electricity and physical chemistry.

[2] With reference to what has been called "Gestaltqualitäten" (Ehrenfels) or "fundierte Inhalte" (Meinong) by modern psychologists, we may say that all cases of individuality—organic or inorganic—would be subsumed under these concepts—which, by the way, are purely psychological — *but not conversely.*

the individual organism, might be said to show us always the same ultimate entity—the ultimate element of matter, in purely external combinations.

But unfortunately the term "teleology" must be understood in the following analysis much more vaguely than it was in our previous descriptive introduction (page 129). We shall not be able either to establish any near analogy with "my acting" or to discover real "purposes of nature" in the sense of Kant; we must be satisfied, if we can discover *anything* whatever like a "whole" or a "unity," or a "purpose," and thus all that is to follow will hardly be more than the statement of subjects for future research.

β. THE PROBLEM OF SUPRA-PERSONAL TELEOLOGY IN THE REALM OF LIFE

History in General

In the first place we refer to the phenomena of human culture once more, as revealed in human history. We have denied on a previous occasion that there is any positive right at present to maintain that any group of cultural or historical phenomena is more than a cumulation of the actings of psychoidal and moral individuals. We quite certainly know nothing at present about such a unity. But it is important to notice that the *problem* is raised even by ourselves. Categorical individuality is at work; it sets us a scientific task—an eternal task perhaps.

As in the study of the individual organism, the problematic categorical theory of culture, of course, would have to begin its analysis by showing, in the first place, that there is *some* kind of descriptive-teleological unity as the subject of further study. I confess we do not even know this yet. We do not see any complication or progress in human history that might not be explained as a cumulation in the easiest way. As far as we *know*, the State—in the widest sense of this word—is the *sum* of the acting of all the individuals concerned in it, and is not a real "individual" itself.

Of course, even if *some* kind of construction or real individual unity in culture were proved, the problem of an *immanent* autonomous cultural and historical factor would still be unsolved. There *might* perhaps some day be found such a factor—in the so-called "unconscious" or "subconscious" sphere, but teleology in history, if there were such a thing at all, *might* also be "machine-like" *qua* teleology. Of course that would not mean to say in this case that human culture is to be understood mechanically—the entelechian individuals which form part of it would contradict such an hypothesis from the very beginning—but it would express that the individual construction at a given state of culture *qua construction* is the effect of a construction of an earlier state, which again follows from an earlier construction, and so on *ad infinitum*; the word construction relating here to the velocity and arrangement of matter in space *and the arrangement of organic individual persons*. In either of the two possible cases just mentioned there would be something above a mere sum of historical individuals, whether it were active at present or had been active at a certain moment of the past.

Thus the problem of historical teleology in any sense must remain an open question—a categorical task.[1]

[1] If history were *evolution* throughout, no place would be left for the concept of a "historical possibility"; if it were partly evolutionary, this concept would be applicable in but a very restricted manner. The discussion

The History of the Individual

But might we not find something like a teleological unity in the *elements* of the historical process, in the life of the single human individual? Is there anything like unity or purposefulness in my own life and in your life, the word life to be understood here as the sum of all, or at least part of all, that has happened to you? I believe that all of us have a certain amount of experience inclining us to give an affirmative answer to this question—but I doubt if it is strong enough to be considered as a scientific fact as certain as Newton's law of gravitation. That degree of certainty, however, would be necessary.

Phylogeny

As to a "phylogeny" or history of the different forms of the Living in general, we have confessed that we know absolutely nothing, except that "Darwinism" and "Lamarckism" are equally unable to solve the problem. There may be a real τέλος to be attained in phylogeny, but there may also be autonomy in phylogeny, and yet the pedigree of the organisms may be a mere cumulation and not a real teleological constellation.[1] Of course, the τέλος of possibility—objective and subjective possibility—as such is, of course, beyond the scope of these lectures, and so is the analysis of the relation of "possibility" to the concepts of determination in general and freedom (comp. Max Weber, *Archiv f. Sozialwiss.* 22, p. 143). I only say here that from the highest point of view there is not much room for objective "possibility" at all, *either* in the face of mere causality *or* in the face of "individuality," since both of these are subclasses of determination—at least in the objective sphere (comp. page 304).

[1] Comp. vol. i. page 305. Bergson, in his *L'évolution créatrice*, also advocates an autonomous but endless phylogeny.

as such might again be due to intrinsic or constellative and machine-like teleology. There are few domains in science where we are so ignorant as we are here.

Thus the category of individuality only establishes tasks in biology, except so far as the personal individual is concerned.

The Significance of Propagation

But is there not one class of facts which seems to show beyond any doubt a purposefulness that exceeds the range of the biological individual as such? Yes, there is a class of organic phenomena, which have been mentioned only quite incidentally so far, since they have nothing to do with what we have studied almost exclusively, the organic personal individual. I refer to the simple phenomenon of *propagation*.

We have already studied inheritance, that is, the fact that the young organism resembles its parents. We have also analysed the significance of the development of the egg of an animal, or any sort of germ or bud whatever. The manifestation of entelechy, as we called it, in an egg or germ was found to be a mere subclass of universal restitution of fragments, in its ontological sense.

But we have not said a single word about the significance of the individual organism's *actively producing* " fragments," to be developed under the control of entelechy. The problem is certainly unique.[1]

Have we not here the very source of all that *can* be teleological or " individual " in a higher than the ordinary

---

[1] This problem, of course, has nothing to do with the problem of *sexual* propagation, shortly mentioned at vol. i. p. 33. I feel unable to add anything positive to the critical remarks there: the problem is beyond us at present.

sense? Does it not seem as if propagation as such were to serve a supra-personal purpose? In any case, in no other sense *can* propagation be understood at all,[1] and it is therefore that we mention it in this connexion and in no other. But here also we know nothing.

γ. HARMONY IN NATURE

Let us now proceed to the analysis of a certain type of problematic teleology which also relates to supra-personal life, but is not historical in any sense.

Nobody at the present day, so far as I am aware, conceives teleologically in any way the origin of islands, mountains, clouds, rivers, or any other form of inorganic combinations on the earth. But such teleology, at least conceived statically, played an important rôle in the eighteenth century. And in the same way the different types of organisms were considered as being in mutual teleological correspondence, animals indeed in their present state being certainly unable to exist without plants. This is the real concept of a *harmony* in nature, both organic and inorganic.

But the concept of this harmony with regard to the Inorganic goes still deeper, from geology and geography to inorganic elementalities: the properties of iron and salt are regarded as instances of "harmony," and so is the fact that water attains its greatest density at $+4°$ C. and not at freezing-point.

I do not hesitate to confess that, apart from historical

---

[1] The only possible objection to this view seems to be as follows: entelechy might know that it cannot overcome inorganic potentials for indefinite time and might therefore secure points of future manifestation. But even this would be "supra-personal" to a certain extent.

THE PROBLEM OF UNIVERSAL TELEOLOGY 349

teleology relating to the sequence of one state of politics or economy upon another, and apart from phylogeny, there seems to me to be a certain sound foundation in the concept of the general harmony between organic and inorganic nature, a something which seems to show *that nature is nature for a certain purpose.* But I confess at the same time that I am absolutely unable to consider this purpose in any other than a purely anthropomorphic manner.

Let us now try to examine in a systematic way to what *classes* of inorganic or organic constellations any kind of teleological *harmony* possibly might relate. Of course, any such harmony would be merely statical in the first place, *i.e.* a given teleological arrangement and no more. But it would be much if even that could be proved.

As to the different types of matter and forces, physics and chemistry try to understand atoms, molecules, and crystals as mere states of equilibrium of one elemental material. The possible forms of equilibrium would be guaranteed by the nature of space from such a point of view. But what about the *specific distribution* and *relative frequency* of the different classes of inorganic materiality? These, of course, are the consequences of a former specific distribution, which in turn is the consequence of a still earlier one. Is there anything in any of these distributions that is of the character of a teleological unity? The only way by which this hypothetic unity might possibly be recognised as such would be the demonstration that it has some relation of purposefulness with regard to organic beings. That certainly sounds very "anthropomorphic," but we must never forget that in no other manner would it be possible here to get even the mere starting-point for a "supra-biological" or "supra-personal" teleology, so to speak, of the future. Of an immanent or entelechian teleology we most decidedly know absolutely nothing in this domain of nature—were it otherwise, our task would not be difficult. Thus the only thing we can do teleologically is to search for *some* point among inorganic specificities of constellation, which *might* possibly relate to *some* imaginable purpose. And the organisms alone can be such purposes. In this way the frequency and distribution of salt and of iron, and the remarkable properties of the ever-present water indeed *do* serve to assist important functions of all organisms and of men, and so does the separation of oceans and continents on the earth.

But we shall postpone the further discussion of this central question until we have reviewed another type of possible individuality or teleology in the Inorganic.

δ. THE PROBLEM OF A REAL INORGANIC INDIVIDUALITY

It is not the specific distribution and frequency of the types of matter to which I refer, but the general distribution of masses in the cosmic universe. And, on the other hand, it is not with a possible mere general "harmony" that we shall deal here exclusively, but with the problem whether there may be found in the inorganic universe such types of constellation—or perhaps even dynamical events—as might allow us to speak of real inorganic individuals, or, strange to say, inorganic organisms. Of course this is quite a different logical problem from the problem of a general harmony of the universe, with man as its purpose. Our new problem, so it seems, is much less "anthropomorphic" than the problem of harmony.

THE PROBLEM OF UNIVERSAL TELEOLOGY 351

Many cosmic constellations of masses, like the single planetary systems, for instance, are very typical in their specificity, as far as we know, and are not reducible to *any* sort of mere symmetry in space, as the chemical elements are on the theory of electrons. Now it certainly is by no means *proved* at present that categorical teleology is applicable to planetary or sidereal systems, that there is anything like individuality to be found in them. But, on the other hand, it must be granted that such a view may be possible and may be proved some day, and we know that not only Fechner, in an almost poetical form, but also other philosophers, regarded planetary systems as real " organisms." This statement, of course, would not prevent a certain sort of " harmony " with regard to life from also being realised in planetary arrangements. We may raise the question in this connexion, whether a bacterium, endowed with human reason and living somewhere in the body of man, would be able to discover the wholeness and dynamico-teleological nature of its host, and would not prefer to say that, as far as it could judge, there was no reason for applying the category of teleology, even in the statical sense, to the very strange and apparently " contingent " constellation in which it was living. It *may* be possible that we are playing the part of this bacterium as regards planetary or sidereal arrangements.

What is actually known about the specificity of sidereal arrangements, apart from planetary systems in particular, relates in the first place to the remarkable formation of the Milky Way and the distribution of many star-systems in its plane. All this proves that there is at least a sidereal arrangement of a rather typical character.

To sum up: *nothing* is *quite* certainly known, either

352 SCIENCE AND PHILOSOPHY OF THE ORGANISM

about a harmony or a truly teleological and individual constellation either in the general distribution of kinds of matter or in planetary or sidereal arrangements. But there are some *approximations* at least to a general statical *harmonious* teleology with regard to living beings and man.

ϵ. CONTINGENCY AND TELEOLOGY

The Concept of Contingency

To *deny* inorganic teleology in *any* form would ultimately be the same as to admit *contingency* as the *exclusive* feature of inorganic specificity of constellation. The term "contingency" has two different meanings in common use. With regard to necessity, philosophy must maintain that nothing happens in nature that is not univocally determined, and that therefore nothing is "contingent"; but as to events at this very point in space and at this very moment of time, philosophy may speak of the contingency of their happening here and now, whenever it is not possible to discover anything like a wholeness or a plan to which their local and temporal appearance is due. Contingency in this sense is the same as non-teleology,[1] whilst contingency in the other meaning is inadmissible to critical philosophy altogether.[2]

If now we wish to express our general result with regard to the problem of any non-biological teleology or

[1] It is worth noticing that the term "contingency" only acquires a clear meaning when opposed to teleology; it is a *negation*. But this proves that teleology (or rather, individuality) is a category.

[2] A fuller discussion of the problem would belong to general philosophy. Comp. also page 304 and page 345, note.

THE PROBLEM OF UNIVERSAL TELEOLOGY 353

individuality by using the term *contingency*, we may say as follows :—With reference to sidereal and planetary arrangements as such,[1] and with reference to phylogeny and history, we are unable at the present day to *prove* the existence of any non-contingency. But this is no final answer at all, the task founded upon the category of individuality remains. With reference to a general harmony between inorganic nature and the organisms, and among the organisms themselves, there seems to be something more than a mere task.

The Concept of a Limited Teleology

For, as we have said, there are *some* inklings of a supra-personal harmony, at least from an anthropomorphic point of view, some inklings of a general sort of statical harmony in the whole of nature, as the old naturalists asserted. In fact, this word "harmony" is the only one that seems to be applicable to the few points we are able to assert positively about our subject. In any case the cosmos is such that organic life (and man's life in particular) is guaranteed in it, at least on the earth's surface.

The common objection to this reasoning is generally a sort of enlarged Darwinism. It is pointed out that any given state of the Organic is not the result of purposefulness but the survivor out of innumerable other states, because —by contingency—it discovered the secret of permanent

[1] This preliminary result is unaffected by certain analytical investigations of the last few years, especially those of V. Goldschmidt, which have discovered something like a general law governing the type of a planetary system as a whole. If the distances of the single planetary orbits from the centre do in fact always follow a comparatively simple formula, it may be owing to the state of aggregation of their material at the moment of their formation, and may be a mere question of probability.

existence under the circumstances that prevailed. But to this objection to teleology as foreboded in mere harmony we again object on our part that this presentment of the facts is powerless to do away with the simple *truth* that, Givenness being what it is, one thing *does* occur in *favour* of the other. In fact, there *are* teleological relations between different organisms, between plants and the sun, and between water and functions of life in general. Things *are* so, we say, and therefore there *is* a certain harmony amongst the elemental constituents of nature, at least with regard to their specific distribution.

As to anything more than a mere harmony of the kind just described there are, of course, no *logical* reasons why the constellation of the inorganic world as such or of history as such should not be regarded as merely contingent throughout and as due to an indefinite line of contingencies in the past, always determined from moment to moment by mere probability. In this case the task propounded by the category of individuality with regard to the Inorganic itself or to history as such would appear as factually insoluble. But since we actually discover *some* sort of harmony between the manifestations of entelechy and the distribution of inorganic realities, do not at least *some* features of the primordial constellation of the inorganic world seem to gain a special teleological importance, do they not seem to be harmonious *for* entelechy, and does not thereby the contingency of inorganic constellation cease to be "contingency" at least in *certain* spheres? Does not the nature of the probability of inorganic constellations seem to be specified in a way that at least suggests a *limited* purpose?

We shall come back to this problem from another point of view, and we will only add here that to admit teleology of only a *limited* character implies a very important conception of the ultimate character of the Given as such.

ζ. MORALITY

Morality as a Standard of Measurement of Universal Teleology

A rather serious objection against the purposefulness of one organism in favour of another follows from the consideration that it does not agree with our ideas of what ought to be, that one class of organisms flourishes at the cost of pains and death to another. This objection is more important than any other, to human feeling at least, though a critical mind would hardly be inclined to call it decisive. For we do not know the *means* that were at the disposal of the hypothetic supra-personal entelechy that must be regarded as having made natural harmony. Nothing, of course, but the solution of the problem of the sense and meaning of the Given could furnish an answer about *any* type of *universal* teleology. We can do absolutely nothing in the face of this problem beyond simply stating that the only sphere in which *we* should be able to conceive such a solution at all would be that of morality and intellectuality. If there were a meaning in the universe with relation to these two purposes—which may be *one* purpose in the last resort—we at least should be able to conceive it.

Thus morality and intellectuality become the standard of measurement of all universal teleology in any sense, and therefore morality once more enters into our theoretical discussions.

Morality as a Category

Let me now say a few additional words about the concept of morality from a merely ontological point of view, so as to accentuate what we have said on this point on a former occasion.

Morality, as a form of judging, is also a category, like causality and individuality.[1] Conceiving it in this way we guarantee the unity of the Given, whereas if we regarded morality as something absolutely different from any other kind of dealing with the Given we should be dividing reality into two parts absolutely irreconcilable with one another. No matter what the special so-called content of morality may be, morality in its most general categorical sense comes into play whenever the relation of two or more active entelechian manifestations to each other is the subject of reflection. And morality as a category is as "constitutive" as any other category, and not merely regulative, since moral acting individuals are real constituents of nature.[2] I finally "understand" morality—just like causality and individuality—psychologically, since I myself may be one of the individuals in question.

Thus morality has its place *first* in the system of categories, *secondly* in nature, *thirdly* in psychology—as all categories have.[3]

---

[1] There is a great difference between morality and moralising. Theoretical ethics is the description of an ideal and is intellectual in the last resort. There is no such thing as "you must," but only "so it ought to be." Therefore the personal moral character of an author has nothing to do with his moral theory.   [2] Comp. page 320 f.

[3] Things would turn out differently if all morality were merely apparent, the community of men being in fact one supra-personal individual unity using the biological individuals as means. See page 121. In this case morality might possibly be regarded as the mere psychological or subjective

It is a very important—and very strange—characteristic of the category of morality that it almost always appears in the form of a negation. We judge that something "ought *not* to happen," but it would in most cases—though not in all—be very difficult for us to say with absolute certainty what "ought to happen."[1] With regard to history in particular, we therefore might say that there was a real evolution in it if we were able to assert that the sum of what ought not to happen becomes less during the historical process in a not merely cumulative way. It is worth noticing that not a word has been said about "freedom," "responsibility," and such like in this short theory of morality.

Morality relates to individuals and to individuals only.[2] Historical cumulations of any kind therefore can be binding in a moral sense only if what they ask does not contradict the immediate relation of individual to individual. This is very important in practical life.

Morality and Vitalism

We now come to a very important relation between morality and all vitalism.

The assertion of morality implies the assertion of entelechy, just as entelechy implies causality and substance.

It seems to me very important to realise that morality and correlate of supra-personal individuality, and not as a category for itself. May we say perhaps that "morality" on its own part *guarantees* the supra-personal unity in history and culture that we are in search of (see p. 344 f.)?

[1] But morality *must* have some sort of content. Mere "formal" morality, like that of Kant, would be as valueless as a statement of the existence of categories of "relation" which did not specify what they are. But a theory of morality is not the business of this work.

[2] Let me add once more: *not* to individuals that form part of a higher truly "individual" constellation, such as the State has been supposed to be. In this case the individuals would only be *means* of the supra-individuum.

entelechy *are* connected in such a way that to assert the former is equivalent to asserting the latter, and to deny the latter is to deny the former. In this sense vitalism is the high road to morality: morality would be an absurdity without it.

How could I feel "morally" towards other individuals, if *I knew* that they were machines and nothing more?—machines, which some day I *myself* might be able to *construct* like a steam engine! To a convinced theoretical materialist, to whom his neighbour is a real mechanical system, morality is an absurdity. This is equally true, whether materialism be held as a doctrine about nature from a point of view which is idealistic and phenomenological at bottom, or professed in the crudest uncritical metaphysical manner. In either case the mechanical theory of life is incompatible with morality. It is of no avail to assume—as some have done—that there might be a something non-mechanical "appearing" under the form of a mechanical system; wholeness can never "appear" in the form of that which is not wholeness but aggregation *per definitionem*.[1] When an author feels morally and considers objective human relations morally in spite of his materialistic conviction with regard to life, he unconsciously gives up his materialism. It is very strange to see what an enormous confusion of thought generally prevails in this region.

There might be vitalism without morality; but the categorical existence of morality implies vitalism as an axiom, *even if it were not yet established by other proofs.*

But enough about a problem that does not strictly belong to our subject. The main reason for our discussing morality has yet to be mentioned.

[1] This was also our argument against psycho-physical parallelism, see p. 289.

PART IV

METAPHYSICAL CONCLUSIONS

Introductory Remarks

Our whole argument has rested so far upon pure idealistic phenomenalism; we have analysed the Given so far as it certainly is my phenomenon. In this sense, forces and entelechies were agents in nature as part of my Givenness, they were concepts auxiliary to the understanding of Givenness.

Is there really no way to escape from phenomenalism to something absolute, to "metaphysics," that is to say, to something that is *not exclusively* "my phenomenon"? And what does all our argument amount to on a metaphysical basis?

It seems to me that there are three possibilities, three windows, as I might say—though *dim* windows only—through which at least we are able to see that there *is* such a thing as absoluteness.

By no means do I believe that I am able to "prove" absoluteness in the proper sense of the word. We cannot "prove" the inconceivable. And absoluteness *implies* unintelligibility in the sense of provableness, otherwise it would not *be* absoluteness but phenomenality. I know very well that the whole of Givenness is my Givenness, whether immediately perceived or conceptually transformed, that all sensations are mine, and all feelings and all concepts and categories. All of this " is " with regard to me, and I properly " know " nothing else about it. In so far critical subjective idealism is quite right. But to adhere to this idealism implies the renunciation of understanding altogether, at least in three fields of phenomenality. There are three regions of phenomenality which never will form part of any true *system* of Givenness, unless the bounds of idealism are broken. But they only can be broken with regard to the *fact* of something which " is " not exclusively with respect to the Ego,[1] just as from a room with windows of ground-glass we may perceive the " fact " that there is something outside without knowing in any way what it is.

Thus we are able at least to *approach* the realm of that which alone deserves the name of *truth* with regard to being. The word " truth " in this sense, of course, signifies something very different from what is called so in logic and mathematics, logical and mathematical truth being only *the validity of relations* with regard to a subject.[2]

[1] Of course, even the words "something" and "is" are only used figuratively in this connexion. If not, the "Absolute" would not be *absolute*. This book is not the place for any attempt to pursue this problem further.

[2] Logical and mathematical truth is certainly "absolute" as to its validity *so long as there exists a subject like the human mind* (comp. the very suggestive address delivered before the Third International Congress for Philosophy, Heidelberg, 1908, by J. Royce). But it falls to the ground with the existence of the subject, and for this reason, though "absolutely true," it is not "absolute truth" metaphysically. In modern philosophy the theory of validity has overshadowed the theory of being.

a. THE THREE WINDOWS INTO THE ABSOLUTE

Morality: the Thou

Morality is one of the windows to absoluteness we have spoken about. For morality towards phenomena or amongst phenomena which are *merely* "phenomena" to my Ego exclusively would be absurd. Morality therefore implies absoluteness, independence of the Ego—though this independence is absolutely unintelligible to me in any detail. Absoluteness in this sense is not identical with "reality" in the sense of "the Given." "Reality" in *that* sense remains a constituent of phenomenality and only means that a certain domain of it is objectified. Reality in this sense is nothing but the product of a certain category—the category subject-object. But morality forces us to regard Givenness, or at least part of Givenness, as a field in which something is to be accomplished—by acting—with regard to the Absolute. In conceiving morality I conceive absoluteness: I conceive the "Thou."

It is here that history acquires its importance, as the field of moral acting. It is here that its general emotional importance may become clear. History is not made of any special *scientific* importance by this consideration, but quite in general it proves to be the groundwork of morality; morality in general being, of course, independent of the specificity of historical constellations.

The Nature of Memory: the Ego

The second "window into the absolute" is constituted by the fact, already mentioned on a former occasion, that there is such a thing as the unity of subjective experience in general and of memory in particular; in other words, the fact that not only self-consciousness itself endures, but also something that is presented to consciousness. This tends to prove the absolute existence of an unconscious or supra-conscious basis of the conscious Ego. Phenomenalism of the *strictest* kind would only allow us to regard as reality what is present to consciousness at one moment. But to say " I " is more than to assert the reality of one moment. It does not imply that the Ego is a " substance," for the Ego creates substances. But it implies the whole of past experience in a partly latent state and therefore implies absoluteness in general — which, of course, must remain quite unintelligible again, since the Ego *could* only explain its nature by means of the categories which in fact are its outcome.

The Character of Givenness: the It

The last window into the absolute is the contingency of *immediate* Givenness and the immanent coherence of the single phases of Givenness in spite of its contingency. Let the reason of immediate Givenness be what it may, " I," as the conscious Ego, *do certainly not create it consciously out of myself;* it is very often contrary to, or at least indifferent to, my will.

And yet there *is* immanent coherence between the single phases of immediate Givenness nevertheless, even if these phases are interrupted by sleep or by my temporary absence, or by something else. A stone happens to begin to fall from a high mountain: I see it, then turn away for a moment, and then look again: the stone in *every* case has arrived just at that point in space where I expected to find it; contingent Givenness, though broken by an interval in its immediateness, is *one*. " I " am not responsible for it, nor are the " categories " responsible.[1]

Therefore, to put it briefly : the contingency of the immediately given phenomena, as far as their non-aprioristic part, that is to say, as far as " sensations " or " presentations " come into account, combined with the immanent coherence of this contingency in itself, tends to prove absoluteness with regard to the " It." " It " is now here and now there, now one thing and now another. This is all with respect to the Ego, it is true; *but not by or from the Ego.*

Our third class of facts that show us absoluteness in general now calls for a further short analysis before we resume from a new point of view our study of universal teleology.

β. THE " POSTULATE "

Immediate sensible Givenness is the material the categorical system has to work with; categories establish axioms with regard to this material and thus render it a system itself. In the first place, it must now be added that the Ego is not content with axioms with regard to Givenness, but from the very beginning also forms some *postulates* concerning it. That is to say : the Ego forms some most general notions, which are by no means absolutely

---

[1] A complete theory of the Absolute would have to consider in this connexion what are generally called "constants" of nature, expressed in the form of quantitative relations ; say the sizes of electrons and atoms. These constants are "contingent" with regard to the reasoning mind ; a theory of matter might reduce them to one or two constants.

inevitable, as axioms are, but which are required in order that the range of our actual knowledge may be self-consistent. We have mentioned the most central one of these postulates whilst dealing with our first proof of vitalism.[1] We can work experimentally only with a few eggs of the sea-urchin, but we *postulate* that what holds for one holds for them all. This postulate is by no means identical with the "axiom" of univocality or necessary determination, whether in relation to causality or to individuality. The axiom of univocality would remain true even if our postulate were given up. If ever two eggs of an animal behaved quite differently, we should not say that circumstances being equal different things had happened; but we should say: the circumstances were not equal. But we *postulate* that nature is so uniform—I do not say "constant"—in itself that when a *certain* number of typical features are present there most probably will be also those, which in many cases have been found to be actually in connexion with them. It is most important that the distinction between this postulate and the aprioristic axioms should be most clearly understood. The *axioms*, based upon the categories as such, relate to the Given as phenomenon in general; they are the prerequisites of *experience*, of "understanding"; they set up scientific tasks. The *postulate* relates to the Given in its specificity and apparent contingency; it maintains that there is uniformity *in* the contingency; it is a question of induction; *it is induction enlarged teleologically with regard to the possibility of science.*[2] As all specificity and contingency of immediate

[1] See vol. i. page 148.

[2] Modern empiricism, economism, humanism, pragmatism, or whatever it may be called, has always confused axioms with the postulate.

Givenness tends to prove the Absolute, *the postulate of the uniformity of nature relates to absoluteness itself.*

γ. TELEOLOGY AND THE ABSOLUTE

The Concept of a Limited Teleology once more

We have said before that applying the category of individuality or teleology to all Givenness forms at least an unending task, and we have raised the question whether the distribution of specific qualities of matter and of specific geographical and geological formations on earth, or the specific distribution of sidereal and planetary masses might some day be found to have some purpose, either in itself or at least for man. And we did not absolutely deny that in history also some unity might be found in the future. The problem of what we called a "limited" teleology now calls for some further elucidation in the first place.

How far *into the Specific of immediate Givenness* does teleology possibly go? Granted that there *is* purposefulness —at least of the statical or constellative type—in the specific distribution of matter and sidereal masses with regard to the welfare of organisms: how far does this purposefulness go? Does it possibly extend to the most minute singularities? Then the whole universe would be one teleological unity in every detail. Nay: then only would it be "one universe" throughout. Only then would there be no "contingency" whatever.

But have we any reason to assume—even granting a good deal of supra-personal individuality—that it is purposeful in *any* sense of the word that a week ago it rained for five minutes, or that this morning I met three dogs of a certain colour, or that a particular stone shows certain irregularities on its surface?

I think hardly anybody, even if inclined to accept universal teleology, would care to push his teleological arguments as far as this, that is to say, right up to immediately "historical" singularities. Teleology must be at least intelligible by analogy in order that it may be admitted hypothetically; and the reason for its being intelligible is absolutely wanting if any event *whatever* is regarded as an outcome of its control.

We have discussed this problem of a "limited teleology" before, though not in relation to the very immediateness of the Given. In fact, *man* is only able to judge about external purposefulness according to *his own* purposes, and the highest purpose of man is intellectuality and morality, both of which are perhaps the same in the last resort. But the universe is not perfect with regard to morality and intellectuality *throughout*, and therefore *cannot* appear to us as teleological *throughout*. Perhaps we may say that it is purposeful so far as it allows of the moral and intellectual perfection of the individual man, that it is a sort of moral and intellectual institution. That would agree with certain doctrines of Indian and Christian philosophy; it would also agree with the metaphysics of the last great moral philosopher—Schopenhauer.

Thus, I believe, we may say hypothetically, summarising at the same time what we have said before: There are probably *domains* of—at least past—entelechian manifestations in the universe, both inorganic and supra-personally organic. The harmony in nature, statical at present, is their result. But the universe is *not in every historical detail* a teleological system; at least the human mind is unable to conceive it as a "universe" throughout. There *is* "contingency," *i.e.* non-teleology, in the universe, not only apparently but really.[1] In other words, real teleological constellations in the Inorganic—if discoverable at all—would only relate to a mutual harmony among different classes of events with special reference to organic life in general, but would not apply to this particular event at this particular time and place. Problematic real teleological constellations in history would only relate to general types of the human mind, but not to the single personalities as such.

It is very important in this connexion to notice well that even in the only field where dynamically effective individuality is known to us—in the biological individual—this individuality seems not to be concerned in the minutest details: the *single cells* of a tissue are *not* as such a really *essential* constituent of organisation.

And another point is very important also: wherever the category of individuality extended so far into the details as to submit *everything* that happens in any system to the immediate control of an entelechy or—in the statical manner—at least to some such control in the past, there would either be *no room for causality* at all,[2] or causality, at least, would always be posterior to individuality. But it is not imaginable that individuality is actively at work—as dynamical teleology or entelechy—or has been at work, if

[1] We have said before that the contingency of *immediate* Givenness tends to show us the "fact" of absoluteness. This concept of the contingency of *immediate* Givenness, of course, must not be confused with the concept of the contingency or non-teleology of "ideal nature."

[2] This would be the mistake of the materialists, only made from the other side!

it finds nothing to work with. It wants "means," and matter including spatial causality is its means—in the manner we have described. Thus, in fact, as we have said, individuality by no means destroys but implies causality; it would be an impossibility without it; it interferes—or has interfered—with causality here and there, but *not everywhere*.

The Domain of Teleology

At this point we shall apply our results about teleology to what we have learnt about the Absolute.

It was known already to Kant that our faculty of creating a real "system" of immediate phenomenological Givenness proves a certain sort of correspondence between the active and the passive part of experience, between categories or rather "ontological prototypes" and sensible Givenness itself. For sensible Givenness *might* be imagined to be such as *not* to allow of any *special* order at all. In this case the mere concept of univocal determination would be awaked by experience in the mind, but there would not even be a field of substance or causality, for causality or substance as categories would not be awakened by a chaotic Givenness.

But this most general question does not affect our bio-theoretical problem as such. Let us therefore turn to a narrower field of analysis.

It would not be impossible to imagine a world in which only the category of substance were applicable—change would be wanting in such a world. And it would not be impossible to imagine a world deprived of entelechy but endowed with causality—there would be no organisms in such a world; the only realm of the category of individuality would be my mind. But there *is* true causality *and* true individuality not only in my Ego but in the world as it is. That is to say: sensible or immediate Givenness corresponds to the categorical system most fully. This is a fact, and this fact relates to absoluteness whenever specific Givenness in its contingency and coherence tends to absoluteness. Might we say perhaps that there exists a common metaphysical basis both of immediate Givenness and of our being able to " understand " it by means of the categories?

But let us come back to our theme.

Certainly, individuality does not govern Givenness in every detail. But the contingency of the universe in certain domains does not exclude non-contingency in certain others—in the organisms and possibly in some other constellations.

What does that mean with regard to the Absolute, now that we know that objectified Givenness tends to show us something about the Absolute?

In the first place we have a *factual* right to say: whereever the reasoning mind finds *organic living individuals,* it finds objectified active reason or *active reason as its object.* *Absoluteness in this respect therefore must be such as to be in some—unintelligible—connexion with something like reason.* Or, if we prefer to say so:[1] absoluteness must be such as to be able to become part of our phenomenological Givenness under the form not only of causality, substance, and inheritance, but also of individuality, *i.e.* objectified reasoning.

And in the second place we have at least a *hypothetic*

---

[1] The following formulation is probably more "Kantian" than is usually admitted. Kant was not an "idealist" to the extent that Schopenhauer supposed. Comp. Riehl, *Der philosophische Kriticismus,* i., 2. Aufl., 1908.

right to speak of certain constellations in givenness, other than organisms, which are teleological in the sense of a statical *harmony of nature*. It is true, this harmony is statical, it is a teleology of constellation, of being, not a teleology *in* becoming as the teleology in organisms is. One state of this statical teleology leads back to an earlier state, which again leads back, and so on, one of these states following from the other mechanically. At least we know absolutely nothing about any real entelechian non-mechanical *act* in the sphere of the Inorganic.

δ. THE PRIMARY ENTELECHY IN THE UNIVERSE—AN ETERNAL TASK OF SCIENCE

But does not this hypothetic statical harmony among certain domains of nature point back to an original primary entelechy that *made* it just as the artist makes an object of art? In spite of the possibility of the indefinite regressus in time that we meet here, it seems to me that the mind is *forced* to assume this primary entelechy in the universe—I do not say "of" the universe—as soon as a universal natural harmony of *any* kind is accepted. This *primary entelechy* would not have created absolute reality, but would have *ordered* certain parts of it, and these parts therefore would show a sort of non-contingent constellation whilst all other constellation of the elementalities of the universe would be contingent.

This is downright "Dualism," the old distinction between ὕλη and νοῦς. But how are we to escape dualism when even the categorical system of relations is dualistic throughout? Passive Givenness also shows us causality *and* entelechy strictly separated, and whenever Givenness tended to absoluteness,[1] absoluteness would do the same. It is true that metaphysical assumptions about the unity of the Ego might seem to guarantee us the possibility of "monism," but as soon as the Ego becomes active, it evolves its unity into manifoldness and therefore is unable to *discover* monism *anywhere*.

In the sense of a *primary entelechy of order of constellation in the world*, as a δημιουργός in opposition to mere "material," the concept of God therefore appears as an eternal task of science; unintelligible in the last resort, as all religions maintain, and only approachable by analogies, like all absoluteness. For it only is through ground-glass windows, as it were, that we are allowed to look into absoluteness; we only know the "fact" of the Absolute absolutely; whilst bound to our categorical system, we only know quite vaguely the "how" of the Absolute.

Thus "natural theology" is possible in the sense of a scientific task, but in no other. There certainly is something that appears to us as reason in Givenness, viz. the

[1] To be quite clear: The problem of the contingency or non-contingency or limited non-contingency of the universe, and further, the problem of the primary entelechy in the universe, relate to *Givenness* as a conceptual *phenomenon* in the *first* place. In *this* field—in opposition to Kant—a clear and satisfying solution of the problem *is* possible; the Kantian "antinomies" are immanent, and are probably soluble in the immanent field. It, of course, is quite a different problem whether and how far the solution relates to anything absolute. Or, to speak in terms of theology: the physico-teleological proof of God, or anything like a God, may be *decisive* with regard to God as an entelechian factor in Givenness; but it is quite another problem whether or not the decision arrived at here relates to the Absolute. This then is the most important thing: all the difficulties and obscurities with regard to the Absolute are not proper to the problem of a "primary entelechy" *as such*, but come upon the scene as soon as *any* attempt is made to refer *any* characteristics of Givenness whatever to the absolute sphere. Comp. page 321, note 1.

organisms; and there probably is more reason than we know decidedly, viz. the harmony, or, to speak in most general terms, the distribution of primordial matter and velocity.

Certainly, the "primary entelechy" that natural science allows us to assume hypothetically, and epistemology allows us to refer by analogy to absoluteness, remains far behind any conception of a perfect absolute Being that man is able to form in his mind. But it does *not* contradict[1] the concept of God as formed by the reasoning imagination.

ε. METALOGICAL CONSIDERATIONS

On a former occasion we made a short excursion into the theory of knowledge, showing how, on the basis of the categorical system, the concept of an "ideal nature" is created, and how "natural factors or agents" are established with regard to the single actual and possible events in conceived Givenness. Our former discussion related to inorganic nature as well as to the domain of life.

In the face of our present metaphysical considerations, the concepts "ideal nature" and "natural factors" acquire a somewhat different aspect. The whole system of "ideal nature," including the relations of individuality and morality, would appear as a description by analogy of what is absolute: in any case the Absolute is such that it may be described by analogy in this way. But "natural agents" with regard to single events in Givenness, say the fall of a particular stone or the morphogenesis of a particular animal,

[1] But science, and the doctrine of entelechy in particular, most strongly contradicts any form of so-called "Pantheism." Entelechy and matter are different and external to one another throughout.

METAPHYSICAL CONCLUSIONS

would now appear as what might be called a sort of *emanation* from the Absolute, as a something that has its source in the Absolute. With regard to causal force and biological entelechy such an emanation may actually happen before our eyes, as it does in inorganic events and in the living organisms.[1] But it also may *have happened*, if our hypothesis of an individualised general harmony in nature is justified. In this case the Demiurgus that science allows to be established as its eternal task would be the highest form of all emanations. In all these questions, of course, the problem of *time* would appear once more.

But our "Science and Philosophy of the Organism" ends here.

[1] On a former occasion (page 261) we have said that the ideal or Platonic existence of entelechy as a constituent of "ideal nature" does not guarantee the permanency of the individuals which are the outcome of its manifestation in any way. It seems to me that the problem must remain open in the "absolute" sphere also. In brief: *individual* immortality is *not provable*; but then, of course, neither is its opposite. And a spiritual eternity that is *not* individual is beyond our comprehension except in a *very* general and unspecified fashion—though this, of course, is no argument against its existence.

Conclusions: The Route Traversed

"The Science and Philosophy of the Organism"—we have tried to analyse what is implied in these words, and now we have finished our task, to the best of our ability.

The science *and* the philosophy—is this "and" really justified? Have we really undertaken two different kinds of analytical studies? It is true the development of the common sea-urchin seems at the first glance rather remote from the concept of categories and morality and universal teleology, and thus it might seem, as many modern philosophers maintain, as if science and philosophy were really two things, only loosely connected.

But there were philosophers in former times—and among them were Leibniz and Hegel—who did not take such a short-sighted view. And I think they are right.

Givenness is One and philosophy is the endeavour to understand Givenness. Part of Givenness is sensations, part of it is categories, part of it is feeling, part of it is memory, and there are many other parts. That domain of Givenness which is formed out of sensations and categories we call Nature. It makes no logical difference, it seems to me, whether nature is studied with regard to what it actually is, that is to say, what really happens in it, or whether we try to discover which elemental parts of our mental organisation come into play in conceiving nature and what "nature" means in the sphere of metaphysics.

The first is generally called science, the latter philosophy.

But in the last resort there is only one kind of human knowledge.

INDEX

Absolute, the, 359 ff., 368 ff.
Acclimatisation, 12, 24 f.
Act of volition, origin of, 62 f.
Action, 33, 52 ff., 193 f., 231 f.
  analogies to, 77 ff.
  of apes, 107
  criteria of, 59 f., 66 ff., 75 ff.
  definition of, 54
  degrees of, 106 ff.
  distribution of, 57 f.
  of invertebrates, 109
  lowest forms of, 110 ff.
  mechanisation of, 55
Action and reaction, principle of, 227 f.
Action system, 21
Adaptation, 143, 229
  functional, of nervous system, 54, 278
Affection of entelechy, 228 ff.
  of psychoid, 231 f.
Animal intelligence, 57
"Answering reaction," 72, 104
Antinomy, 304, 321, 371
Ants, 109
Apes (acting of), 107
A priori, 43, 86, 159, 201 f., 206
Aristotle, 83 f., 255, 297
Art, works of, 133, 138
Asher, 89
Assimilation, 242, 245 ff.
Association, 58, 64 ff., 97 ff., 111
Atwater, 166
Autonomy of life, 50, 71 ff., 80 f., 88, 92, 136, 233, 266 ff.
Autotropism, 13
Avebury, Lord, 109
Axiom, 301, 364

Basis, historical, of reacting, 59 ff., 78 f., 97, 99, 103, 107 f., 117, 277 ff.
  different types of, 63 ff.

Basis, elements of, 80, 107 f.
Becher, 78
Bechterew, 94, 167
Becoming, principle of, 171 ff., 200
  and entelechy, 176 ff.
Bees, 46 f., 58
Bergson, 66, 74 f., 99, 114, 280, 292, 295, 305, 313, 318, 328, 330, 332
Berkeley, 117
Bethe, 27, 96, 102
Bodies, classes of, 146
Bois-Reymond, E. du, 85, 255
Boldyreff, 113
Boltzmann, 200
Born, 95
Brain, centre, 4, 27, 33, 87, 95 f., 102
  connecting function, 91 ff.
  functions of, 89 ff., 96 ff.
  lower, 102 ff.
  relation to elements of Givenness, 275 ff.
  spheres, 93 f.
Braus, 96,
Bredig, 186
Busse, 74 f., 114, 218, 295

Carnot, S., 171
Catalysis, 185 ff., 192, 232
Categories, 296 ff.
Causa finalis, 315 f.
Causality, 154, 156 ff., 161 ff., 233, 286, 296, 306 f., 316 ff., 335
Cause, 158, 233, 317
Centre, brain, 4, 27, 33, 87, 95 f., 102
  lower brain, 102 ff.
Cerebral physiology, 89 ff.
Chain-reflex, 29, 40 f.
Chemistry, physiological, 247 ff. 254 f.
Christian philosophy, 366

378   SCIENCE AND PHILOSOPHY OF THE ORGANISM

Chromotaxis, 24
Clausius, 171 f., 198
Clifford, 126
Cohen, 302, 309
Connecting function (of brain), 91 ff.
Consciousness, 37 f., 105, 141 f., 294, 320
Constants, 202 ff., 363
Contingency, 352 f., 363, 365 ff., 371
Continuity of life, 181, 221 f.
Co-ordination, 29 f., 51
Correlation, non-causal, 157
Correspondence, individuality of, 66 ff., 80, 85, 88, 103
Criterion of acting, first, 59 ff.
  second, 66 ff.
  union of both, 75 ff.
Crustacea, 112
Crystals, 133, 146 ff.
Cumulation, 118
Cuvier, 328

Darwin, Ch., 42
Darwinians, 36, 106
Darwinism, 353 f.
Death, 184, 261 f.
Definition of action, 54
  of instinct, 38 f.
  of organism, 338 f.
Degrees of acting, 106 ff.
Demiurgus, 371, 373
Descartes, 222
Descent, theory of, 262 f.
Determination, univocal, 153 f. 303 f.
Development, 189 ff.
Differentiation, 192 f.
Directed agents, 11
Dissimilation, 245 ff.
Dissipation, 171, 174 f., 181
Diversity, 160, 176
  of distribution, 191 ff.
Divisibility (and entelechy), 257 f.
Dualism, 370

Economy of thinking, 151 f., 297
Ehrenfels, 343
Elastic after-effect, 78, 99
End of life, 260 ff.
Energetics, qualitative, 208
Energy, catenation of, 175 ff.
  conservation of, 159, 162 ff.
  and entelechy, 164 ff.
  intensity of, 172 ff., 177 ff., 202
  potential, 163 f.
  principles of, 158 ff., 195 ff., 308
  specific, of sensory nerves, 84 ff., 92, 95

Energy, supposed vital, 167 f., 177, 205
  transformations of, 174 f.
Engramma, 98, 122
Entelechy, 137 ff., 320, 335 f.
  and catalysis, 186 f.
  and causality, 161 ff., 235, 316 f.
  and chemism, 181 f.
  and constants, 204
  and divisibility, 257
  and energy, 164 ff.
  and inorganic world, 161 ff.
  justification of, 153 ff., 264 ff., 266 ff., 284
  and localisation, 258
  and mechanics, 208 ff., 218 ff.
  order of, 150 f.
  primary, in the universe, 370 ff.
  and substance, 238 ff., 256
Epiphenomenon, 288
Equilibrium, 149, 175 ff.
Erréra, 184
Evolutio, 154
Evolution, 120 f.
Exercise, 55
Experience, 25 f., 32, 54, 56 f., 60, 64, 107, 110 ff., 113, 140 f., 301
Explaining, 206, 324 ff.
Extensity, 241 f.

Fatigue, 55, 78
Fechner, 351
Fertilisation, 230
Finality, 313 f.
Fitting, 10
Flourens, 102
Forma essentialis, 149
Francé, 16
Freedom, 154 f., 304 f., 357
Function, mathematical, 303, 314 f.
  physiological, 144
Functional adaptation (of nervous system), 54, 278

Geissler, K., 218
Geotropism, 10
Giardina, 102, 105
Givenness (the Given), 125, 201 ff., 267 ff., 281, 283 f., 292, 306 f., 321 ff., 355 f., 359 f., 362 ff., 368 f., 374 f.
Glaser, 56
God, 371
Goldschmidt, V., 353
Goltz, 6, 58, 72, 87, 103 f.

Haberlandt, 10
Hanel, E., 42

INDEX

Harmonious equipotential system, 189 ff. 310 f., 333
Harmony in nature, 348 ff., 353 f., 370,
Hartmann, E. v., 142, 222 f., 302, 308, 318
Hauptmann, C., 89
Hegel, 118, 125 f., 138, 213, 302, 374
Heidenhain, 4
Heliotropism, 10
Helm, 172
Hering, 87
Hertz, 215 f.
Heterogeneous induction, 12
Historical basis of reacting, 59 ff., 78 f., 97, 99, 103, 107 f., 117, 277 ff.
 different types of, 63 ff.
 elements of, 80, 107 f.
History, 117 ff., 344 ff., 353, 357, 361
Hobhouse, 106
Hofmann, 148
Hume, 297
Hypnotism, 98

Idealism, 116, 201 f., 292
Identification, 279 f.
Immortality, 373
Indian philosophy, 366
Individualised stimuli, 41, 43, 66, 72 f., 101, 232
Individuality, category of, 296 ff., 310 ff., 335 f.
 of correspondence, 66 ff., 80, 85, 88, 103
Individuum, 145 f.
Inheritance, 181, 221 f.
Innate ideas, 44
Instinct, 33, 35 ff., 83 f., 109 f.
 definition of, 38 f.
 regulation of, 46 ff.
 stimuli of, 41 ff., 48
Intelligence, animal, 57
Intensity (of energy), 172 ff., 177 ff., 202
Interaction, category of, 306
 psycho-physical, 115 ff., 143, 226
Intra-psychical series, 231, 280 ff., 293 f.

Japp, 226
Jennings, 4, 16 ff., 24 f., 28, 31 f., 50, 55 f., 62, 103, 111, 113, 141
Jensen, 176
Joest, 96
Justification of entelechy, 153 ff., 264 ff., 266 ff., 284

Kant, 43, 115, 117, 125, 132 f., 141, 143, 257, 297 ff., 302 f., 306, 308, 312, 319 ff., 332, 344, 368 f., 371

Kelvin, Lord, 171, 225
Kinnaman, 106
Klebs, 330
Klein, A., 75
"Knowing and willing," 140 ff.
Korschelt, 96
Kries, v., 74

Lamarckism, 36
Langley, 95
Leclair, 295
Leibniz, 117, 297, 374
Lewandowsky, 89, 104
Life, end of, 260 ff.
 origin of, 260 ff.
Limits of regulability, 182 ff., 236
"Living" substance, 246 ff.
Locke, 44, 297
Locomotory organs, 4
Loeb, J., 15 f., 18, 29 f., 40 f., 96, 105, 230
Lotze, 231, 256, 288
Lubbock, Sir John, 109
Luciani, 105

Mach, 126, 206
Machine-theory, 26, 341
MacKendrick, 184
Manifoldness, extensive, 137, 157
 intensive, 138, 151, 157, 197, 283, 316
Maxwell, 184, 198 ff., 225
Mayer, R., 159
Mayer-Soule, 43
Means, 131, 140, 143
Mechanics, 162, 209 ff.
Mechanism, 283
Meinong, 343
Memory, 78, 279 f., 361 f.
Mental disease, 98
Metaphysics, 202, 294, 320, 359 ff.
Metschnikoff, 19
Mimosa, 8
Minkiewicz, 24
Moment of regulation, 237
Monakow, v., 89
Monism, 80, 283, 371
Morality, 119 ff., 205, 305, 320 ff., 355 ff., 361
Morality, as a category, 356
 and teleology, 355 ff.
 and vitalism, 357 f.
Morgan, Lloyd, 41 f., 106
Morphogenesis, 143, 148 f., 157, 191 ff., 229 ff.
Movement, organic, 3 ff.
 at random, 20 ff.

Müller, J., 45, 85 ff., 93
My own body, 266 ff., 282 ff., 293 f.

Nagel, 89
Nature, 116, 120, 281 ff., 318 ff., 321 ff.
  harmony in, 348 ff.
  ideal, 324 ff., 372 ff.
  philosophy of, 125 ff.
  purpose of, 132 f., 344
Necessity, category of, 303 f.
Nemeč, 10
Nervous conduction, 4
Noll, 10, 12, 243
νοούμενα, 320 f.

Ontological prototype, 319
Ophiurids, 56
Order of entelechies, 150 f.
Organism, definition of, 338 f.
Origin of life, 260 ff.
Ostwald, 126, 206, 235
Oxidation, 242 ff.

Palágyi, 269
Pantheism, 372
Parallelism, psycho-physical, 114 ff., 287 ff., 358
Paramecium, 17
Pauly, 143
Pawlow, 58, 113
Pearson, 126, 206
Pfeffer, W., 11
Pflüger, 103
Phases, principle of, 158, 234
Phenomenalism, 201 ff., 210, 362
Philosophy of nature, 125 ff.
Phonograph, 59 ff., 99
Phylogeny, 346 f., 353
Podmore, 122
Poincaré, 319
Possibility, 345 f.
Postulate, 302, 363 f.
Pragmatism, 364
Preyer, 31 f., 50, 56, 101
Propagation, 347 f.
Prototype, ontological, 319
Przibram, 147 f.
Pseudo-psychology, 53 f., 105
Psychoid, 82 f., 96 f., 116, 139 f., 231 f., 282 f., 293 f., 320, 335
Psychologism, 298 f.
Psychology, 53, 62, 65, 72, 115, 139 f., 231 f., 278 f., 283, 298
Purpose, 130 ff.
  of nature, 132 f., 344

Radiolaria, 4
Rádl, 58, 157, 328
Rauber, 147
Reflex, 8 f., 20, 27 ff., 32, 40 f., 44
  freely combined, 44
Regulation, 5, 7, 90 f., 100 ff., 119
  of instincts, 46 ff.
  limits of, 182 ff., 236
  moment of, 237
Rehmke, 280
Relation, categories of, 305 ff.
Respiration, 242 ff.
Restitution, stimuli of, 229
Retro-differentiation, 196
Reversion (of tropisms, etc.) 12, 23 f.
Rhumbler, 4
Rickert, 288
Righting reactions, 31, 50, 113, 141
Rubner, 166
Ruttloff, 96

Sameness, 97, 110
Schelling, 125 f., 328
Schneider, 143
Schopenhauer, 45, 125, 305, 328, 366, 369
Schrader, 58, 103
Schroeder, Chr. F., 49
Schwarz, 218
Self-motion, 198
Self-purpose, 131
Semon, 98, 122
Sense (of tropism), 11, 23 f.
Sense organs, 4
Sherrington, 30
"Shock," 92
Siphonophora, 4
Soul, 285, 288
Space, 43, 234 f.
Spaulding, 112
Specific energy of sensory nerves, 84 ff., 92, 95
Spheres (of the brain), 93 f.
Spinoza, 117, 287
Spiritualism, 122, 261
Spitzy, 102
Spontaneous action, 85
Starfish, righting reactions of, 31, 50, 113, 141
State, the, 118 f.
Stentor, 24 f., 56 f., 103, 111 f.
"Stimmung," 13
Stimuli, individualised, 41, 43, 66, 72 f., 101, 232
  of instincts, 41 ff., 48

INDEX

Stimuli of restitutions, 229
  simple, 41, 66
Strecker, 143
Subconsciousness, 98, 105
Substance, 238 ff., 286, 296, 306 f.
  as a category, 256
  inorganic, 239 ff.
  "living," 246 ff.
Supra-personal factor in history, 117 ff., 344 ff., 356 f.
"Suspending" action of entelechy, 179 ff., 221 f.
Systematics (of entelechies), 327 f.

Tait, 225
Taxis, 8 ff., 13 ff., 24, 41
Teleology, 129 ff., 308 f., 335, 343
  dynamical, 135 f., 138, 151, 341
  limited, 353 f., 365 ff.
  statical, 135 f., 151, 341
  supra-personal, 344 ff.
  universal, 340 ff.
Telepathy, 122
Theology, natural, 371
Third proof of vitalism, 75, 80 f.
Thorndike, 106 f.
Time, 149, 329 ff.
Transplantation, 95
Treviranus, 45
"Trial and error," 23, 56, 113

Tropism, 9 ff.
Truth, 360

Uexkuell, v., 27 ff., 35, 40, 51, 56, 73, 98 f., 102
Unconscious, 37 f., 141 f.
Universal teleology, 340 ff.
"Unterschiedsempfindlichkeit," 18

Verworn, 176, 292
Vitalism, 43 f., 50, 54, 72 ff., 75, 80 f. 88, 92, 281 ff., 296
Volition, act of, 62 f.
Vulpius, 101

Walter, 19
Ward, J., 114
Wasmann, 84, 106, 108
Weber, law of, 12
Weber, Max, 346
Weismann, 36
Wentscher, 221
Winterstein, 243
Wundt, 63, 87, 107, 115

Yerkes, 112 f.

Zwaardemaker, 166

THE END

Printed by R. & R. CLARK, LIMITED, *Edinburgh.*

HEREDITY AND SELECTION IN SOCIOLOGY

BY

G. CHATTERTON HILL

Demy 8vo, Cloth, 600 pages.

Price **12s. 6d.** net.

Post Free, Price **12s. 11d.**

SOME PRESS OPINIONS

"A most praiseworthy and suggestive work—should certainly be studied by every serious thinker."—*Morning Post.*

"Mr. Hill is decidedly doctrinaire, but his book is packed with scientific and sociological facts, and it gives the reader healthy intellectual exercise."—*Christian World.*

"Shows wide reading, is written in a forcible and clear style, and contains much that is interesting, fresh, and acute."—*Aberdeen Free Press.*

"It is a book of equal calibre with Mr. Kidd's and goes even deeper than that remarkable production into the springs of life and conduct."—*Methodist Recorder.*

"This most suggestive and valuable work, which contains abundant sociological data."—*Aberdeen Journal.*

"Mr. George Chatterton Hill has written a volume of surpassing interest not alone to scientific but to theological students."—*Catholic Times.*

Published by A. & C. BLACK, SOHO SQUARE, LONDON, W.

RUDOLF EUCKEN'S PHILOSOPHY OF LIFE

BY

W. R. BOYCE GIBSON

LECTURER IN PHILOSOPHY IN THE UNIVERSITY OF LONDON

SECOND EDITION

Crown 8vo, Cloth, with Frontispiece Portrait of Rudolf Eucken.

Price **3s. 6d.** net.

Post Free, Price **3s. 10d.**

SOME PRESS OPINIONS

"Mr. Gibson has given us in small compass a lucid exposition of the philosophical system of Eucken, who is Professor of Philosophy in Jena. . . . This is a most suggestive and stimulating book. In a very real sense it has brought philosophy down to earth and is deserving of serious study."—*Aberdeen Free Press.*

"To it the interested reader will turn with expectation, and his expectation is likely to be more than realised. For Dr. Boyce Gibson is himself a scholar, as well as an enthusiastic lover of this great scholar."—*Expository Times.*

"No reader should fail to find pleasure in a book so full of fresh and stimulating thought, expressed with great felicity of language."—*The Scottish Review.*

"It is done with just the proper combination of sympathy and criticism."—*British Weekly.*

"This little book on Eucken's Philosophy is of quite exceptional interest and importance."—*The Inquirer.*

"Professor Boyce Gibson . . . has performed a real service in promoting the acquaintance of English and American students with a thinker whose distinctive views give him a special claim to their attention. . . . Professor Gibson has achieved a notable success, writing briefly, lucidly, and sympathetically."—*The New Age.*

PUBLISHED BY A. & C. BLACK, SOHO SQUARE, LONDON, W.

**PLEASE DO NOT REMOVE
CARDS OR SLIPS FROM THIS POCKET**

UNIVERSITY OF TORONTO LIBRARY

```
B           Driesch, Hans Adolf Eduard
3218            The science and philosophy
S5          of the organism
1908
v.2
```

ImTheStory.com

Personalized Classic Books in many genre's

Unique gift for kids, partners, friends, colleagues

Customize:

- Character Names
- Upload your own front/back cover images (optional)
- Inscribe a personal message/dedication on the inside page (optional)

Customize many titles Including
- Alice in Wonderland
- Romeo and Juliet
- The Wizard of Oz
- A Christmas Carol
- Dracula
- Dr. Jekyll & Mr. Hyde
- And more...